Contents

Preface   2

1   Introduction   6
Dr Chris Bolton

2   Theory and Pedagogy   28
Dr Adam Bethlenfalvy

3   Challenging Theseus, challenging the curriculum   44
Dr Kostas Amoiropolous

4   The impact on young migrants   70
Balbir Sohal and Gilroy Brown

5   The impact on learners with Special Educational Needs and Disabilities   96
Dr Gill Brigg

6   The impact on teacher development   122
Rebecca Taylor and Emma Davis

7   Informal mentoring   148
Rebecca Patterson and Alison Ramsay

8   Beyond the school gates   168
Miranda Ballin and Ian McAndrew

About the contributors   186

In June 2024, the people involved in the project leading up to this publication gathered at The STEAMhouse, Birmingham for a sharing that took them through the experience of the project since its inception in January 2022.

From the pandemic ...
This project grew out of Big Brum's experiences during the 2020-21 lockdowns. The Covid-19 pandemic aggravated and worried at existing faultlines in our schools and communities, exposing dissonances and inequalities, and creating a widespread sense of malaise, anxiety and instability.

As teachers and children began to cautiously return to school from the first lockdowns, the language of 'recovery' began to be widely used. For some, not least the UK government of the time, this was especially about a return to 'the new normal', about catching up on studies and rebooting the economy. For others, there was a recognition that the faultlines that had been exposed by the pandemic should not so easily be glossed over: that real trauma and damage had occurred and that real recovery might take a long time and a great deal of care.

As successive waves of fresh crises broke over the schools and communities still struggling with the aftermath of Covid (including, but not only, around the cost of living, war in Europe, political instability, climate chaos), it became clear to Big Brum that 'recovery' was going to need creativity, imagination, care and a great deal of time. As so often, the impact of these successive crises were being felt most acutely by those who were most vulnerable and least well-protected: the young, the poor, those already-marginalised by wealth or culture or geography. We recognised that this situation would require a significant rethink for ourselves and the way we engaged with those around us.

Developing a model
During lockdown, Big Brum had begun experimenting with film-making and digital Theatre in Education programmes, especially the Monodrama 'Socially Distant' (Cooper, 2020). We used a version of this programme to create a model where primary teachers could experience the feelings and concepts of our artistic work for themselves before we brought it to their children. We then invited them to 'tune in' to the children's experience of the work ... and to follow it up with the children in school as they felt most appropriate (see page 10). We tested the model at Benson Community Primary School, with a single year group, in the very first days after children returned to school ... and it proved to be a tremendously powerful approach (Ballin, 2021).

But what if we were to upscale this model to a whole primary school? What would the impacts then be? Might it have a similarly powerful affect, not only on the individual children and their teachers, but on the whole school culture ... and perhaps the community beyond its gates? And what if we were to do this not just with one inner-city school, but with several schools in levelling-up areas and other places facing significant socio-economic deprivation within the West Midlands (the very places most in need of support in their 'recovery')?

We took this proposal to the Paul Hamlyn Foundation, who responded to it warmly and with enthusiasm. With their support, we then invited a team of expert evaluators to support us in understanding the impacts and efficacy of the model: on additionally vulnerable groups of children; on teachers; on curriculum and pedagogy; on the community beyond the school gate. It is the tremendous and insightful work of these evaluators that is shared in this publication: they tell us that we have got many things right, but that we are still on a journey; they advise us that there is a significant job still to be done and they suggest some of the things that we, the schools and the others we work with might want to bear in mind as we carry this job out.

Some of these evaluators, such as Balbir Sohal and Gilroy Brown (see page 70), have based these findings and recommendations on their experience of multiple TIE programmes in several schools. Most evaluators have chosen to focus on their experience of a single programme with a particular age group. Others, such as Gill Brigg (see page 96) have extrapolated their findings from the experience of a specific programme in an individual school.

For Big Brum, this advice and understanding is not an abstract question. Heartened but challenged by this experience, and by the company's restoration as an Arts Council England National Portfolio Organisation, we are already beginning to further develop the 'Schools of Recovery' model for all twenty schools in North Solihull, one of England's most socio-economically deprived communities. We believe that this ambitious plan is a little scary but absolutely necessary ... and we are determined to learn from the ideas and advice in this book to make it work as well as it possible can.

The Artistic Work

Big Brum is an artistically-led Theatre in Education company, so it would be remiss for us not to say a little bit here about the principal TIE programmes involved in this project.

Romeo and Juliet toured for Y5/6 children in the first year of the project. A digital version was then made available for classes working on 'Ripped' in the second year. Chris Cooper's adaptation of Shakespeare's tragedy used live theatre with filmed moments to make the story resonate with children's lives today and ask, *"who is responsible for this bloody mess?"*

The Giant's Embrace was used throughout the project as a stimulus and CPD opportunity for teachers, who went on to use the storybook and film with their children. It was based on a former very popular 'live' TIE programme and took the form of an unfinished fairy tale that subtly explored questions about our wants and needs and the difficulty of deferred gratification.

Along the Silk Road (by Chris Cooper) toured to Y5 and Y6 children in Autumn 2022. The play and TIE programme were set in historic China and the UK of today, inviting children to think about whether people say what they mean at a time when narratives were (and still are) bitterly polarised. The statement early in the play, *"there is more to value than profit, child,"* was used by several schools as a stimulus for exploring values.

Ripped took the form of a series of workshops for Y5 and Y6 children, created by Richard Holmes and centred on the story of a troubled girl who has ripped a dictionary and placed it outside her headteacher's office. The children were invited to give advice to the headteacher about how he should best help meet her real needs and wants. In both 2022 and 2023, the programme was used alongside – or as an introduction to – 'Romeo and Juliet'.

Minotaur (by Chris Cooper) used the classic Greek myth to explore what makes a monster, a king, a hero? The programme toured to Y4 children in 2023 as part of a training and work placement for Applied Theatre students at Birmingham City University. This experience informed a further short tour and placement programme in May 2024.

Rumpelstiltskin told the classic Grimms fairy story to Y3 children, supported by props and a simple stage set. The adaptation, by Richard Holmes, invited the children to think -in an age-appropriate way - about power, property, control and the value of a child's life.

References

Ballin, B. (2021), 'Socially connected: the displaced teacher and the displaced child', in Jozifek, Z. et al, *To Be – researching connections between drama, well-being and education.* Budapest: To Be Consortium. Research report, curriculum and guidebook accessible online at https://bigbrum.org.uk/projects/to-be

Cooper, C. (2020) *Socially Distant.* Birmingham: Big Brum TIE

Introduction

Dr Chris Bolton

'Creating "Schools of Recovery"' (SoR) was a two-year project to explore and evaluate a project model developed around the work of Big Brum Theatre in Education Company. Whilst there are a number of useful and insightful evaluations that exist about the important work of the company, such as 'Engaging, Exploring, Expressing: The case for Theatre in Education' (2019), the 'More and Better Project' (2019), and 'Human Spaces: An evaluative case study' (2018), SoR happened in a very different, transient and emergent context. This context has enabled a form of transformation for the company. Via the SoR project, and during this transformative period, Big Brum continue to hold true to their artistic policy in that human beings have to know and re-know themselves, individually and socially.

What follows in this publication is important for everyone connected to the arts, education, and more importantly young people. It seeks to build on previous work created by the company to explore how Big Brum's approach to, and model for, Theatre in Education (TIE) might be extended and applied in a post-Covid period of recovery and tests a 'project partnership model' with theatre at its heart. This partnership model involves not only the company itself, but also primary schools, their leadership teams, teachers, and the communities that those schools serve.

Emerging out of the global Coronavirus pandemic, which not only disrupted, damaged, and affected humanity on an unprecedented scale but also gave rise to new and different opportunities to *"rethink what matters most in education"* (Azorin, 2020:2), Big Brum's project exists as evidence of their further transforming themselves. SoR sees the company moving themselves toward a hub for the development and practice of child-centred theatre- and drama- in education, and this is an essential element of survival for both the company and their approach to Theatre in Education.

Usefully, evaluative contributions from seven organisations, from here defined as the 'commission', present a well-rounded picture of how Big Brum's approach has been applied to seven different areas and gives value to the diverse impact of Big Brum's model and approach. The members of the commission included:

- **Dr Adam Bethlenfalvy**, Associate Professor at Károli Gáspár University and CEO at InSite Drama, Budapest
- **Dr Konstantinos Amoiropoulos**, Artistic Director of Diadromes, Athens
- **Balbir Sohal** and **Gilroy Brown**, Education Consultants
- **Dr Gill Brigg**, Additional Needs Officer for National Drama
- **Rebecca Taylor,** Senior Lecturer and **Emma Davis**, Lecturer at University College Birmingham
- **Dr Rebecca Patterson**, Senior Lecturer in Education and **Alison Ramsay**, Lecturer in Primary Education at Manchester Metropolitan University
- **Miranda Ballin**, Artistic Director at Sparc, Penygraig and **Ian McAndrew**, CEO and Joint Artistic Director at Think Creatively CIC, Ponyclun

The work of the commission was also supported by Big Brum's Advisory Group of educators and artists.

The commission's varied expertise, experience(s) in education and understanding of different elements of the educational landscape enabled them to focus on particular lines of enquiry that Big Brum wanted to evaluate. Whilst there are a number of other areas that could have been evaluated in terms of the project model's impact, the different aspects evaluated by the commission in this report include the following:

Theory and Pedagogy- Big Brum's key theoretical and pedagogical components and their impact on teachers and actor-teachers (see page 28)

Challenging the Curriculum- the use and application of Big Brum's model in a school curriculum, and how this is communicated to teachers and students (see page 44)

The impact on young migrants- the impact of Big Brum's approach on newly arrived children and migrant children (see page 70)

The impact on learners with Special Educational Needs and Disabilities (SEND)- the impact of Big Brum's approach on children with SEND (see page 96)

The impact on teacher development- Big Brum's role in the continuous professional development of teachers and their work in relation to teaching practice (see page 122)

Informal Mentoring- the process of mentoring between participating teachers in Big Brum's project and between the different participating schools (see page 148)

Beyond the school gate- the impact of Big Brum's approach on the engagement of school communities (see page 168)

In forming the commission, the main aim was to help establish the model presented in the SoR project as a means of meeting children's needs, whilst creating a future for child-centred and artistically led theatre in education in the United Kingdom (UK). Supporting the commission, whose role was not only to evaluate the project but also to advocate for the project's outcomes, Big Brum aimed to draw on high-level and long-standing advocates of the company and their work, such as their patron Baroness Shami Chakrabarti.

Creating Schools of Recovery - Aims

Big Brum were clear in defining to the commission what they intended to learn from an evaluation of the project and Big Brum's transformative approach. The aims of the project, and thus foci for the commission, included:

- Testing and extending a collaborative model of working to give value to the potential of this model for Big Brum, schools with whom they worked, and the teachers and children within those schools.

- To explore the value and significance of Big Brum's model and approach for schools in areas of socio-economic deprivation.

- To explore the value and significance of Big Brum's model and approach for children who were disproportionately affected by the Coronavirus crisis.

- To build on previous important work developed from the To Be Project (2021) with a larger number of schools.

- To learn about how the SoR project might impact on specific children and groups of children, through to teachers' professional development, and on to larger impacts, such as whole school and mentorship strategies.

- To learn about the impact of the SoR project on SEND children, newly arrived children and migrant children, and school communities more generally in socio-economically deprived areas.

Inevitably, and given the outstanding practice of the company, evidence of Big Brum's 'Nine Principles of Working' with children and young people became clear! These principles are outlined in Fig 1, on page 9 and can be read about in more detail throughout the evaluation.

Fig 1: Big Brum's Nine Principles of Working

1. Trust every child
Big Brum vows to treat young people not as undeveloped adults but as human beings in their own right, respecting their experiences and understandings, getting to the heart of what it is to be human.

2. High teacher-young people ratios
We facilitate small group work with up to 30 young people to ensure a high ratio of actor teachers to young people, maximising participation and inclusion.

3. Free for all audiences
A very important factor in breaking down the normal socio-economic factors that prevent young people from accessing the arts, especially theatre and drama.

4. Be crystal clear
We have clear and candid discussions with schools before we perform, identifying any special approaches that may be required.

5. Make art accessible
We're bringing art into a familiar space that young people already inhabit, breaking down a common barrier of arts engagement: attending arts venues and the 'alien' effect that has on young people.

6. Build safe spaces
We are carefully crafting every drama session so young people can place themselves into theatre and respond to reality a safe distance from their own experience.

7. No wrong answers
Big Brum demonstrates that there are no wrong answers because we are interested not in what is 'correct', but in what young people think and the process by which they come to these conclusions.

8. Ask the big questions
We question effectively and are renowned for our ability to utilise poignant questioning with young people to open up imaginative responses and help them think in new ways.

9. Get lost in the moment
We work in the moment, entering sessions with the goal to respond to the ideas of the young people present as they process what they have seen and want to discuss with our people.

The 'To Be' Project

Whilst not the intention to rehash the extensive work of Big Brum's involvement in the 'To Be' project, it is worth contextualising the relationship between it and the current SoR project. The 'To Be' project was an international project that used elements of drama and theatre to promote and support the wellbeing of teachers and young people. As part of this, Big Brum worked with primary school teachers in an inner-city primary school in Birmingham (UK) and used Chris Cooper's monodrama 'Socially Distant' (2020) as a stimulus.

This pilot project to SoR, enabled the company to explore their unique method and approach to education, and saw the company gather qualitative data from teachers to explore how they sought to meet the needs of the 'displaced child' by engaging teachers in a creative and felt manner. There were a number of benefits linked to children's wellbeing, teachers' wellbeing, and in terms of collaborative and creative practice. Overall, however, the findings clearly showed that the 'To Be' project benefited all children including those identified as being most at risk of school exclusion. The findings also created a space to reconsider the impact of creative collaboration, the development of 'felt understanding' in teachers' practice and the facilitation of a space to connect Big Brum's approach to the authentic emotional and educational needs of teachers and children (Fig 2). Notably, this project also saw the creation of a curriculum for wellbeing called 'Socially Connected' (Ballin, 2021). This comprised of digital and downloadable resources for present, future, and aspiring teachers, TIE and Drama in Education practitioners.

Fig 2: Simplified schema of the SoR project model

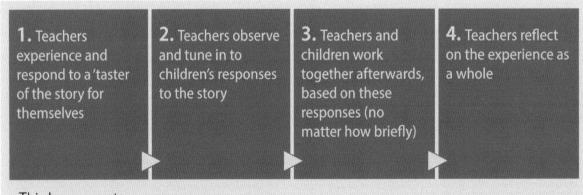

1. Teachers experience and respond to a 'taster of the story for themselves

2. Teachers observe and tune in to children's responses to the story

3. Teachers and children work together afterwards, based on these responses (no matter how briefly)

4. Teachers reflect on the experience as a whole

This happens at:
- the individual class level
- in the whole school across several TIE programmes
- across all the participating schools

Thus, the stage was set for Big Brum to apply this model and approach on a wider and larger scale. In doing so, the SoR project aimed to work collaboratively in this manner. In 2021-22 the project engaged with three primary schools with this number increasing to six in 2022-23 (Fig 3). The primary schools were located in the West Midlands of the United Kingdom, and each has specific socio-economic factors.

Fig 3: The plays and programmes involved in SoR – a timeline

All schools are in areas of socio-economic deprivation and/or levelling-up areas in the West Midlands. John of Rolleston and Outwoods are in the same locally-based Multi Academy Trust. 'The Giant's Embrace' is a CPD programme for teachers supported by a film and storybooks for children. This programme was taken up by five of the schools.

Date	Schools	Programme
Spring/Summer 2022	Benson Community School, Birmingham	**The Giant's Embrace**
	Fordbridge Community Primary School, North Solihull	**Ripped**
	John of Rolleston Primary School, Burton-on-Trent	**Romeo and Juliet**
Autumn 2022 - Autumn 2023	Benson Community School, Birmingham	**The Giant's Embrace**
	Fordbridge Community Primary School, North Solihull	**Along the Silk Road**
	John of Rolleston Primary School, Burton-on-Trent	**Ripped**
	Outwoods Primary School, Burton-on-Trent	**Minotaur**
	Rookery School, Birmingham	**Rumpelstiltskin**
	Stoke Heath Primary School, Coventry	

Evaluation Context

It is important to contextualise the educational landscape from which the SoR project emerged and currently sits, particularly given the trauma caused by the Coronavirus pandemic. Although much has been written about the impact of the pandemic, and in no way is this introduction attempting to re-present what we have all experienced, known, and felt, the project's origins are firmly rooted and located in that context. Using the themes of the commission's aims, what follows is a brief contextualisation in order to foreground the commission's evaluative work.

Pedagogically, the impact of the pandemic on teachers' 'normal' practice was significant and profound. It saw a move away from traditional face-to-face spaces to virtual and online platforms with many pedagogical changes arising out of necessity rather than design. This forced all teachers, regardless of subject specialism or age-phase, to adapt their pedagogical approach to teaching and learning. For drama pedagogy, which often relies on live action and a co-creation of meaning in a social space, this move to virtual spaces was challenging. Despite this, creative adaptations in drama pedagogy emerged in a variety of ways, such as the creation of online process drama (Cziboly & Bethlenfalvy, 2020: Po-Chi, 2020), Verbatim digital storytelling (Gallagher et al., 2020), and we saw moves toward more hybrid approaches as the world started to return to a sense of normality, such as the Socially Distant Stories project (Bolton & Patterson, 2022). These divergent approaches re-affirmed a fundamental aspect of drama pedagogy as one that requires a human dimension, a human connection. Questioning what this 'human dimension' means now as we are emerging out of this context, provides a foundation and grounding for the SoR project particularly by focusing on Big Brum's model and approach to learning in light of this context.

Inevitably, these shifts toward virtual spaces and hybrid practices impacted on school curriculum, both in terms of form and content, and forced teachers to re-consider their curricula in terms of the reality of their context and the unrealised virtual world. Evidently, the impact on curriculum time, quality, and experience was negatively affected, with the examination regulator in England, Ofqual (2021) worryingly noting that *"disadvantage and deprivation appear to be most associated with less effective learning"*. More specifically, the research from Ofqual also found that *"Teaching and learning for primary-aged students also appear[s] to have been negatively impacted"*. Linked to this, the inspectorate Ofsted (2022) found that subject-specific knowledge and skills continued to be affected by changes in access to school curricula because *"content had not been taught when schools were partially closed or because pupils did not learn well remotely"*. The relationship between socio-economic deprivation and primary aged children's learning is well documented, and whilst not aiming to solve this challenge, SoR sought to evaluate the impact of a project partnership model on this particular area.

During the pandemic, particularly (but not exclusively) in the UK context, education was adrift and needing leadership. This need for leadership was not adequately met, with the UK government's guidance *"often appear[ing] ill-informed and unhelpful"* (Moss, 2021: 6) and this left schools and their teachers often having to fathom out how to deal with *"pressing issues quickly and directly"* (ibid.). This lack of leadership also revealed much about the fragility of the UK education system, with Moss (2021: 6) insightfully suggesting that these issues stemmed from *"over-centralisation, a lack of awareness of problems on the ground, and a preference for pressure-driven management linked to testing and inspection that ignores the material impacts of poverty on schools and communities"*. It became clear that what was being revealed by this unprecedented context was that education was not fit for purpose, was brittle, and that there was a disconnect between policy initiatives and experiences 'on-the-frontline' of education. Further to this, the International Literacy Centre (2020), focussing on the role of primary schools, critically pointed out that primary schools play a crucial role within their local communities, particularly in terms of support for young peoples' health and welfare.

Whilst the support that primary schools offer is widely known, sadly under-acknowledging this support is evident through *"... funding formulae for schools and in our testing and inspection regimes"* (ILC, 2020). This evidence was further strengthened through the use of *"high-stakes accountability and norm-referenced testing as the drivers of system repair [which] risks seriously distorting schools' priorities at this critical time"* (ibid.). This lack of acknowledgement from 2020, about the role of primary schools, persists in 2024 and can be seen in more recent literature reports. For example, school funding will see reductions (Cruikshanks, 2024), the impact of testing and a narrowed curriculum continues to impact children's mental health and well-being (Hargreaves et al., 2023), and the impact of school inspection regimes on school leaders and teachers, such as those conducted by Ofsted, remains (Perryman et al., 2023). The picture seems to show that despite the lessons from the pandemic the outcomes are still the same!

Clearly, the pandemic affected all children in a variety of ways, but particularly in terms of their mental health and well-being (Office for Health Improvement and Disparities, 2022). However, one aim of the SoR project was to explore the value and significance of Big Brum's model and approach for children who were disproportionately affected by the Coronavirus crisis. Specifically, this aim focussed on young migrant children (YMC) and children with SEND. However, all participating schools were also in areas of socio-economic deprivation and/or levelling-up areas in the West Midlands.

It was reported that children with SEND found lockdown 'boring' and 'lonely' (Ashworth et al., 2022: 1772) and that changes in routine had impacted on friendships. For many children with SEND this *"exacerbated underlying social and communication difficulties"*. Linked to this, Asbury et al., (ibid.) found that for both children with SEND, and their parents, the impact of the pandemic led to experiences of *"loss, worry and changes in mood and behaviour as a result of the rapid social changes that have occurred"*. Therefore, there are links here between children with SEND and the wider school communities of which they were a part.

For YMC no doubt there were similar experiences. Importantly, schools for YMC *"are not just places where knowledge and skills are acquired, but also fundamental spaces for the development of their sense of self, belonging and citizenship"* (Manzoni & D'Angelo, 2021: 60). However, lockdowns and school closures in response to the pandemic acted as *"multipliers of educational inequalities"* (2021: 57). Some of the main reasons for this multiplication are connected to familiarity with education systems and life in the UK, alongside challenges around language, and limited resources, not to mention *"the traumatic personal experiences of migration"* (ibid.). Strengthening the significance of this issue, the OECD (2020) reported extensively about the impact of the pandemic on children, particularly those most vulnerable, in over 188 countries finding that:

> *"School closures have a very real impact on all students, but especially on the most vulnerable ones who are more likely to face additional barriers. Children and youth from low-income and single-parent families; immigrant, refugee, ethnic minority and Indigenous backgrounds … and those with special education needs suffer by being deprived of physical learning opportunities, social and emotional support available in schools and extra services such as school meals. They risk falling further behind and becoming isolated with school doors closed."*

Internationally, PISA (2023) found that *"across the OECD area, disadvantaged students' sense of belonging at school deteriorated between 2018 and 2022"*, and through the enforcement of protective measures, such as social distancing, the global pandemic arguably had a role in this sense. Added to this, PISA's call for a transformation in education in which students are no longer seen as consumers of prefabricated educational content and that teachers are viewed as more than 'service providers' potentially moves the paradigm of education toward the aims of the SoR project itself. These aims align well with PISA's stated vision for education, which sees *"a world in which education becomes a shared enterprise geared towards helping the next generation build a reliable compass and the tools to navigate with confidence through a rapidly changing world."*

In this evolving context, the development of teachers' identity and practice was unavoidably affected also. Much has been written about the impact of the pandemic on in-service teachers' mental health (Kim et al., 2022; Education Support, 2021), in-service teachers' wellbeing and workload (See, 2024), and their professional development (Ofsted, 2023). With most development activities taking place online during the pandemic, research from Ofsted (2023) found that *"teachers thought that it was lower in quality"*, which in turn had an impact upon their practice. To some extent, the brittleness of education fed into questions about the purpose of education, and no doubt led some teachers to question the purpose of their endeavours as teachers. Inevitably, feelings of anxiety, depression, and isolation in combination with elements such as panic attacks, mood swings and insomnia were all common features affecting teachers and their commitment to continued development during the pandemic (Education Support, 2021). The increasing demand on teachers' time during this period meant that teacher development opportunities, and the quality of those opportunities, were significantly reduced.

Linked to this, the relationship between teacher development and retention is well researched (NFER, 2024; McJames et al., 2023) and shows that investment in teachers' professional development positively impacts on retention within the profession. Despite the Department for Education's (DfE) (2023) 'spin' on teacher retention in 2021/22, the data showed that 39,930 teachers left teaching during the pandemic for reasons other than retirement. Worryingly, this represented 8.8% of the workforce, which was the highest number since records began in 2010. Data from the Education Policy Institute (2023) show that *"The overall picture is, unfortunately, a fairly gloomy one"* with more teachers *"quitting the profession before retirement"* and it *"becoming harder to recruit"*. However, whilst the pandemic clearly exacerbated this problem, it was not the only cause. Thus, exploring new(er) ways to support teacher development, as explored through the SoR project becomes increasingly important.

During this unstable and changeable time, the DfE (2019)[1] introduced the Core Content Framework (CCF) and Early Career Framework (ECF) in an attempt to establish a foundational entitlement to a structured package of support for future generations of teachers over the first three years of their career. As part of this, mentoring and support from 'expert colleagues' was intended to form a key element of this multi-year entitlement. Given the context described above, the timing of these changes to Initial Teacher Education (ITT) and for Early Career Teachers (ECT) placed significant, and additional, pressure(s) on school-based mentors and ITT providers. Essentially, ITT

---

[1] The CCF and ECF became mandatory for all ITT providers in 2020-21 academic year.

providers, such as Universities and School-Based Initial Teacher Training providers, had to adapt their traditional practices to a more prescriptive and didactic form of teacher education and mentoring, which in-turn affected school-based mentors and their practice when supporting new teachers into the profession. Hordern & Brooks (2023:800) insightfully summarise this change as one that was *"orientated towards a scientism that (1) marginalises longstanding traditions of educational thought, and (2) technicises and instrumentalises teaching practice."*

These changes have since recently been reviewed, with the DfE (2024) announcing the results of a review into the CCF and ECF. The revisions see a reduction in duplication, a focus on subject specificity, a stronger focus on SEND and an attempt to lighten mentor workload. Despite this, mentoring in school and the mentoring of those in the profession is potentially infected by these moves toward technicality and instrumentalisation. As described above, one aim of the SoR project was to explore how notions of mentoring might be developed 'informally' and between schools who were taking part in the project.

Undoubtedly, the changes brought about by the pandemic context affected school communities both within the school gates and beyond. Many schools during the lockdown period(s) became important, if not vital, in terms of community cohesion. Findings from the NFER (2021) unsurprisingly showed an overwhelming need to support school communities with much more than academic and curriculum provisions. For example, pupils in primary schools were reported to be *"struggling with social skills, confidence and self-esteem"* (Nelson, et al., 2021:ii) and that whilst this was the case, access to working with outside agencies faced additional challenges, such as a lack of funding and the capacity to facilitate this type of support. School leaders within the research made strong calls for 'early-intervention' and 'multi-agency' approaches to *"mitigate an escalation in poor mental health and learning incapacity, to support families, and to minimise staff workload and stress"* (ibid.).

Ofsted (2022) clearly stated that the context of a school's community had presented challenges and difficulties for school leaders with many 'disadvantaged communities' having *"been particularly hard hit by the pandemic"*. Further to this, they reported that for some of these school communities there has been a need to provide support to parents with mental health or substance abuse issues and that across a range of different community contexts, schools have reported that they have had to *"help parents deal with COVID-related anxiety"*.

Despite this, many teachers working in school communities went beyond their 'traditional roles' and adopted new facets of their responsibilities. Moss et al., (2020: 6) suggested that some of these new responsibilities included running food banks, delivering food parcels, and distributing meal vouchers to support families in socio-economically deprived communities. This meant that given the stress on support from welfare organisations on the ground *"schools remain[ed] an important part of the fabric of social care within local communities"* and that schools generally during the lockdown period *"acted as important hubs for children and their families"*. Whilst this change in traditional views of teachers no doubt caused additional stress, the crisis also afforded teachers the space to re-consider their perspectives on home-school relationships.

Interestingly, in the survey of 1,653 primary school teachers *"...about half the teachers working in the more disadvantaged schools said they felt more aware of how poverty and overcrowding impacts on students lives"*, with over two thirds of those teachers also recognising how difficult home learning was. Evidently, meeting the needs of children from the most disadvantaged contexts is challenging, and whilst education alone cannot fix wider structural societal inequalities, providing these children with diverse educational spaces in which to understand the world is vital. Perhaps sharply concluding this, Moss et al., (2020: 20) suggested that:

> *"Covid-19 has in many senses been a national disaster. Its effects will ripple on into the next year, not least as the government struggles to get the economy back on its feet – an unprecedented task with few clear options. Our poorest communities are likely to feel the economic effects most sharply. The basic food insecurity they already face has been quite rightly highlighted through the crisis."*

This brief contextual overview sets the scene from which the SoR project developed. As Big Brum were faced with this context, the importance of developing the SoR project became stronger, particularly as the company were exploring how they might respond to this context in a meaningful and developmental way. This attempt by the company not only deserves commendation but should also be celebrated as an attempt to change educational paradigms as a result of the global pandemic.

Themes Emerging from the Project
Given the depth and breadth of the evaluations available here, it would be beyond the limits of this introduction to truly delve into the insight offered and nuance provided by the commission's work. However, there are a number of important considerations and themes that emerge in light of the different evaluations. The diverse evaluations about the SoR model and approach intersect on various and complex levels. Despite this, there

is a sense of coherence demonstrated in the project and there exist a number of common 'threads' that emerge through the commission's work.

1. Safe Space- Braver Spaces

Clearly emerging from the commission's work is that the SoR model and approach creates space. Considering space as a concept, one might rightly think of literal and physical spaces, for example the performance of 'Minotaur' took place in the school hall, some preparatory work for 'Rumpelstiltskin' took place in the classroom. However, there are other types of spaces facilitated by the project model and approach. It is clear that through the SoR project there are social spaces for young people, teachers, and actor-teachers in which to discuss, learn and explore. The types of social spaces evaluated in the SoR project go some way in transforming traditional school-based learning spaces, moving them beyond traditional transmission-of-knowledge spaces towards more social constructivist spaces.

Alternatively, we might consider these social spaces as pedagogical spaces that work in multi-layered and complex ways. For example, the physical space created by the programmes offered - such as 'Minotaur or 'Rumpelstiltskin'- open up spaces for social connections, whereby participants are connected through the fiction of the drama. As this happens, this space becomes pedagogical as young people have the space to learn in an aesthetic and visceral context. Alongside this, teachers also have a space to learn - either about the pedagogy employed by Big Brum or even about the young people with whom they work. However these spaces operate in practice, and whatever use they provide for participants in the project, the space created also facilitates for them a space to re-imagine, re-consider, and re-cognise themselves and to varying degrees the commission's evaluations reflect this.

In creating spaces, such as those described above, the SoR model and approach to learning, and thus Big Brum's artistic and pedagogical practice in this context, is firmly underpinned. This underpinning is not only supported by Big Brum's 'nine principles', which themselves are a common theme emerging from the commission's work, but also the notion of a crucible paradigm. This paradigmatic view of teaching and learning subverts a traditional-didactic relationship between teacher and students and instead replaces it with a much more collaborative approach that rests on a more authentic human relationship. This relationship is democratic. It gives space to inclusion, agency, and equality. It promotes feelings of belonging and empathy. Clearly, the notion that 'no wrong answers/no right answers' are being sought provides a philosophical foundation that supports the SoR project. In effect, this philosophical foundation helps to facilitate safe spaces, a common theme emerging from the evaluations. However, given the educational context briefly described above, I might push this notion of 'safe space' a little further to suggest 'brave space'- a space in which teachers are asked to re-consider their view(s) of teaching and learning, and young people are asked what they think, rather than what they think they should think. Taken in this way, the SoR project provides a sense of freedom and liberation through the fictional contexts, whereby the artistic approach employed becomes a holding frame for this freedom of thinking.

It is recognised that this approach, therefore, can become inclusive. Whilst it should be acknowledged that there are some challenges around the definition of 'radical inclusion' used by Big Brum as being 'too broad' (see page 107), the emergent theme from the commission's evaluations is that the SoR project's approach and model seeks to include all participants and goes beyond statutory forms of inclusion, such as the Department for Education's (2015) SEND Code of Practice. By connecting with children on a human level, however marginalised and/or excluded, Big Brum's practice within the SoR project can be recognised as another way toward inclusive approaches. As the company are not governed necessarily by educational policies it means they have a freedom to approach inclusion in an artistic, creative, and human way. This is brave and should be noted.

2.Student Voice, Student Agency & Relationships

Clearly, Big Brum's promotion of a pedagogical model that is based on dialogue and meaning making is evident in all of the commission's evaluations. Whilst this is demonstrated through the work in different ways, the voice of the student remains a central focus that is respected. This not only adds to the brave spaces created through the SoR project but also means that this child-centred approach goes some way to re-positioning the student and their expertise in the world and experience(s) of the world. In doing so, the SoR project connects the students' reality to the fiction of the drama and thus re-values them as active citizens in the world. This creates, for them, a sense of agency in which their opinions, ideas and thoughts are valued and respected. Evidently, through the commission's evaluations, the use of questioning to promote a social constructivist paradigmatic view of teaching and learning removes the dominance of voices, such as the voice of the teacher. That is not to say that teachers' voices and ideas are removed completely, rather that they become equal in terms of their value to the learning process. Student agency, through the SoR project, enabled many of the participants to not only access the work of Big Brum's programmes, but also enabled them to actively participate. Through the brave spaces that the project created, young people, and in some cases their teachers, evidently felt that they had a right to express themselves and influence decisions through the dramatic experience(s). This activated students within their learning experience and again enabled them to potentially re-imagine and re-know themselves as young people.

By placing the student at the centre of the work, the SoR project evaluations show that this process changes relationships. These changing relationships were evident in terms of the teacher-student relationship, the student-student relationship, and both students' and teachers' relationship to Big Brum. In collaborating and connecting with each other, the SoR project was able to promote a sense of belonging for the participants, however long-lasting that might be (see pages 76-78). In essence, and through these relationships, belonging to each other meant that the participants had a sense of responsibility either to each other or toward the characters in the fictional stories that were being shared and explored. In this sense, it was evident that students within the SoR project were able to develop a sense of empathy. The development of these empathic relationships is a meaningful and sophisticated finding and provides an example of a way to support recovery from the educational context previously described whilst adding to the exemplary work that already exists in the schools involved.

The SoR approach and model, however, is not without its challenges, as noted through the commission's evaluations. Whilst schools, teachers and students within those schools felt this sense of belonging, challenges such as accessibility to materials presented, preparedness for the model, confidence to apply and use the approach as modelled, and understanding of the pedagogical rationale were noted as potential threats to the longevity of this type of work in schools (see pages 122-123). Linked to this, connections between the artistic content - such as 'Minotaur' for example - and a statutory curriculum were not always apparent. This is not surprising, particularly given the strong focus on 'catching up' that faces all schools in the UK context. Nor is it impossible! Alongside this, the pressure on teachers' time means that connecting their curricula to artistic interventions, such as those provided through the SoR project, is difficult, but again, not impossible. However, what is important here, is that the project evaluations show a strong impact on young people and teachers who took part in the work, with evidence of participants making their own connections and associations. This may well go beyond 'normal' teaching and learning.

3. Teachers' identity & practice
In terms of 'recovery' and given the need for new and different approaches and opportunities in education, creating these brave spaces is no doubt a challenge; it requires teachers developing new(er) skill(s) and commitment, whilst recognising that this is simultaneously threatened by the aforementioned educational context. However, if the challenge of creating these spaces is not felt and experienced by teachers, they will not change them, and this emerges as a key theme in developing the SoR model and approach.

Arising from the commission's work, we can see that there is a real need for teachers generally, but teachers within the SoR project specifically, to move their professional frame of thinking toward more of a personal and human way of being. No doubt, this move in the psyche of teachers is challenging, particularly given the pressure, stress, and accountability they face whilst working in the education profession. Workload expectations no doubt play a large part in teachers' difficulties with this shift (see pages 132-133). Despite these challenges, when teachers do approach and re-focus their frames of thinking and being, the impact on their students can be profound, and this might be considered as a key feature of teacher development within the SoR project. In doing so, teachers can thereby create brave spaces within their pedagogical practice. Whilst it is recognised that pressure from operational structures connected to the reality of day-to-day teaching demands, such as marking, planning, and providing data might hinder this way of thinking and being, the success of the SoR approach rests on teachers and Big Brum collaboratively working to adapt deeper and more implicit views of education.

Another potential threat to teacher development through the project, was the way that the drama work was valued. Evidently, and on one level, the commissions' evaluations demonstrated that the artistic input provided by Big Brum's actor-teachers was affected by the physical environment in which the work took place. Perhaps underlying this issue was a lack of understanding about the environmental conditions needed for this type of model and approach to be impactful (see page 130). On another level, the demands on teachers' time, as briefly noted above, might also be considered as a factor impacting on the value of the work provided and how it is perceived (educationally) by teachers. This is worrying and shows that the potential of brave spaces for teachers to re-think and re-consider what is important in education are potentially being suppressed by the demands of 'being' a teacher. Adding to this complexity is that despite teachers seeing the many benefits of the SoR approach in terms of their learners' engagement and behaviour, they were unable to implement what had been modelled in their own practice. In some cases, teachers were so time-poor that they were unable to attend brief follow-up discussions with the commission! That is not to say teachers were not committed: rather, it demonstrates the pressure being faced by them. There may be a number of reasons for this, linked to the day-to-day demands of teaching, but this suggests that more work on collaborating with teachers and supporting them to develop their practice might be needed following the SoR project.

The commission's evaluations indicate that the need to provide support for teachers - whether that be in terms of their pedagogical approach, curriculum development, inclusive practice, or professional growth - is vital. Emerging as a theme to varying degrees implicitly or explicitly throughout the commission's work, the notion of mentoring exists as a useful form of teacher development. Interestingly, the notion of 'informal mentoring' has arisen from the project evaluation (see page 148). Despite the day-to-day constraints that are a reality for many teachers, this form of mentoring for teachers and their practice *exists in the in-between spaces*'. And this approach to mentoring is fuelled by ongoing communications between all parties and participants - within a school context and beyond! Whilst this has potential there are threats to this, not to mention the teachers' own willingness to engage. However, this form of mentoring could resist more 'professional' frames of thinking and support teachers' moves toward more human ways of being. In this sense, the mentoring process potentially becomes more organic, meaningful, and long(er)-lasting.

Conclusions

Undeniably, there is much to learn from the SoR approach and model. This learning is not only important for Big Brum but also for teachers, artists and those connected to working with young people. The SoR project provides an alternative way of thinking about 'recovery' from the pandemic context and its aftermath, which gives rise to new ways of working with young people that are meaningful and go well beyond more traditional advice about what young people and teachers need in a post-pandemic world.

Evidently, the SoR project and the commission's evaluation(s) below give value to the extension of Big Brum's collaborative model of working and demonstrates that despite larger systemic and social challenges, this type of approach to learning and teaching is possible, has value, and can impact on various stakeholders. This means that the model promoted by Big Brum through this project is significant, particularly for those schools serving socio-economically deprived communities. As we have seen, children coming from those communities have tended to be disproportionately affected by the global pandemic, but the SoR project goes some way to reducing that affect, if not addressing it in a way that is unique.

By building on international work, such as that evidenced in the 'To Be' Project (Ballin, 2021), the SoR model and approach demonstrates that there is an element of universality in attempting to address the needs and wants of young people and teachers. The need to meaningfully address issues around wellbeing, inclusion, and what it means to be human is a clear link between the two projects and demonstrates that Big Brum are transforming into a hub for the development and practice of child-centred theatre- and drama- in education. Personally, I have always viewed the company so! This view is particularly strengthened through the extensive collaborative work between them and my own masters level students working and researching as drama teachers. This has resulted in insightful and creative approaches to drama research evidenced via their success and the Drama Hub blog[2]. However, this transformation is even more concentrated at a time when the world is emerging from the devastation caused by the global pandemic.

It is clear that the effect of the SoR project is multi-layered and there is evidence of intersectional impact between the various participants connected to the project. SoR has impacted on specific children and groups of children in various ways, and this has been captured to a large extent through the commission's evaluative work. It is also clear that the model and approach has challenged, changed, and affected teachers' development to varying extents. This perhaps is the hardest area to change given the almost overbearing pressure facing many teachers today. No doubt, the project has also affected mentoring strategies within school and relationships with wider school communities, and this is commendable.

We know, have felt, and experienced the world change around us as a result of the global pandemic. As we emerge from the trauma of that time it is vital that society does not return to normality and potentially ignore the felt understanding of that time. This is crucial for us all, but particularly for young people who might potentially need space, time and opportunities to share their experience(s) through drama. Drama, theatre and the imagination in action are what help us to understand what it means to be human, and it is through the other - character, situation, dramatic world - that we can come to know ourselves. This is important to note as this drives to the core of the SoR project itself.

References

Asbury, K., Fox, L., Deniz, E. et al. (2021) *How is COVID-19 Affecting the Mental Health of Children with Special Educational Needs and Disabilities and Their Families?*. J Autism Dev Disord **51**, 1772–1780. Available at https://doi.org/10.1007/s10803-020-04577-2 [Accessed 3/05/2024]

Azorín, C. (2020) *'Beyond COVID-19 supernova. Is another education coming?'* Journal of Professional Capital and Community, 5(3). Available at: www.bit.ly/3EGKz92.

Ballin, B. (2021), 'Socially connected: the displaced teacher and the displaced child', in Jozifek, Z. et al, *To Be – researching connections between drama, well-being and education*. Budapest: To Be Consortium. Research report, curriculum and guidebook accessible online at https://bigbrum.org.uk/projects/to-be

Big Brum TIE. (2019). [online] *Engaging, Exploring, Expressing: the case for Theatre in Education*. Available at: https://docs.google.com/document/d/1EBSkjdv4iehF6xW5Qjyt-R1Pm9KEb6WhTFw47vayHsg/edit

---

[2] For the Drama Hub blog, see https://dramamtl.wordpress.com/

Bolton, C (2018) *Human Spaces - An evaluative Case study. Creating spaces for young people to explore what it means to be human.* Birmingham City University Report.

Bolton, C. and Patterson, R. (2022) *Socially Distant Stories from Beyond the Screen.* (Online) https://www.bcu.ac.uk/education-and-social-work/research/projects/socially-distant-stories

Cooper, C. (2020) *Socially Distant.* Birmingham: Big Brum TIE.

Cruikshanks, R. (2024) *School funding model: Effect of falling school rolls.* Education Policy Institute. Available at https://epi.org.uk/publications-and-research/school-funding-model-effect-of-falling-rolls/ [Accessed 15/04/2024]

Education Policy Institute. (2023) *Six charts that explain the state of the teaching workforce in England.* Available at https://epi.org.uk/publications-and-research/six-charts-that-explain-the-state-of-the-teaching-workforce-in-england/ [Accessed 2/05/2024]

Hargreaves, E., Quick, L. and Buchanan, D. (2023) 'National Curriculum and Assessment in England and the continuing narrowed experiences of lower-attainers in primary schools', *Journal of Curriculum Studies*, 55(5), pp. 545–561. Available at https://www.tandfonline.com/doi/full/10.1080/00220272.2023.2253455 [Accessed 1/5/2024]

Hordern, J. & Brooks, C. (2023) *'The core content framework and the 'new science' of educational research'*, Oxford Review of Education, 49(6), pp. 800–818. Available at https://www.tandfonline.com/doi/full/10.1080/03054985.2023.2182768 [Accessed 4/05/2024]

International Literacy Centre [ILC]. (2020). *Written evidence submitted to the Education Select Committee Inquiry into the impact of COVID-19 on education and children's services.* https://committees.parliament.uk/writtenevidence/9081/pdf/

Manzoni, C., & D'Angelo, A. (2021) *Migrant students in the UK pandemic – Impacts, school responses and community approaches.* National Institute of Economic and Social Research. Available at https://ddd.uab.cat/pub/caplli/2023/274949/supmigstuthrpanbey_a2023p57.pdf [Accessed 04/05/2024]

Moss, G. (2021) *The fragilities in the English education system revealed by Covid-19, & how to put them right.* BERA Bites, issue 7: Exploring the impact of Covid-19: Pedagogy, curriculum & assessment. Available at https://www.bera.ac.uk/publication/bera-bites-issue-7-exploring-the-impact-of-covid-19-pedagogy-curriculum-assessment [Accessed 4/05/2023]

Moss, G., Allen, R., Bradbury, A., Duncan, S., Harmey, S., and Levy, R. (2020). *Primary teachers' experience of the COVID-19 lockdown – Eight key messages for policymakers going forward.* UCL Institute of Education, London. Available at https://discovery.ucl.ac.uk/id/eprint/10103669/1/Moss_DCDT%20Report%201%20Final.pdf [Accessed 7.05.2024]

Nelson, J., Lynch, S. & Sharp, C. (2021). *Recovery During a Pandemic: the ongoing Impacts of Covid-19 on Schools Serving Deprived Communities*. NFER. Slough. Available at file:///C:/Users/id118087/Downloads/recovery_during_a_pandemic_the_ongoing_impacts_of_covid_19_on_schools_serving_deprived_communities.pdf [Access 7.05.2024)

OECD. (2020) *The impact of COVID-19 on student equity and inclusion: Supporting vulnerable students during school closures and school re-openings.* Available at https://www.oecd.org/coronavirus/policy-responses/the-impact-of-covid-19-on-student-equity-and-inclusion-supporting-vulnerable-students-during-school-closures-and-school-re-openings-d593b5c8/ [Accessed 3/05/2024]

Ofqual. (2021) *Learning during the pandemic: review of research from England*. Available at https://www.gov.uk/government/publications/learning-during-the-pandemic/learning-during-the-pandemic-review-of-research-from-england [Accessed 3/05/2024]

Ofsted. (2022) *Education recovery in schools: spring 2022*. Available at https://www.gov.uk/government/publications/education-recovery-in-schools-spring-2022/education-recovery-in-schools-spring-2022#the-current-state-of-childrens-education-and-personal-development [Accessed 3/05/2024]

People and Organisation Ltd. (2019) *More and Better Project – External Evaluators Report*. (Online). https://bigbrum.org.uk/projects/the-case-for-theatre-in-education

Perryman, J., Bradbury, A., Calvert, G., & Kilian, K. (2023) *Beyond Ofsted an inquiry into the future of school inspection*. London: NEU. Available at https://beyondofsted.org.uk/wp-content/uploads/2023/11/Beyond-Ofsted-Report.pdf [Accessed 1/05/2024]

PISA (2022) *PISA 2022 Results*. Available at https://www.oecd.org/publication/pisa-2022-results/ [Accessed 13/03/2024]   For more on (Programme for International Student Assessment (PISA) see www.oecd.org/pisa/

Bibliography

Ashworth, E., Kirkby, J., Bray, L. and Alghrani, A. (2022). *The impact of the COVID-19 pandemic on the education, health and social care provision for children with Special Educational Needs and Disabilities (SEND): The Ask, Listen, Act Study. Listen, Act Study*. Available at https://www.ljmu.ac.uk/-/media/files/ljmu/research/centres-and-institutes/rcbb/qualitative-evidence-briefing.pdf [Accessed 3/05/2024]

Cziboly, A. and Bethlenfalvy, A. (2020) *'Response to COVID-19 Zooming in on online process drama'*, Research in Drama Education: The Journal of Applied Theatre and Performance, 25(4), pp. 645–651.

Department for Education. (2024) *Outcomes of the review of the Initial Teacher Training Core Content Framework and Early Career Framework*. Available at https://assets.publishing.service.gov.uk/media/661d24ba08c3be25cfbd3e62/Outcomes_of_the_review_of_the_Initial_Teacher_Training_Core_Content_Framework_and_Early_Career_Framework.pdf [Accessed 2/04/2024]

Department for Education. (2023) *School workforce in England Reporting year 2022*. Available at https://explore-education-statistics.service.gov.uk/find-statistics/school-workforce-in-england [Accessed 1/05/2024]

Department for Education. (2019) *ITT Core Content Framework*. Available at https://assets.publishing.service.gov.uk/media/6061eb9cd3bf7f5cde260984/ITT_core_content_framework_.pdf [Accessed 5/08/2020]

Department for Education. (2019) *Early Career Framework*. Available at https://assets.publishing.service.gov.uk/media/60795936d3bf7f400b462d74/Early-Career_Framework_April_2021.pdf [Accessed 5/08/2020]

Department for Education (2015) *SEND Code of Practice: 0-25 years*. Available at https://assets.publishing.service.gov.uk/media/5a7dcb85ed915d2ac884d995/SEND_Code_of_Practice_January_2015.pdf [Accessed 8/05/2024]

Education Support. (2021) *State of teachers' health remains worrying despite emergence from Covid pandemic*. Available at https://www.educationsupport.org.uk/news-and-events/news/state-of-teachers-health-remains-worrying-despite-emergence-from-covid-pandemic/ [Accessed 3/05/2024]

Gallagher, K., Balt, C., Cardwell, N., & Charlebois, B. (2020) 'Response to COVID-19 – losing and finding one another in drama: personal geographies, digital spaces and new intimacies'. *Research in Drama Education: The Journal of Applied Theatre and Performance*, 25:4, 638-644

Kim, L.E., Oxley, L., Asbury, K. (2022) '"My brain feels like a browser with 100 tabs open": A longitudinal study of teachers' mental health and well-being during the COVID-19 pandemic.' *British Journal of Educational Psychology* (2022), 92, 299-318. Available at https://bpspsychub.onlinelibrary.wiley.com/doi/pdfdirect/10.1111/bjep.12450 [Accessed 2/05/2024]

McJames, N., Parnell, A., & O'Shea, A. (2023). 'Factors affecting teacher job satisfaction: a causal inference machine learning approach using data from TALIS 2018.' *Educational Review*, 1–25. Available at https://doi.org/10.1080/00131911.2023.2200594 [Accessed 4/05/2024]

National Foundation for Educational Research (NFER). (2024) *Teacher recruitment and retention crisis shows no signs of abating, new report reveals*. Press Release available at https://www.nfer.ac.uk/press-releases/teacher-recruitment-and-retention-crisis-shows-no-signs-of-abating-new-report-reveals/#:~:text=NFER's%20new%20Teacher%20Labour%20Market,workload%20pressures%20since%20the%20pandemic. [Accessed 4/05/2024]

Po-Chi, T. (2020) *Response to Covid-19 'Now I send you the rays of the sun': A drama project to rebuild post-Covid-19 resilience for teachers and children in Hong Kong*. Research in Drama Education Vol. 25, Issue 4. Pp 631-637

Office for Health Improvement and Disparities (2022) *COVID-19 mental health and wellbeing surveillance: report*. Available at https://www.gov.uk/government/publications/covid-19-mental-health-and-wellbeing-surveillance-report Chapter 4. [Accessed 3/05/2024]

Ofsted. (2023) *Independent review of teachers' professional development in schools: phase 1 findings*. Available at https://www.gov.uk/government/publications/teachers-professional-development-in-schools-phase-1-findings/independent-review-of-teachers-professional-development-in-schools-phase-1-findings#:~:text=Most%20training%20during%20the%20pandemic,had%20received%20during%20the%20pandemic. [Accessed 3/05/2024]

See, B. H. (2024) 'Insights into UK Teachers' Wellbeing and Workload during the COVID-19 Pandemic Lockdown: Testimonies from the Silent Voices and Lessons Learnt.' *Education Sciences* 14, no. 4: 344. Available at https://doi.org/10.3390/educsci14040344 [Accessed 4/05/2024]

"Drama, theatre and the imagination in action are what help us to understand what it means to be human, and it is through the other - character, situation, dramatic world - that we can come to know ourselves. This is important to note as this drives to the core of the SoR project itself."

Evaluation of Theory and Pedagogy in the Schools of Recovery Project

Dr Adam Bethlenfalvy

Executive Summary

This evaluation report examines the pedagogy and theory applied by Big Brum Theatre in Education Company in the 'Creating "Schools of Recovery"' Project. The evaluation examines the key tenets of Big Brum's Artistic Policy and reports on how these are present in their practice.

The evaluator found that:

- The company is extremely consistent in implementing its theory in practice.

- This is most apparent in the complex content offered to students and the thorough and layered facilitation that opens space for the participants.

- Engaging teachers in the content and the students' reflections – a central aim of the project – was only partly achieved in this case, the reason behind this could be the limitation of moving teachers out of their professional teacher perspective.

- The evaluation makes some recommendations concerning the engagement of teachers and also the updating of the Artistic Policy with regards to engagement with teaching staff. The recommendations include:

    » Further developing enactive modes of engagement with students;

    » Offering specific tasks to teachers that allow them to connect on a more personal level to the content and the reactions, thoughts of the students;

    » Offering some specific guidelines to teachers, related to questioning, that would help them develop a more varied strategy for the follow-up of the programmes.

Background and contextual information

Big Brum has based its work on an Artistic Policy (Big Brum, 2011) that articulates the theoretical and pedagogical foundations of its practice. The document has been revisited and developed over time by company members, the latest version is dated January 2011, and is still considered the basis of the company's activities[3]. Some key elements of this four-page document have been re-worked for more effective communication of the company's core values into nine Principles of Working (see page 9). I will be evaluating the pedagogy and theory placed into practice within the 'Creating "Schools of Recovery"' Project based on this document, looking at how its key components appear in the practice of the company and how they are reflected in the feedback of teachers and also the actor-teacher training work done by the company.

First, I shall review the document and then reflect on how its key tenets are apparent in the company's work. I will offer a short overview of the methodology employed in this evaluation and then articulate some recommendations.

Theory and pedagogy

It is useful to briefly discuss the two concepts that are at the centre of this evaluation. I shall be following the widely accepted understanding of theory as the general set of principles that are the basis the company's work. Pedagogy is referred to as the *"art, science, or profession of teaching"* (Merriam-Webster Dictionary), but Harry Daniels suggests that it *"should be construed as referring to forms of social practice which shape and form the cognitive, affective and moral development of individuals"* (2001:1). This later definition, besides placing the affective and moral side-by-side with the cognitive, also places the focus on the impact and hence the aim of teaching, clarifying that Daniels is referring to teaching practices that *"are understood as those which influence the formation of identity as well as learning outcome"* (ibid). While Daniels's definition encompasses a fairly open and holistic understanding of pedagogy, a number of approaches to teaching have more specific agendas set as the aim of their educational methods. I will not deconstruct Big Brum's pedagogy to place its elements on the complex map of pedagogies but will make some connections with current educational theories after the process of analysing Big Brum's approach.

Big Brum's Artistic Policy (AP) articulates a well-defined materialist philosophical premise

---

[3] I have vivid memories of company days spent examining, discussing and developing the Artistic Policy collectively when I was a company member in 2004-2005 so all staff members have an understanding and ownership of the document.

and the role of art as a mode of knowing, exploring and understanding the knowable world in a safe, imaginative and enactive way. The Company sees the TIE programme as a *"point of mediation between the young people and the world they inhabit"* (2011:2) and understands its role as using *"the art form to enable young people to educate their own minds not in **what** to think but **how** to think"* (ibid, emphasis in the original). So, while the theatre image and dramatic action of the performance element of the TIE programmes compact reality and resonate a segment of it that is relevant for their audience, the artist-educators offer structures for the audience-participants to make meaning of these images and the reality compacted within them socially. *"Image enables us to cognise apparently different aspects of reality in their essence and in relation to each other"*, explains the AP, pointing out the importance of artistic representation as human-situation centred, complex but accessible representation of the world. It is clear from Big Brum's Artistic Policy that they examine the world from a critical stance, but also that they aim to offer genuine freedom to audiences in exploring the theatre image and dramatic action and deciding for themselves what to think of these. It is useful to point out here, that the Company aims to create opportunities for young people to experience felt understanding. This concept stems from Walter Benjamin's 'feeling thoughtfully' and 'thinking feelingly' (Davis, 2014:90), aiming to connect different faculties in enhancing complex meaning making.

Big Brum's Artistic Policy incorporates key theories such as Heathcote's 'crucible paradigm' which considers students as collaborators (Matusiek-Varley, 2016:220), and Vygotsky's Zone of Proximal Development (ZPD) that emphasises the importance of meaning making processes reaching beyond existing knowledge, happening through social activity and engagement in the surrounding world (Daniels, 2001:56). The AP also emphasises the importance of conceptual learning in contrast to the issue-based approach that has become widespread in applied theatre. The significance of coherence within the TIE programme – including follow-up materials offered to teachers – is also emphasised.

These key tenets of their pedagogy are also expressed in Big Brum's nine principles of working, especially in points such as: Trust every child; Build safe spaces; No wrong answers; Ask the big questions; Get lost in the moment (see page 9).

In an interview conducted for this evaluation report, Richard Holmes, the Artistic Director of Big Brum, talked about the importance of the AP for the company. He said: *"I think that this document has kept the company on a straight path since 2015 when the majority of the company left"*, as it captures profoundly the key pillars of the company's work. Discussing whether it has lost its relevance since the last rework in 2011 Holmes said that *"the theoretical underpinnings of the materialist standpoint, the Vygotskian theories and the Crucible Paradigm, I think these have possibly become even more relevant since COVID"*. Holmes talks about the significance of the document in the school context that was severely impacted by the pandemic. He explains that *"the new normal was a return to the old normal, but in a more severe manner. There was lots of money given to engage young people in their learning, in what they missed out on during the pandemic, which wasn't maths and wasn't necessarily subject matter, but they had actually missed out on really coming to understand what it was that they were experiencing during the lockdown."* Holmes states that *"putting the child at the centre of the work and the schools became more pertinent after those two years of lockdown"*. Holmes places emphasis on the importance of really listening to the students and offering them space for exploring the troubled world around them.

Holmes also states, that *"if I was to add anything to this document, then it would be a section recognising teachers as a displaced people as well, besides identifying young people as displaced."* The Artistic Director explains that *"the teacher's disconnection, isolation, alienation was a trend, not only in schools, but I think it was a trend that we all experienced very fundamentally and very objectively in that period"*. This realisation is also discussed in the research report of the To Be project. *"Big Brum has also come to recognise that the same forces affecting children in schools also displace teachers, that they too are increasingly and aggressively being denied 'their historical sense of self and community … the art of living freely in the world as social historical beings'. They are also increasingly being denied spaces where they can be their authentic 'teacher selves', enabling young people to live freely and socially: the gap between their 'have-to-be' and imagined teacher selves becomes ever-harder to close"* (Ballin, 2021: 67). Isolation appearing both among students and teachers has become one of the most precarious problems of our time, according to Big Brum, and so they have placed it as one of the cornerstones of the 'Creating "Schools of Recovery"' Project. Building connections between people in different ways is one of the aims of the project according to Holmes.

I have reflected on some of the key components of Big Brum's Artistic Policy but have not entered into a detailed analysis of the document as that would leave too little space for the evaluation of the practice implemented in the project. However, it is useful to connect the theories above with some influential pedagogies to reflect on its connections with current educational thinking. The social criticism engrained in Big Brum's pedagogy can be seen as analogous to Freirean pedagogy which aims to critically explore the world and intends *"to provoke a critical consciousness in the audience"* (Neelands, 2006:21). Charles N. Adams Jr. argues for Theatre in Education to be seen as critical pedagogy, which, he explains, *"is a bricolage of approaches and philosophies of teaching and learning that view education as a practice of freedom and work in opposition to forms of schooling that, as bell hooks states, serve to reinforce domination"* (2013:291). The connection with Big Brum's pedagogy is evident.

Gábor Takács argues that TIE has strong connections with constructivist pedagogy, as *"both state that supporting children in creating adaptive knowledge, i.e. understanding how to relate to the world surrounding them, is an important role of education. This entails teaching children how to be independent, supporting them in creating their own notions, theories and in making their own decisions"* (2021:18). These aims are clearly present in Big Brum's policy document.

The concept of felt-understanding can be connected to Laura I. Rendón's Sentipensante Pedagogy, which *"guided by a nondual epistemology and ontology, is based on integration and consonance, representing the union of sensing and thinking processes and the balance between inner and outer knowing. The model includes six dialectical spaces expressed as a difrasismo where two concepts, critically examined to reveal how they differ and how they complement each other, illuminate a larger reality. In this fashion, intellectualism is united with intuition to reveal a holistic view of teaching and learning"* (2009:142). While the methodology of this approach differs in major ways from Big Brum's, the association in the aim of enhancing holistic learning is an important connection.

Big Brum's pedagogy and approach, expressed theoretically in its Artistic Policy, connects with significant educational thinking. The evaluation will continue by looking at in what ways and to what extent these concepts appear in the practice put in place in the Schools of Recovery project and project model.

Evaluation of Big Brum's pedagogy in practice
The focus of this section of the evaluation will be based on the observed TIE programmes in May 2023. Four performances of 'Minotaur' were observed in two different schools, one in a rural context, while the other was in an urban surrounding. The rural school was a smaller institution, while the one in a city was a much bigger one. There was an apparent difference in the school staff's relationship to Big Brum's contribution; while the village school staff seemed more welcoming, at the other school the staff seemed less engaged. The latter school was new to Big Brum whereas the company had already done work at the former. This evaluation will not go into a more detailed exploration of these differences, as data was not collected directly from staff or pupils by this evaluator: this information has been shared in order to give a sense of the varying contexts that the programmes were

realised in.

The sessions of 'Minotaur' were facilitated by Big Brum's permanent lead actor-teacher Zoe Simon, who also directed the production that was performed by five trainee actors from Birmingham City University, working with the company on an internship. The trainee actors performed the full tour and engaged with participants in the interactive parts of the programme. I interviewed them to find out which elements of Big Brum's pedagogy they had become consciously aware of and what were they able to apply during their internship. Their situation is also interesting, because they are still students as well, so their sensitivity towards the participants in the schools would be higher. Some of their key points were the following:

Freedom and space: The student actors thought that Big Brum offers children freedom. *"I think there's a real freedom in the conversation that they don't get in the classrooms"* said one of the students. Another added that *"giving kids space is a really key thing that they do"*. When asked to specify she said *"I think Big Brum has a lot of questions, but you also feel very much like there is space to consider that and not always have to give an answer. Rather you can sit and think about it."* When probed further on this issue, she added *"they don't really push the narrative onto the kids and kids are not obliged to actually answer back, they answer back because they choose to."* These comments connect with the Company's perception of children and young people expressed in the Artistic Policy.

Collaboration and hierarchy: One of the students explained that *"Big Brum recognises children as independent individuals. They are talked to seriously: they are talked to just like how you would talk to another adult."* Another actor discusses working against hierarchy in the facilitation: *"I think it's centred on a dialogic approach. It's centred on that everyone is on the same level. Just because Zoe leads it doesn't mean she's the teacher and the way that Zoe and the others do it is so clear that it's like an open space and anything can be said."* Another actor added that, *"I think it's the partnership. We're going to work together. We're all on the same level."* This can be seen as a clear reference to the Crucible Paradigm that is central to the Company's work.

Inclusion: One of the actors said that Big Brum *"is one of the only environments where every day I knew I came in, I was accepted for what I was"*. She described a moment in the rehearsal process when she was struggling so much that she had an emotional breakdown *"and Zoe [the director] was like: it's fine. And that's something I think I like carry with me that you should feel like yourself in a space. I think that carries through on tour as well for the kids."* Another actor added that *"I would say not just for the kids, but I think overall Big Brum cares a lot about everyone. I think especially for us throughout this process, there* *was so much support, which I haven't seen a lot through the theatre industry. I haven't seen that level of support. I think just generally they care for theatre and they care about the children. As well, the people that work for them. It's just that level of care that I personally haven't seen anywhere else."*

Material: Another element that the actors reflected on as an important feature of Big Brum's work was that the material they use is *"not censored for the children. It's not adapted for the children. It's just very good."* They agreed on this being a positive approach, because *"the children will take from it what they will, and it is a good thing that they don't automatically assume what children will and won't want to see."*

While these reflections serve as useful pointers and reveal as much about the training process offered by Big Brum for the implementation of the project in schools, it is important to match them with the observations and the content of other documents related to the TIE programme. I will be doing this by going through three distinct elements of the realisation, discussing what content was offered in this specific programme and how theatre was used in this process, how and what space was offered for the participants/ students in this programme and what spaces were opened for teachers by Big Brum.

Offering content

The TIE programme is centred around Chris Cooper's play, a rework of the Greek legend of the Minotaur, that tells the story in nine episodes. The myth itself has several variants, and Cooper's version builds less on the Athenian versions and shows Theseus – the killer of the half-bull, half-human creature – as a cold and manipulative politician, who reaches his goal through using his beauty and the vulnerability of others. Meanwhile, the Minotaur appears as a child-monster, trapped in its mingled body and the Labyrinth. Cooper's version of the story is clearly centred around the concept of power and use. This itself is an important element related to the content offered by Big Brum, it has a clarity concerning its focus on the metatext level which reappears through specific action, dialogues and objects on the plot level. Using Edward Bond's theatre terminology, the play has a clear, definable centre: this is *"when you have reduced the dramatic problem to its essential confrontation"* (Bond, 1996:166). Bond explains in the following quote how the centre appears in the drama in a structured way, exploring and testing the central confrontation in various ways.

"A play consists of one speech which is repeated in increasingly searching ways. Each character takes the speech and reworks it. This speech is the central speech (CS)

34

- it contains the basic theme of the play and also - in its utterance - the way the characters relate to the theme. At each occasion a character will take the speech and then push it as far as he can in exploration of the theme. It will search for the truths the play wishes to tell. Usually in the speech there will come a line which is the furthest that character can take the speech - for himself - at that time. Often the speech will continue for a while. It will then reflect on what it has discovered in the central line of the central speech....as the play progresses the CS and the CL [central line] will develop, becoming more clarified, revealing and definite. The speaking of the speech will define the characters: for some the CL will become more human, in others more inhuman." (1996:161)

Big Brum clearly follows and uses this structure as the Centre, the central speech and central line appear in the beginning of the internally used programme structure as well. There are also a number of contradictions offered within the text and its performance that can create productive engagement with the content. We can see the contradictions appearing on various levels. There is a contradiction already on the level of the popular/expected narrative (Theseus as a hero) and the narrative of the fiction (Theseus appears as a manipulative, inhuman narcissist). The conceptual level (the concept of hero) is also juxtaposed with the actual actions of Theseus in the drama, and similarly, the concept of monster is juxtaposed with the actions of the Minotaur, for example when he plays like a child with a toy ship inside the Labyrinth. The performance, as directed by Zoe Simon, also contrasts words said by the characters with their actions at some points, opening space to examine their real intentions. These contradictions widen the spectrum on which both the concepts and the actions can be analysed, they provoke meaning making, which can be made social and conscious through effective facilitation. Big Brum's commitment to conceptual learning is realised through such material, that put the conceptual and the particular (action, image, sentence) side-by-side and allow the audience to make sense of it for themselves. Evidently, the story is not dumbed down for younger audiences, but the complexities are not in the plotline, but are structured into the relationship of the different layers in and behind the plot, and in its performance.

Big Brum' pedagogy is based on the tenet that we can understand the world surrounding us - and ourselves as well - through fiction. The Bondian concept of Site plays an important role in building a coherent and conscious relationship between the actual world and the fictional reality of the drama. Chris Cooper argues that *"Bondian drama is distinguished by the concept of the Site. Sites are used in Bond's drama primarily to establish the dramatic logic of the situation in order to illuminate our social reality and forge the direct connection between the play and the experience of the audience. Site is a tool for practice and analysis that can enrich all drama work. There are many sites in drama but we can identify four main categories based on Bond's own definitions:*

- *Site A – The social sites, our era.*
- *Site B – The specific sites of the drama/play through which the story is told.*
- *Site C – The action, images and objects that activates sites A and B in site D.*
- *Site D – the audience/participant as the site of the imagination – the source of human value and meaning, humanness.*

*Each Site is dialectically interconnected or contained in the other. Each site is specific and in playing the play it is the responsibility of the actor to resist both **generalising** 'joy', 'anger' or 'fear', and **commenting** on the situation they are enacting"* (2013:132). Cooper's explanation reflects on how the artists' awareness of the sites and their reflection in all the elements of the performance (including set, props, images and actions besides the text) becomes key in offering a coherent and resonant performance.

Dorothy Heathcote explains that *"people have most power to become involved at a caring and urgently involved level if they are placed in a quite specific relationship with the action, because this brings with it inevitably the responsibility, and, more particularly, the viewpoint which gets them into an effective involvement"* (1984:168). In her seminal essay 'Signs and Portents' (1984) Heathcote offers frame to be used as the concept that offers the participants a specific position or task in relation to dramatic action offered by the TIE company. The concept was originally used by the sociologist Erving Goffman in his groundbreaking study 'Frame Analysis' (1986) and was then developed by Heathcote to be used in DIE and TIE. While often connected to the concept of 'frame distancing' that *"involves taking the optical idea of a new angle one step further, recognising the possibility of looking at an object from various 'distances', which is also a device for making situational perspective shifts in the drama"* (Eriksson, 2022: 25), the concept of frame – in itself – need not be considered a distancing device. It can be used without offering participants an explicit role and even an explicit task, but to offer some reference concepts, questions and thus focus their attention on specific dimensions of the play. Big Brum start their programme by looking at the table of King Minos which is placed at some distance from the set of the play. The children then see some actions of the King and a soundscape connects this to what then develops into the narrative of the arrival of Theseus to Knossos. While this scene allows the facilitator to give some context for the play, the discussion following it also offers a question that can frame the participants' observation of the following scene: What is it like being a King? Though Minos does not appear later in the play, the participants are invited to observe the nature of power and politics that is omnipresent in the metatext of the plot and also in the world surrounding them.

Two of teachers of the Year 4 groups commented that they thought that the language of the play was too difficult for some of the children in the group. This is possibly true and the play (and in some cases the noise created by canteen staff in the hall) sometimes made it difficult to hear the actors: it is important to see the performance as a complex unity of words, actions, images and space and the experience and comprehension of the audience is based on the combination and interaction of these elements in performance. While students with language competence challenges might have found some of the text alienating, the actions, images, emotions could have engaged them on different levels. The play is written so that scenes that are based on almost solely action – episode one, three, five and seven, out of the nine episodes – alternate with scenes that carry more, complex dialogues. The performance of 'Minotaur' also aimed to open space for engagement through slowing down or extending actions. These moments can either draw the attention of the audience or lose them, as noise and tiredness can lead to distraction. However, my observations during the four performances were that these were the exceptions and not the majority. The teachers' observation might also be based on the centrality of language in their own pedagogy.

As can be seen from the analysis above Big Brum offers the possibility for conceptual, complex learning by presenting a narrative that has been analysed and made coherent through a defined centre. The fiction and reality are consciously connected in the performance that is framed through action and questions that direct the attention of participants on concepts that are in the realm of the aimed understanding. The complexity of the narrative invites students to step into their Zone of Proximal Development, where the frame and structure of the whole programme offer the scaffolding that helps participants to *"stand a head taller than themselves in everyday life"* (Artistic Policy, 3).

Opening space for the participants

Opening space for the participants to engage with the theatre production is a defining element of Theatre in Education. I will look at how this space is created in the 'Minotaur' programme through its structuring, through the activities offered and facilitation.

The frame discussed above is an integral component of the overall programme structure. The performance is halted several times, and the facilitator engages the students in discussion. These breaks in the performance allow students to clarify any questions they have about the plot, but their main aim is to open space for the audience to reflect on the play. The interactions develop the concepts set up at the beginning, examining the concepts of monster and hero in relation to authority ('kingness'). The conceptual and the concrete are examined in light of each other in these interactions. While the performance offers the concrete, the specific, the questions asked by the facilitator offer the conceptual. The two work in a dialectical structure, allowing participants to clarify the concepts for themselves socially and evaluate actions and events in the play. Connecting conceptual and practical levels is also key in developing a higher level of thinking.

While the modes of possible interactions in a TIE programme can vary on a wide spectrum, encoding meaning making in the symbolic, the iconic, or the enactive modes (Bruner, 1996:155), the 'Minotaur' programme offers primarily the symbolic mode – discussion – as the form of meaning making. The major reason behind this could be the time constraint, engaging in other types of activities could be more time consuming, while the performance of the play uses up a considerable portion of the full session. However, there are specific qualities to these discussions that make them very different from usual classroom teacher-student communication. One of the key differences is the content, the subject-matter that is at the centre of the discourse: this has been analysed in the previous section. But there are also important differences in how the interactions are facilitated. The five actors and the facilitator often change from whole group discussions into five or six groups to continue the exploration in smaller groups. This creates a smaller teacher-student ratio and allows many more participants to speak. The actor/teachers also have the opportunity to gently invite students who are quiet to share their views. Although this seems evident, it is important to point out as larger groups and an overburdened curriculum lead to less space for those students who are less sure of their ideas or have linguistic constraints and are afraid to talk in front of the whole group. All contributions are taken seriously by the teachers, giving value to independent thinking and the student's personal perspective. This approach validates out of the box ideas, imaginative responses or emotions-based reflections, so focus is not only on the cognitive, rational thoughts, which is also an important difference with the usual classroom discourse.

The above is also very consciously facilitated by the questioning used by Big Brum. While there is a fairly large body of literature on questioning used in drama education with some arguing for its growing importance in the changing world (Saxton et al, 2018), it is useful to not try to squeeze Big Brum's practice into already existing taxonomies. I could differentiate three categories of questions used by the facilitator based on their pedagogical aim based on my observation of the four sessions of the 'Minotaur'. The audience was invited to respond cognitively about how they understood what they had seen through the reasoning questions asked by the facilitator, for example when she asked *"did you see a hero?"* Students could explain their understanding of the concept of hero through contrasting it to the action of the play, explain why or why not they saw a hero: they were reasoning. Another type of question invited students to immerse themselves imaginatively in the space and situation of the fiction, for example *"what do you think it feels like to be in that Labyrinth?"* or *"where does she feel the fear inside her?"* These immersive or sensate questions invite students to respond to the fiction feelingly, reflect on the bodily and emotional impact. While both of the previous types of questions rely on the use of the imagination, the third category explicitly aims to move the imagination into action. For example, there was a scene in the performance when the Minotaur was sitting in the heart of the Labyrinth and playing with a ship. The ship's sail had a sun painted on it. The facilitator asked the students *"what does the Minotaur see when he looks at the sail?"* One girl responded: *"He sees an eye looking at him"*. The facilitator probed further: *"and what does that eye see when it looks at the Minotaur?"* A fruitful interaction followed. The *imaginative* question specifically moves the thinking into a more poetic, philosophical direction, allowing participants to express themselves outside the usual rational discourse, articulating profound thoughts and insights in new ways. Altogether the three layers that are opened up through the questioning offer an holistic and multidimensional understanding of the examined situation and connected concepts. Together with the dialectic dynamic between the specific and conceptual discussed earlier, Big Brum offers the students space to engage with theatre in an accessible but complex, holistic mode that connects the specific and the universal/conceptual aspects of the content and opens the rational, the sensate and the imaginative modes of resonating on them within one process. Mike Fleming sees this type of space created for meaning making as a key opportunity for arts in education, he states that *"understanding is not an event and certainly not an 'all or nothing' affair but more akin to an extended process. When we see understanding not as a form of colonisation of knowledge but more as a process of refining and deepening, of seeing things from new angles and making fresh connections there are important implications for education in general and more specifically for pedagogy"* (2012: 1).

Opening space for teachers

The 'Creating "Schools of Recovery"' project has a specific focus on teachers, Artistic Director Richard Holmes explains how Big Brum set out to do this:

> *"I think that the aim from the outset was to engage the staff in the TIE experience so that they had a felt relationship to the work. In the same way as I think that we try to give the young people a felt relationship. So, their felt relationship to the material becomes the thing that drives reason or seeks logic to uncover or explain the situation to ourselves and to others. I think that's what we want to do, sort of connect teachers to their students through the material. So, we're connecting the teachers to the*

material that the young people are striving to understand or to explore."

Following the quote above, the project aims to create a connection between teachers and students through human engagement, besides the institutionalised relationship that is based on professional responsibility. Holmes explains the connection between the story of the Minotaur and this aim: *"The Minotaur is driven by hunger, this is what the children were saying. He can't not eat children. Theseus is driven by revenge, hatred. But the two things, they're the barriers to being able to see the other. And I think that's what's at the heart of the artistic policy, is that ability to see and hear each other as human beings rather than the other. And that's, I think, what we set out to explore with teachers, how can we help teachers see young people as not the other but as humans seeking meaning in the world."* Though the aim set up by Big Brum seems fairly straightforward, it is actually quite complex, as teachers are present primarily in their professional capacity in the sessions and carry this frame into how they are present in the sessions happening in an institutional context.

Big Brum engaged with teachers directly primarily through the pre-performance and post-performance teacher meetings and used all opportunities to enhance communication with school staff within the project. This aspect of the project is being evaluated independently, so I will only reflect on two elements here. As access to teachers was limited by understandable time constraints within the project my evaluation relies primarily on data collected and documented by the Company at their reflective meetings with teachers.

There is evidence that teachers noted elements of Big Brum's pedagogy: there are many reflections on the types of questions asked, for example, in the document recording what teachers were able to adapt into their own practice. The importance of asking open ended questions clearly stuck with a number of teachers, and also the need of not putting pressure on children to give the 'correct response', giving them time to think. As curriculum teaching is largely language based this element of the Big Brum's pedagogy can probably be included in daily practice if deemed important by the teacher. Teachers also reflected on the possibility of *"putting a specific problem or classroom issue into a fictional social story"*, which again is at the heart of Big Brum's work. The Company reflects on these elements in their nine Principles of Working, but it might be useful to go further and offer teachers more explicit and practical assistance in their formulation of questions and also in the choice of fictional stories through written materials offering them guidelines.

Interestingly there is much more evidence of teachers engaging on a personal level with

'Ripped', a TIE programme centred around a school incident, than with the 'Minotaur' programme, which is set in a more distant fictional context. Perhaps this is so, because teachers feel personal connection to the school context, or the problem offered within that fictional narrative. While there is more data from teachers regarding other Big Brum performances there is not so much in relation to the 'Minotaur' programme: the same is true concerning follow-up work done by teachers. Many of the teacher comments are related to behaviour, but also others that were noted down, like *"children found it good as it was a 'treat' – not followed up with written work"* or *"mixed response: some children did not understand"* suggest a professional, rather than a personal engagement. This is understandable as teachers are present in an institutional context and the ethos of the school has an impact on how and what they focus their attention on. If the school places an emphasis on behaviour, teachers can find it hard to focus on the children's creativity. It was also clear from the observation that teachers were – understandably – paying attention primarily to their students and not the performance. Perhaps this was a barrier in engaging on a personal level with the content.

Although Big Brum framed the session for teachers, asking them to observe the participants, perhaps in some cases a more specific focus or task that is related to specific performance and the possibilities it offers to the participants could be offered to the teachers. For example, in the case of the 'Minotaur' TIE programme it could be a focus on the poetic or philosophical language of the students or inviting teachers to create more imaginative questions – a type of question that is not used very often in classroom interactions.

Research methodology

The methodology of this evaluation was developed to compare theoretical principles and the praxis of the company. Hence, it is partly based on already existing company documents (Artistic Policy, programme structures, etc.) that have been put side by side with data derived from various sources. The data collection methods used for this evaluation were: observations of theatre in education programmes delivered in schools; interviews conducted with trainee actor-teachers and the Artistic Director; feedback from teachers of participating students; and art and written materials created by participating students.

Four performances were observed of the 'Minotaur' TIE programme in May 2023 with Year 4 children in two schools that had visibly different connections to the company and its work. While one of the schools had an ongoing relationship with Big Brum and the teachers had some understanding of their work, the other school was new to their practice. As a practitioner and academic working in a different country I was unable to attend more performances, but data collected by fellow evaluators was shared and examined for this evaluation as well. The analysis of data was based on the finding the key theoretical tenets' recurrence in the practical work and the responses of key stakeholders to Big Brum's practice in this project. The project itself encompassed such a large body of work that the evaluator was unable to cover its entirety, so the choice was to focus in more depth on a limited body of work.

Conclusion and recommendations

The quality of both the theatre performance and the interactions in the 'Minotaur' programme are unquestionable. Big Brum's practice embodies its well-articulated theoretical and pedagogical groundings. The consistency of Big Brum's work is also reflected in the fact that the principles outlined in the Artistic Policy are applied also in their work done with interns, besides the programmes realised in schools. As Big Brum's work has been building towards impacting on teachers as well as students it would be timely to incorporate these developments into the Artistic Policy in more detail.

The specific programme that was at the centre of this evaluation offered a complex and engaging performance, while the primary mode of interaction was discussion that opened space for students to engage dialectically in the conceptual and the specific. The facilitation focussed not only on rational understanding, but also on the affective and the imaginative: this is a specific strength of the company's way of working. While there is more evidence of teachers' personal engagement in other programmes, in the case of the 'Minotaur' the staff did not connect powerfully on a personal level.

Concerning the interaction with the students, it would be useful to develop the discussions further into other enactive modes of engagement that allow students to do and create more. The engagement of teachers depends highly on the specific programme and in some cases it would be advisable to offer specific tasks to teachers that allow them to relieve their professional frame of mind and connect on a more personal level to the content and the reactions, thoughts of the students. It would also be useful for the company to offer some specific guidelines to teachers, related to questioning, that would help them develop a more varied strategy for the follow-up of the programmes.

Bibliography

Adams, C.N.Jr. (2013) 'TIE and critical pedagogy', in A. Jackson and C. Vine (eds) *Learning through Theatre*. Oxon: Routledge, pp. 287–304.

Ackroyd, J. (2006) 'Introduction', in J. Ackroyd (ed.) *Research methodologies for drama education*. Stoke on Trent, UK: Trentham Books.

Baldwin, P. and Fleming, K. (2003) *Teaching Literacy through Drama*. London: Routledge Falmer.

Ballin, B. (2021) 'Socially connected: the displaced teacher and the displaced child', in Jozifek, Z. et al, *To Be – researching connections between drama, well-being and education*. Budapest: To Be Consortium.

Big Brum (N.D.) *Our nine principles of working*. Birmingham: Big Brum Theatre in Education Company. https://bigbrum.org.uk/9-principles-of-working

Big Brum (2011) *Artistic Policy*. Birmingham: Big Brum Theatre in Education Company. https://static1.squarespace.com/static/60d061bcd571dc3fb7554ef9/t/60da28adc343fd57d8339fd4/1624910001086/Big+Brum+Artistic+Policy.pdf

Bond, E. (1996) *Edward Bond's Letters 3*. Amsterdam: Harwood Academic Publishers.

Bruner, J. (1996) *The Culture of Education*. Harvard: Harvard University Press.

Cooper, C. (2013) 'The Performer in TIE', in A. Jackson and C. Vine (eds) *Learning Through Theatre: The Changing Face of Theatre in Education*. Third edition. London: Routledge.

Daniels, H. (2001) *Vygotsky and Pedagogy*. London: Routledge Falmer.

Davis, D. (2014) *Imagining the Real: towards a new theory of drama in education*. Stoke on Trent, UK: Trentham Books.

Eriksson, S.A. (2022) 'Distancing as topos in process drama', in M. McAvoy and P. O'Connor (eds) *The Routledge Companion to Drama in Education*. London: Routledge, pp. 18–31.

Fleming, M. (2012) *The Arts in Education*. London: Routledge.

Goffman, E. (1986) *Frame Analysis: an essay on the organization of experience*. Northeastern University Press edition. ed. Northeastern University Press, Boston.

Heathcote, D. (1984) *Collected Writings on Education and Drama*. Northwestern University Press, Evanston.

Heathcote, D., (2012) *The Fight for Drama – The Fight for Education*. The JOURNAL for DRAMA in EDUCATION. Volume 28, Issue 1.

Matusiak-Varley, B. (2016) *Dorothy Heathcote: A Model for Alchemical Leadership*, PhD thesis, Durham University. Available at Durham E-Theses Online: http://etheses.dur.ac.uk/11775/

Merriam-Webster. (n.d.). Pedagogy. In Merriam-Webster.com dictionary. Retrieved March 17, 2024, from https://www.merriam-webster.com/dictionary/pedagogy

Neelands, J. (2006) 'Re-imaging the Reflective Practitioner: towards a philosophy of critical praxis', in J. Ackroyd (ed.) *Research methodologies for drama education*. Stoke on Trent, UK: Trentham Books.

Rendón, I.L. (2009) *Sentipensante (sensing/thinking) pedagogy: educating for wholeness, social justice and liberation*. Sterling: Stylus Publishing.

Saxton, J. et al. (2018) *Asking Better Questions: Teaching and Learning for a Changing World*. 3rd edition. Pembroke Publishers.

Takács, G. (2021) 'Constructivist Drama', in *Pedagogy and Politics in Hungarian TIE*. Budapest: Káva Kulturális Műhely, pp. 18–39. Available at: https://kavaszinhaz.hu/wp-content/uploads/2021/02/pedpol_kkonyvek6_jav4.pdf.

Challenging Theseus, challenging the curriculum: how the TIE programme of 'Minotaur' relates to the school curriculum

Dr Kostas Amoiropolous

Executive Summary

This research is a small-scale evaluative case study developed to evaluate the theatre in education programme 'Minotaur', created and applied by Big Brum TIE Company for students in KS2. The evaluation focuses on how the programme relates to the school curriculum, what pedagogical model is being applied, and how it is communicated to teachers and students.

The research included observing the programme in two primary classes in Birmingham, interviewing the programme producers, and receiving feedback from teachers' focus groups.

The research explores Big Brum's pedagogical model, as described in the company's official documents and its team's interviews and situates it in the area of Heathcote's crucible paradigm and the critical pedagogy movement. The research then evaluates the programme results by analysing the collected data against the company's theoretical claims. The company primarily offers a challenging work model for approaching the curriculum and the pedagogical praxis based on the crucible paradigm.

However, some important points need to be made about how Big Brum's aims and method are communicated and shared with the teachers. This includes recommendations about:

» More frequent meetings and programme-specific written information for teachers (especially in advance of the programme coming in and including dialogue about the school's curriculum and topics/themes being taught);

» An explanation to teachers of the crucible paradigm;

» Providing indicative follow-up activities, including some which allow schools to share selected children's work with the company;

» An advance presentation of the programme to teachers[4].

"The programme will challenge a school's overt and hidden curriculum, based on the 'banking model' where children are seen as learners whose ignorance is gradually lessened."

Introduction and background

This study presents an evaluative case study examining how Big Brum Theatre in Education (TIE) Company's work relates to the school curriculum. It is a part of the larger project 'Creating "Schools of Recovery"' and evaluates the model of work that Big Brum Theatre in Education company has applied in engaging teachers with the TIE programmes produced by the company so they could be able to offer sustained and inclusive support to their students who also experience these programmes. The evaluation focuses on a specific TIE programme, 'Minotaur', which is addressed to students of Key Stage Two, between 8 and 9 years old.

The 'Minotaur' TIE programme is based on the ancient Greek myth of Theseus and the Minotaur, and it develops in nine episodes. Big Brum specifies the focus of the programme as:

> *"What makes a monster, a monster?' It's the question that 'Minotaur', a play by Chris Cooper, aims to answer. Gods and monsters, heroes, and kings – these are the main focuses of Greek mythology. But what about the perspective of the 'monster' inside the labyrinth?"* (Big Brum, n.d.a)

Chris Cooper wrote the play, while the TIE programme was initially directed by the current artistic director of Big Brum, Richard Holmes, in 2019. The programme was later recreated by the current facilitator of the programme and the lead Actor Teacher of the company, Zoe Simon, who had taken part in the first production cycle as an actor/teacher. Zoe Simon redirected 'Minotaur' under the guidance of the initial director, Richard Holmes, and followed the same, central guidelines and structure of the first cycle. It is this second cycle and recreation of the programme, which took place in 2023-24, that this case study describes and evaluates.

Cooper's play has kept the traditional myth's basic plot, but adjusted the main characters' attitudes, stances, and actions. Thus, Theseus is not merely the familiar hero who kills a

---

[4] Editorial note. While this is a feature of the project model, this did not happen with 'Minotaur.'

villain and relieves a city of its bloody obligation. He appears instead as a self-centred, brutal chauvinist. On the other hand, Ariadne appears naïve, an easy target for a devious manipulator such as Theseus. She falls in love with him and betrays the law of her father, to whom she was initially faithfully devoted. Subsequently, assured by Theseus that he will take her back to Athens, she helps him to kill the Minotaur; he ultimately however abandons her on his way back (Cooper, 2019:17). Pasiphae, meanwhile, the mother of Ariadne and Minotaur, wife of King Minos, demonstrates her disapproval of Minos and his deeds, while Minotaur is appreciated and loved by her as her son.

The Minotaur emerges in the text as a complex, individuated character, rather than the vicious creature traditionally imagined in versions of the myth, functioning only as the occasion for Theseus to accomplish his destiny. Cooper portrays a character who is like a child, who cannot speak and who, although monstrous and murderous, still, when he is alone at his retreat in the seventh episode, plays with a miniature, model Pentecontar and performs other actions reminiscent of a child's symbolic play.

In the climactic confrontation in the labyrinth, Minotaur when attacked by Theseus declines to fight back or defend himself, or even to try to avoid his adversary's blows. He instead *"walks straight onto"* Theseus' sword, killing himself as he pushes his body further onto the blade. Theseus and Minotaur end up holding each other, and Minotaur *"feels Theseus's face with one of his bloodied hands"* (Cooper, 2019:14).

As Cooper and Big Brum's team have explained, the intention is to present the story in a novel way, different from traditional presentations where Theseus is solely a hero and Minotaur merely villainous adversary. As the facilitator argued, the roles of the hero and the monster seem reversed where Minotaur does not seem to be a threat to Theseus. Minotaur, for the playwright, is denied his freedom. In a sense, he is made into a monster by being imprisoned in the labyrinth by King Minos, something opposed by his mother Pasiphae, who regards it as a strategy of Minos's to terrify and control his citizens. The Minotaur, according to the director, is a case of arrested development, because he doesn't see the world beyond the quarters into which he has been thrown. And yet, according to Cooper, *"this extraordinary creature is able to cling onto his childhood"* while he turns his chamber into a ship; he is trying to understand, by piecing together glimpses of the world that is denied for him. In a sense, the programme attempts to challenge the customary ways this myth is used in the curriculum and in that way to challenge established concepts relating to heroes, monsters and kings.

The programme thus is intended, according to the author, to address questions such as who is responsible for making a monster out of Minotaur? How did a monster become monstrous? This question, according to the director of the programme, connects particularly to a world that demonises the other and turns it into a monster, and is closely related to heroes and kings since *"you can't have the one without the other".* How, also, do we understand heroes like Theseus, and how heroes are made? This question again is related to the everyday world, which *"is surrounded by the iconic and those effigies of superheroes",* and where it feels *"that societies are in need of heroes and part of the question of the story is why?",* the director mentions. What does it mean to be a hero in our world today, a world where, for example, Boris Johnson is heroised because the UK claims to have created 'world-beating inoculations' when thousands of people were dying of Covid, but this is treated *"as if it's not to be shared"?* From *"whose perspective is someone a hero and whose perspective a monster?"* And what then about kings? What is a king? In the same fashion the facilitator of the program, Zoe Simon, explains that the programme attempts to *"challenge the thoughts on who those people and the story are and why they have come to be the way they are. And then what that means for the people I know, or the world I know."*

According to Holmes, the adult world imposes a meaning on the story of Theseus and the Minotaur *"which isn't necessarily the experience the young people get from reading it or hearing it";* Big Brum aims to give *"young people the authority to read it in their own way, to say the story from a child's perspective rather than telling them the morality of the story".* The aim is to engage the students emotionally, but in a way that challenges the traditional reading of the myth, resonating with children's personal stories and realities and relating to young children's well-being. The director adds that if you are making a story taken from a remote or mythical past, it has *"to be relevant and resonate today";* such stories *"beg us to explore the human condition".* The director doubts that if the company was telling the story as *"it is always told"* it would *"resonate and engage students as it did"* (ibid). Hence, the programme intends to allow *"children to question in a different way or to think differently about the world and what they are being taught"* and to *"have autonomy over their own thoughts".*

On the other hand, Big Brum explicitly acknowledges that its work is not *"geared to specific areas of the national curriculum"* (Big Brum, 2011:2). The defining concern of the company is to *"use theatre and drama to work alongside young people to make meaning of their lives and the world around them"* (Big Brum, 2019:1). Likewise, the company states that:

> *"We are passionate about helping children and young people develop new ways of thinking, problem-solving, and confidently interacting with the dilemmas of the complex world around them. Our mission is to teach young people not what to think,*

but how to think" (Big Brum, n.d.b)

In line with this vision, the company has formulated nine Principles of Working (see page 9), which guide its work and describe its intentions.

However, the company has explained in collaborative, evaluative research with other European TIE companies, that while it of course values education, it values particularly the learning that prepares active future citizens, which is *"necessarily socially and historically grounded"* (Cziboly & Union, 2021:21). It is argued in that regard that *"logical-scientific thinking and narrative thinking are equally needed to be cultivated by the educational systems and need to be fused"*. According to the rationale of the collaborative research, the narrative mode is the one through which human beings *"construct an identity and find a place in one's culture"* and relates to drama and theatre (ibid).

According to their principles and their description of their general concerns, Big Brum seek to promote a pedagogical model based on dialogue around problem-posing processes where the voice of the students is respected as central. They describe a process of meaning-making with immediate reference to students' reality. These statements would seem to comprehend the educational act theoretically as dialogic engagement with problems, where there are no right or wrong answers and hence no dominant voices from any single part of the educational process.

It should be noted that, in theoretical terms, this rationale resonates on the one hand with some of the basic principles of the theory of critical pedagogy, as developed by the educational philosopher Paulo Freire, and on the other with those of drama pioneer Dorothy Heathcote.

Similarities to Critical Pedagogy lie in the problem-posing method where dialogue and respect for the participants' voices are crucial for helping students comprehend the world they live in, as in Big Brum. In the problem-posing method, the traditional relationship between the teacher, and student, where the one is the sole teacher while the other is taught, is undermined. Critical pedagogy's view of this traditional relation is captured in the term 'banking education', where *"knowledge is a gift bestowed by those who consider themselves knowledgeable upon those whom they consider to know nothing"* (Freire, 1970:58). Critical pedagogy practice is based on a joint responsibility for the process of meaning-making in which *"all growth is established and nurtured between teacher and students"* so *"the knowledge, texts, and materials introduced become objects of reflection by teachers and students alike, brushed against the realities of our lived histories"* (Darder, 2018:113). Both students and teachers thus become equally responsible for a process in which all knowledge develops, and any reference to an assumed 'authority' is no longer valid (Freire, 2018:80). Children are regarded not as docile listeners or passive receptors, but as critical co-investigators in dialogue with the teacher (Darder, 2018:113-114). In this model, although a teacher may present specific material to the students for their consideration, he/she is also open to re-considering his/her prior *"considerations as the students express their own"* (Freire, 2018:81). In contrast to the traditional model, in the critical problem-posing model teachers are also students.

For critical pedagogy, an *"authentic dialogue acknowledges different positions and allows a process of the unveiling of realities"* (Nieto, 2020:148). This process, through the dialogical, problem-posing pedagogy, directs attention to discovering and rethinking the social and material conditions that impact the world of the students and the teachers alike (Darder, 2018:114-115). First and foremost, the pedagogy is informed by a humanising praxis where the relationship of human beings to the world is central to teaching and learning (ibid:112); this echoes the theoretical approach of Big Brum, where exploring 'what it is to be human' constitutes a significant theme in their principles.

Furthermore, in the critical model of pedagogy:

> *"... people develop their power to perceive critically the way they exist in the world with which and in which they find themselves; they come to see the world not as a static reality, but as a reality in process, in transformation."* (Freire, 2018:83)

For educators in the tradition of critical pedagogy, 'naming' the world (Freire 2000:88) which students inhabit is crucial for education because:

> *"When people lack a critical understanding of their reality, apprehending it in fragments which they do not perceive as interacting constituent elements of the whole, they cannot truly know that reality."* (Freire, 2018:104).

For critical pedagogists, so-called 'banking education' anaesthetises and inhibits creative power, whereas critical problem-posing education involves a constant unveiling of reality (Hill & Kumar, 2015:81). Critical pedagogy is thus not merely a ready-to-hand and quickly replicable method, but a process that could ensure 'conscientisation,' – that is, the coming to critical consciousness of the learning subject (Baral, 2015:209).

Connecting the educational praxis to social and material reality is crucial for critical educators because understanding the world and the possibility of changing it constitutes a central purpose of the critical paradigm. Critical pedagogy is therefore critical and suspicious of any educational model that does not challenge existing social and material conditions; or as Shor (2018) articulates this suspicion: *"Any pedagogy or curriculum which does not question the status quo tacitly or actively endorses it"* (p.187).

Paulo Freire has outlined seven basic principles guiding critical pedagogy. The first highlights *"the importance of pedagogical space"* (Freire, 1996: 127). According to this first principle, any educational process should take place in a positive pedagogical space that should be beneficial to learning. An educationally beneficial space is not confined to actual, physical space, but refers also to acknowledging and appreciating students' contributions. The work model should demonstrate to them that they are valued as thoughtful contributors who can create new ideas and possibilities. Freire (1998: 89) has also conceived of this beneficial space as including an ability to *"understand the meaning of a moment of silence, of a smile, or even an instant in which someone needs to leave the room."*

While Freire acknowledges that teachers hold a position of authority, his sixth principle states that teachers should not manipulate the situation for their own cause even if, as his fifth principle maintains, there is no neutral educational praxis. The seventh principle states in this regard that students' autonomy, their cultural identities and their experiences should be respected: *"a fundamental starting point is respect for the learner's cultural identity"*, which even includes *"language, syntax, prosody, semantics, and informal knowledge"* (Freire 1996: 127). The rest of Freire's principles concern the importance of content (the third principle), a direction to a specific objective in the fourth principle, and the existence of educators and learners with specific, demarcated but flexible roles which complement and do not nullify each other (Freire, 1996:127).

The basic ideas and guidelines of critical pedagogy could be captured in the below two strategies for practice:

- Educators should seek to create conditions in which students can develop personally meaningful understandings of the world and recognise they have agency to act on the world, to make change.
- Education is not about showing life to people, but bringing them to life. The aim is not getting students to listen to convincing lectures by experts, but getting them to speak for themselves in order to achieve, or at least strive toward an equal degree of participation and better future. (Ross, 2015:152)

The relevant literature offers some suggestive models of work that could be incorporated into critical pedagogy practice. Wallerstein (as cited in Nelson & Chen, 2023:139), for example, suggests that educators working with young learners should:

- *"Represent an everyday problem situation that is easily recognisable to students and to which they have emotional connections.*

- *Illustrate as many sides to the contradiction as possible yet be simple enough for students to project their own experience.*

- *Focus on one problem at a time while suggesting links to other themes in people's lives.*

- *Not provide solutions to the problem but rather stimulate dialogue.*

- *Not present a problem which is overwhelming to the student, such as one where the actions required to solve it are out of reach for the students. There should be capacity for small actions that address the problem, even if they do not solve it."*

Dorothy Heathcote directly evoked Freire's theory when in 1996 she explained her views on drama and education. She offered an illustrative list of paradigmatic views of children by adults/teachers to help educators to clarify and reflect on the 'operant paradigm' (Heathcote, 1996:26) that they or a school followed, and disclose possible forms that the hidden or overt school curriculum might therefore take. This list of paradigms makes apparent the essential differences between, on the one hand, various banking-like education models, and on the other the more creative and liberating model of drama and education. Heathcote, who seemed to endorse Freire's ideas (ibid: 33 & 34), appears somewhat indebted to them in her adumbration of nine such paradigms:

> *Child as flower – given enough time and care …*
>
> *Child as candle – you can rely on me to keep you lit up.*
>
> *Child as echo – no, do it the way I've said/shown to you.*
>
> *Child as friend - if I'm nice to you, will you …*
>
> *Child as adversary – the trouble with you (lot, class, etc.) is …*
>
> *Child as clay – in time you'll turn into the class I want …*
>
> *Child as crucible – me and you have to keep stirring everything around.*
>
> *Child as machine – by October they should all be able to …*
>
> *Child as vessel - We did the towns yesterday, today we're going to do Indian crops …*
> (ibid: 27)

Some of the illustrative metaphors in this list capture aspects of the banking model of education. For example, the child as vessel is regarded as a receptacle to be filled up by the teacher or the school; it disregards the fact that children bring to their learning existing knowledge, ideas and abilities, which contrasts with Freire's respect for students' culture or Big Brum's first principle of trusting and regarding children *"as human beings in their own right, respecting their experiences and understandings"*. These paradigms can make manifest aspects of the hidden curriculum in educational settings, which serve:

> *"the tacit teaching to students of norms, values, and dispositions that goes on simply by their living in and coping with the institutional expectations and routines of schools day in and day out for a number of years."* (Apple, 2019:13)

Heathcote avowedly favoured the paradigm of the 'child as crucible' for drama, and for education in general, where the pattern is *"me and you have to keep stirring everything around"* (Heathcote, 1996:28). By 'me and you' she of course means the teacher and the students. She even claimed that she does not ever consider knowledge to be complete. Knowledge, for her, is an open, never-ending process, and students' pre-understandings and pre-attitudes should be disclosed and engaged, in preference to *"laying some new thing upon them"* (ibid). It is evident that, as in Freire, Heathcote favours an approach for educators that acknowledges their lack of absolute, correct knowledge, which 'stirs' knowledge, ideas, and conceptions together with the students. The teacher appears an equal partner in a relationship where no party claims absolute knowledge. Heathcote clarifies the chosen paradigm by arguing that:

> *"Now in the drama framework, the teacher contributes and participates, the children co-operate with the participating teacher as well as they can, and they all end up explaining the world to one another. What you have then is, a classroom working as a laboratory. If, after exploring, we do not keep explaining to each other, we cannot really own our own knowledge. So if we explore, and then explain, we will automatically be drawing upon our final draft work, the best we can explain, in the best way, at this given time. This recognises that we may explain differently tomorrow because we shall perhaps participate differently tomorrow. This is the crucible paradigm, where we are stirring our knowledge, together."* (ibid:31)

Gillham (1995) has elaborated on the crucible paradigm for drama, placing it at the heart of his 'curriculum for living' proposal (p.61). For Gillham, the crucible paradigm counters the 'syndrome' of right and wrong answers and its implied pedagogy. Instead, to encourage curiosity and the desire to know, a curriculum should be developed around questions *"to which we do not know the answers"* (ibid). At the centre of such an approach is a *"problematic: enigmas, puzzles, riddles, paradoxes, ambiguity, ambivalence, and contradictoriness"*. Problem-solving is regarded as central for this approach, so it becomes crucial to identify the questions that are worth asking and to find ways to present worthy problems *"suggestively, alluringly, provocatively"* so students can feel the urge to solve them. As with Heathcote and critical pedagogy, Gillham's curriculum for living insists that a curriculum must refer to the real world by using practical activity, and transform the classroom *"into a combination of a laboratory, a library (...), and a theatre"* where young people are truly empowered (ibid:62).

There are many clear parallels between Heathcote and Freire, especially if we comprehend the act of 'explaining' the world as a kind of naming it, as in Freire's approach. The same theoretical orientation can be discerned in Big Brum, in the company's ambition to help children *"to make meaning of their lives and the world around them"* while focusing on a process rather than an end-product.

Big Brum, although it does not purposefully target curriculum areas, aims by its focus on children's wellbeing to challenge the traditional hidden and overt curriculums. It claims that *"the content of a TIE programme offers an exploration which can be used to access all aspects of the curriculum. Skills and knowledge are acquired with and through meaning making"* (Big Brum, 2011:2). The company in fact claims that it is part of its ambition *"to help benefit the curriculum through culture and creativity"*.

All the above, including Big Brum's pedagogical model, offer possible directions and serve to delimit the critical context for examining their work in practice through the 'Minotaur' TIE programme.

Method
This research is a small-scale evaluative case study developed to evaluate the theatre in education programme 'Minotaur', created and applied by Big Brum TIE Company for students in KS2. The evaluation focuses on how the programme relates to the school curriculum, what pedagogical model is being applied, and how it is communicated to teachers and students.

Data were collected first by interviewing the primary producers of the program, Chris Cooper, the playwright of 'Minotaur', Richard Holmes, the initial director, and Zoe Simon, the main facilitator of the program. Chris Cooper was interviewed twice; the first time was before the observation of the application and the second afterwards. The director was interviewed three times, before, during and after the programme's application; and the facilitator once, during the observation.

The first cycle of interviews offered the opportunity to collect data, clarifying the company's intentions with this specific TIE programme, related to how the programme is intended to connect to the school curriculum and on which pedagogical paradigm the programme is developed. The data included the company's rationale, as it is described in the company's official documents, to clarify the theoretical and pedagogical grounds on which the company stands. Their rationale is used to detect possible theoretical underpinnings that ally the company with pedagogical theories such as the critical pedagogy model. Accordingly, all these preliminary, theoretical data were used in the evaluative stage of this research by formulating the critical context for observing and evaluating the programme's application in schools.

After the observed applications, the second and third cycles of interviews were used to evaluate the programme and further clarify critical moments that the researcher selected as relevant for developing the evaluation.

Interviews were semi-structured, to allow interviewees to develop their own thinking (May, 1997:111) on the programme's aims and on how they understand and describe their pedagogical model of work concerning the school curriculum. All interviews were recorded on camera with the participants' consent and transcribed. All videos were then erased.

Data for evaluation purposes were also collected by observing two applications of the programme in two classes of the same school in the Birmingham area. First-hand data were important for understanding how the programme worked in practice in live situations (Cohen et al., 2017:542) and for evaluating how the programme engages the participants in a real-life context (Yin, 2009:18). The observation included recording the programme's performative parts, but because of certain safeguarding restrictions, the camera focused only on the stage and not on the participants.

Since recordings could not include students, data were also collected by keeping detailed notes on students' responses, ideas, and verbal expressions during the regular discussions developed between the facilitator and the participants. However, due to a mixture of ethical and methodological considerations, the research could not gather other data generated by the participants, such as written texts or interviews with students.

A third source of data was the feedback from teachers' focus groups that the company contacted. These focus groups evaluated various of the company's TIE programmes and generated some brief data which, hence, were not detailed and not entirely focused on the specific programme. The company recorded the feedback, and the relevant parts were transcribed.

The data analysis was developed by comparing data from the above sources against Big Brum's rationale and intentions, as described by its team, and further analysed by the researcher.

The presentation of the findings is structured as a narrative following the development of the programme during its application, but titles are given for each section to help distinguish the most dominant, surfaced characteristics that seemed relevant for the evaluation.

Findings and analysis

The 'Minotaur' TIE programme develops by alternating between watching the play and, between each of its nine episodes, prompting discussions among the facilitator and participants. Participants in the programme do not have prescribed roles in either the play or the discussions.

Creating a safe space: After the first introductory meeting, where it was explained that the programme would explore 'what makes a monster', the young students were asked to talk about things that frightened them. Participants were sitting on chairs in a semicircle. The facilitator did not make any comments when children expressed their fears; but, with gestures like nodding and giving direct attention to each child, the facilitator acknowledged all contributions and displayed acceptance and understanding of all the responses. The facilitator kneeled so as to be at the same level as students, and implied with stance and gesture that she understood the children's fears and indeed shared some of them.

It was thus made clear from the very beginning that in the forthcoming work, all responses and contributions would be heard and valued, including those coming from the teacher, and that children should feel safe in sharing relevant personal feelings, thoughts, and understandings. This activity can be seen as establishing for participants that the programme activities would take place in a safe space where all feelings are welcomed, valued, and respected. This same mode of interaction continued through the whole application in both observed classes, by the facilitator and by the rest of the Actor-teachers when they were participating in later small group discussions; the teachers' focus group felt that acknowledging every contribution made by the participants had a positive impact on them.

Practical activities: Immediately after the introduction, the Big Brum team presented the room of King Minos, which included *"an ornate, regal table"* with two maps – of Crete and the Labyrinth, respectively – a small cup, a king's crown, and an orange. Participants were invited to see, comment on, and even touch the displayed objects if they wanted. So, these props were accessible and could be explored by observing or interacting with them. This meant that the props were not seen as alien objects, separated from the participants and displayed only for viewing. Availability of the props for hands-on interaction was intended to connect participants in a more immediate way to the context of the play and, potentially, encourage them to project onto or even invest in the props something from their own understanding. And indeed, according to the feedback from the teachers' focus group on this activity, *'students loved it'* and it hooked them in.

Curriculum related: The facilitator then narrated some background information based on the original myth, such as who King Minos was and the city and social structure over which he reigned. For example, the narration mentioned that Minos *"is the great king of Knossos, his influence reaches far and wide, he trades with the world. All fear his power, enemies, and friends alike ... he lived 3,000 years ago, on an island called Crete, which was considered the most advanced civilisation in Europe ... the king lived in his beautiful palace of Knossos"* etc.

The half-imaginary, half-historical material of the background narration communicates historical fact, such as the power of ancient Crete, and is an example of aspects of the programme that could serve statutory curriculum requirements: for example, *"increasing [children's] familiarity with a wide range of books, including fairy stories, myths and legends"* (Department of Education, 2013:35); *"listening to and discussing a wide range of poems, stories and non-fiction at a level beyond that at which they can read independently"* (ibid:21); or *"writing narratives about personal experiences and those of others (real and fictional)"* (ibid:32). For example, as one of the teachers' focus groups mentioned, at the time 'Minotaur' was applied in their school, the class happened to be doing the myth of Theseus in the English lessons for Year Four, and the teacher gave children the task of rewriting the story. According to the focus group, the programme helped students to engage with the myth of the Minotaur and showed that they had a very good understanding of the scenes. Yet the teachers' focus group at the same time felt they could not say for sure whether the children had integrated something from the programme into their story, because this would have demanded a high-level skill which it

56

was thought that children lacked.

Students' voice/trust every child: As mentioned above, the programme as a whole did not allot the participants a role, with the main interaction with the facilitators through discussions which were conducted after every one or two episodes of the play. The central activity of the programme consisted of asking participants to select objects which were used in the performance by the characters, interpret them and then place them in the room of King Minos, created and presented before the play's beginning.

According to the members of the production team, the purpose of this central activity is to use these objects as visual cues to suggest aspects of the kingdom, showing what kind of a king Minos is and what he allows in his kingdom. It is expected that the activity will help participants to ground the story in one place and develop their understanding of it. The activity is intended to constitute a useful tool for the imagination because all important objects for the participants are placed there. Which objects are selected may change in different applications of the programme (as has been observed in the two observed applications of this study). This indicates that participants are not expected to discover a given meaning in the object or directed to choose pre-selected ones, but may focus on, interpret, and pick out what is important and meaningful for them. In other words, they are called to interpret the objects in a way that relates to their own thinking, experience, and understandings. Programme participants are getting involved actively in the construction of the meaning of the programme for themselves, even though they do not assume a prescribed role in it.

Connecting to reality: In the opening scene, students watch a hooded, bound young man edging into the labyrinth which is made of *"solid pale stone"* with some *"bloodyhand [sic] prints and streaks where a hand has slid down the wall"* (Cooper, 2019:3). The youth, who wears a *"white body-length tunic and a bay leaf laurel crown over the hood"* (ibid), is trying to navigate in the labyrinth while unable to see because hooded.

In Cooper's interpretation, the scene is intended to engage the kids *"instantly"*, because it is assumed it resonates *"with a lot of fears they have"* (C2). The aim appears to be to open up a space onto which young people will project their own experiences of the world they inhabit. Drama calculated to resonate with participants' realities illustrates the sixth principle of Big Brum, whereby young people are encouraged to *"respond to reality"*, in this instance, their own reality with its fears and dilemmas. This intention presents a straightforward link to critical pedagogy praxis, where discovering and rethinking the social conditions that impact the world and the relationship of human beings to the world are pivotal.

Critical pedagogy's model of work, however, ordinarily requires, as mentioned above, an everyday problem situation that is easily recognisable to students and to which they have emotional connections. Big Brum's 'Minotaur' does not present an everyday problem; it does not evoke or refer to a one-to-one relationship between factual world and the fictional situation. A young, hooded and bound man wandering in a labyrinth can be understood in this context only as an analogy. Working through analogy is one of the ways to protect participants into emotion related to their own personal experiences (Bolton, 2010:89); such protection of participants recalls Big Brum's sixth principle, which states that responding to reality should be done at a *"safe distance from (participants') own reality"*. Davis (2014), for example, asserts the ability of drama to resonate at levels deeper than immediately understood by participants, levels which children may not be immediately conscious of, just as fairy tales can do (ibid:78-79). In this view, the opening scene might resonate in an analogical fashion with the feeling of helplessness, of being abandoned to a world that belongs to and is shaped by others, where children are struggling to find their way, and to bear witness to life (Bond, 1992). As Holmes interprets children's modern reality, *"the adult world does do awful things to children, but adults were children that had awful things done to them."*

The teachers' focus group seemed to agree that, in general, Big Brum TIE programmes resonated with children's own lives by offering potent connections; children related to the struggle of the characters even if they sometimes found it hard to understand the language or the full context of the company's interpretation in the programmes. Participants seemed to recognise themselves in the struggle of the characters.

There was at the same time no hard, observable evidence that participants made definite connections with their realities during the two observed applications of the 'Minotaur' programme; the teachers' focus group did however note that children *"wanted freedom for the characters"*(which may indicate a measure of identification with the characters of the play, like the Minotaur).

Sustaining a safe space: The facilitator's first question to the participants, after watching the first and the second scenes, including the wandering hooded youth, was to ask what they noticed. The facilitator repeated almost every response, allowing all members of the group to listen to all contributions. The facilitator at the same time used gestures and expressions that signalled a sincere effort to understand students' comments on the play, communicating to the children that their suggestions were meaningful, and deserving of serious consideration. She would for example regularly hold her chin, nodding, maintaining eye contact with each of the speaking participants, and use expressions like *"hang on for a second, let me think about it again"*. She then compared different responses, connecting them to the play and combining them to form a clearer picture of what had been watched, according to students' understandings.

When participants mentioned the hooded young man, the facilitator asked students to break up into groups and discuss what this hooded person might have been thinking or imagining while wandering in the labyrinth. All the actors/teachers of the company took part in these groups, questioning children and provoking deeper consideration and understanding. This exercise helped the children to feel safer before later speaking publicly in front of the whole class, and to go deeper into the meaning of the hood for themselves. Again, all the members of the company valued children's contributions in their groups, concerned to maintain a safe space for a dialogue.

Focusing on contradictions/developing dialogue: Participants suggested that the young, hooded man would have tried to *"do the right thing"*, *"behave well"*, *"beg for forgiveness"* and *"try not to be eaten"*. These responses seem to signify a contradiction: the character, the hooded young man, as well as the participants, all know very well that he is about to be devoured by Minotaur, but still, in the students' interpretation, he is thinking of how to behave well and beg for forgiveness. The response of *"try not to be eaten"* could be interpreted reasonably in the context of trying to escape death. The response of *"do the right thing"* is ambiguous, being interpretable in different ways: *"do the right thing for surviving"*, for example, or *"doing the right thing so as to behave well"*. But to *"beg for forgiveness"* and to *"behave well"* seem to mean something enigmatic which, unfortunately, the programme did not manage in the moment to tarry with for further elaboration, although the facilitator seemed to have spotted the apparent contradiction and highlighted it with more questions. It is interesting to keep in mind that the young, hooded man was not a volunteer; he was chosen, according to the myth, to be sacrificed for the sake of the rest of his society. He therefore found himself in a situation over which he has no control, but still behaves obediently, not even attempting to remove the hood despite the fact that, according to the text, he could have done so at any moment, since his hands are bound in front of him.

There was no opportunity to investigate through other means what the children might have meant; but trying to interpret these responses in a general way might lead us to assume either that participants did not understand what was happening and why, or that they were projecting something of their own experiences onto the young man and the situation he found himself in; in more complex cases, both options could have been true. In the second case, the way these responses were formulated seem to place the young, hooded man in a position of answerability, to carry with them a sense or assumption of his being guilty of some misbehaviour or misdeed, even though he is chosen by lot to be sacrificed for the sake of his community. Could it be that some of the participants have interpreted the situation in a way that approximates their own experiences of feeling answerable to others, adults or peers, while finding themselves in analogous situations? Have they taken the hooded man at a deeper, unconscious level as an image of their own socially imposed guilt, of the feeling of being punished for a vague reason that they do not even understand? Have they connected to the situation as powerless young people who sense themselves submitting to social situations that they do not understand, but to which they are obliged to submit without question? And could this interpretation be the case even if the group did not understand the action of the scene in terms of the drama's plot? There is, as mentioned, no firm evidence to support these speculations for the specific class; but they are lent credence by the emergence of a comparable, but more complex, contradiction observed in the second application of the programme in a different class which is presented below.

Crucible paradigm/dialogue/no right or wrong answers: This time in the second observed application of the programme, the facilitator did not simply discuss the hood with participants, but began by asking any of the children to put on the hood and the bay leaf laurel and to describe what it felt like.

At the same time the facilitator queried the meaning of the hood in a way that appeared sincere to the children. She claimed to be *"puzzled"*, unable to understand why *"in this kingdom, King Minos would send young people with a hood into the labyrinth to be eaten"*. The facilitator in this way has raised the question of the possible meaning of the hood, while at the same time communicating that she doesn't know the answer to this question and needs the help of the participants to understand. This moment in some ways exemplifies the crucible paradigm in Big Brum's practice, where the teacher does not assume power or possession of the absolute, correct knowledge, but rather constructs an answer together with the children, in dialogue, being open to being taught by children and reconsidering her own ideas and understandings. As the focus group mentioned, one of the most useful elements of the programmes in general for teachers, which they have adapted in their practice from the work of Big Brum, was the posing of open-ended questions without any feeling of pressure to offer 'correct' answers.

Revealing contradictions: This hands-on activity, inviting the wearing and describing of the hood, provoked novel responses which directly articulated tensions or contradictions. These responses included, for example, noting that the hood felt *"warm"*, *"comfy"* and *"cosy"* but at the same time the *"young man cannot see"*; the hood *"may make the youth forget about the monster"* and so *"feel safe"*, but the likely eventuality, that the *"Minotaur will come suddenly as a surprise"* and *"kill him"*, is still recognised. The contradiction relates to the meaning of the hood, interpreted as comfortable at the same time as it prevents the young man facing his own reality. This connects, according to the director of the programme, to a more general social situation related to what *"stops us seeing the world"*. The facilitator emphasised the emerging contradiction by repeating the conflicting responses and presenting them together. Revealing and exploiting contradictions for meaning-making, as is practised in critical pedagogy, seems a primary concern of the company's that is well exemplified in this activity.

Creating metaphors/naming the world/making the material accessible/focus on one problem at a time: It is worth mentioning in this regard that in the same activity, one of the participants referred to the bay leaf laurel on the top of the hood, as a *"sacrificial crown"*. The response evidently comes from the realm of metaphor. The participant has created this rather complex metaphor, seeing the bay leaf laurel as a symbol which is at once something related to a sacrifice and a symbol of power or honour. In this sense, the participant has explained the world of the myth to and for himself in a new way, indicating that the company's work with 'Minotaur' did help participants to think in new and creative ways about the imaginary world of the myth.

Selecting and discussing important objects, and then placing them one at a time in the room of King Minos, may simplify the story and make it easier for the participants to distil their thinking about and understanding of the situation while holding the most important, meaningful objects in one place. The activity at the same time seemed to offer the possibility of anchoring certain views on the play in tangible objects which hold special meaning as symbols.

Objects in this way seem to acquire a symbolic function; they can stand for something different from what the object is in reality, a different object or idea that participants have chosen and created themselves and are not given by the company. Symbols, according to Vygotsky, are mental tools which are used to construct an understanding of the world (Vygotsky, 1986).

The group did not return to the room of Minos with the chosen objects all together, in the end of the programme; this might have been made the basis for an exercise that helped sum up or reflect on the whole of the play or the myth.

Practical activities: The activity in which a volunteer put on the hood and reported how it felt seemed to prompt more complex reflections, on more complex contradictions, and more conscious meaning-making, as seen in the metaphor of the "sacrificial crown". Such an action is nevertheless closer to an experiential, hands-on activity and so to young children's way of experiencing and doing things than it is to abstract reasoning and reflecting on words alone. Although participants did not assume a role in the drama, the activity aligns in it effect with Gillham's appeal for practical activities and Heathcote's laboratory classroom. Big Brum on the whole relied mainly on discussion or asking participants to place the chosen objects into Minos's room, and not on these hands-on exercises. The director's explanation for this was the lack of time, citing the fact that the company had only two hours to develop the whole programme in each class.

Some of the comments of the teachers' focus group suggested more active, physical engagement for the students, like re-enacting of the story, so participants could connect with the material more productively instead of sitting and watching the play and then discussing it. In fact, teachers thought that children were sitting too long on the floor and more activities were needed. They would prefer, for example, if children could experience and understand the story from within, and even proposed popular techniques and conventions, such as 'freeze frame' and 'hot seating', as outlined, for example, in the work of Neelands (1990 & 2015). They had corresponding reservations about the pauses between the scenes which were used for discussion, with some teachers feeling that children were not engaged enough with the conversations, even though others found the discussions and the dialogue between the facilitators and the students interesting. Similar requests for more active engagement on the part of the students were made with other programmes like 'Ripped' and 'Romeo and Juliet'.

Further contradictions: Later in the same, second application of the programme, a discursive approach was developed which encouraged detecting and highlighting of possible contradictory senses or meanings, centred on questions like *"what makes a hero?"*, *"what makes a monster?"* and *"what is a hero; what does a hero look like?"* – some of the central questions of the programme. The discussion followed episodes six and seven. In the sixth episode, Ariadne explains to Theseus her plan for helping him to kill Minotaur. Theseus in the scene exhibits his customary manipulative, self-centred behaviour, flattering the daughter of Minos, overconfident that he is going to kill the beast. Ariadne, for her part, makes it clear she has fallen in love with Theseus. Earlier, in the play's second episode, Ariadne has a heated encounter with her mother, Pasiphae, insisting on obedience to the rules laid down by Minos for the kingdom, while Pasiphae, defending her son Minotaur, scorns Minos for his brutality and Ariadne for her blind loyalty to him. In the seventh episode, we see Minotaur in his retreat among remains of his victims, including bloody tunics, clothes, shoes, and bones, playing with his toy, a miniature of a Pentecontar. Among the participants' responses to the question of what makes a hero and what a hero looks like, were words and phrases like: *"brave"*; *"have an opinion"*; *"follow what you want to do"*; *"saves someone's life"*; *"has responsibility"*; *"resilience"*; and *"never give up"*. The facilitator continued the discussion by asking if participants have seen *"all these things in the scene where Theseus was talking to Ariadne"*.

The responses were again contradictory and conflicted but not as eloquent as with the hood above: Theseus was *"rude"*, but he was at the same time *"kind"* and *"generous"* because he offered a *"peeled orange to Ariadne"*. He was *"sneaky"*, but also *"brave"* because he was resolved to kill Minotaur. As before, the facilitator emphasised the apparent contradictions, summarising (without inviting or expecting a response to the summary): *"So we have a hero who is sneaky and rude, but he also does good things"*.

Crucible paradigm: The next question asked whether participants had seen *"any similarities or differences between the Minotaur and Theseus"*. Children seemed to interpret the Minotaur as *"nice"*, whereas Theseus was *"bad"*. The facilitator once again, in the same fashion as before, highlighted the paradox whereby the monster, habitually expected to be the villain, was nice, and the hero, habitually expected to be nice, was rude and bad. She indicated surprise at the response, and paused for a while showing that she needs time to understand the children's opinions. She ended up by declaring that she was learning a lot of new things about this world which she hadn't known before; this dialogic approach, respecting the children's input, accorded with the crucible paradigm and with the critical pedagogy principle whereby a teacher is also a student.

After the final episode, in which Theseus, having killed Minotaur on Crete, abandons Ariadne on the island of Naxos on his way back to Athens, the facilitator asked participants to reflect on *"what is being launched to Athens"*. Theseus has left Ariadne, and embarked for return to his father, but he has strictly prohibited a sailor from changing the sails of his boat from black, their colour at the beginning of his expedition, to white – a change he had promised his father he would make if he succeeded, so the sign of success and victory could be seen from afar. In the traditional myth, Theseus forgets to change the sails and his father, Aegeus, on seeing the black sails, and assuming that his son has failed and been killed by the Minotaur, commits suicide by leaping into the Aegean Sea. Cooper has changed this detail of the myth and made Theseus purposely keep the black sails. One of the participants from the beginning of the discussion on what is launched responded interestingly that it is a *"bomb"*; another, that although Theseus' ship, before it left Naxos, was a *"slow ship"*, it is now transformed to a *"war ship"* – a danger taken back to Athens by Theseus himself, as the facilitator noted.

Curriculum related: The facilitator at the end of the programme asked the participants to imagine that they could write a letter to the Athenians: what would they include in it? Children and their teachers were asked to work on this letter after the programme and send it to the company. The activity was an opportunity to reflect on the whole programme and at the same time cover other aims of the curriculum related to writing, such as *"writing narratives about personal experiences and those of others (real and fictional)"* (Department of Education, 2013:32).

None of the schools, unfortunately, completed this activity. The teachers' focus croup has also reported that the programme was not necessarily linked to the material of the curriculum, or to what the class was occupied with when the programme was applied. Any activity given from the company therefore represented extra tasks for the teacher and the class for which there was insufficient time.

There were additional issues for some teachers with how the programme related to their overt curriculum. One of the focus groups commented that, although the programme was a 'treat' for the children and they enjoyed it for what it was, participants had difficulties in understanding the play well enough; it was felt that the programme would be more suitable for older years such as Year Six. That was the main reason teachers did not do any follow-up activities after the application of the programme. Another focus group commented that Big Brum needed to be more aware of the demands that the curriculum places on teachers and felt that the programme should have been addressed to older year groups, the fifth year in particular; the younger children were either ignorant of the story or were not on the whole mature enough for such a programme; that the programme did not complement the school curriculum; or even that some of the children felt scared.

Other teacher groups stressed a need to be better informed beforehand about what the company was trying to do with the programme, so they could try to incorporate them to their own teaching. It would be much more useful, for instance, if they had the content of the programme and the themes that Big Brum consider relevant for the children in advance, so they could plan in relation to their curriculum.

Discussion

The 'Minotaur' TIE programme is developed according to a model of work based on the crucible paradigm, where the voices of the children, their experiences and understandings are respected and taken account of seriously. Throughout the whole process, there were no wrong or right answers given to or solicited to participants; the paradigm offered to students and teachers a different form of working, which was considered its most useful aspect by the teachers' focus groups.

In this paradigm, the facilitator/teacher assumed the role of the co-investigator, who poses questions but does not assume knowledge, remaining all the time open to rethinking his/her preconceptions. The facilitator shares with the students the role of a learner in the process.

Participants play a key role in meaning-making and interpretation of the play, based on their understandings and experiences, and are thus empowered. Fixed and traditional readings of the story that might come from familiarity with tellings of the myth are challenged through the exploitation of contradictions built from the play, especially where they were reflected in participants' responses.

The programme created a safe space for participants to explore and express their feelings, ideas, and understandings in a dialogue with the facilitator and the play.

The programme will challenge a school's overt and hidden curriculum, based on the 'banking model' where children are seen as learners whose ignorance is gradually lessened. It challenges habitual readings of the myth by offering a new way of approaching its story, relevant to present social circumstances and questions.

The programme did create conditions for participants to try to explain the world of the play, and hopefully their own world, which in some cases took the form of complex and expressive metaphors created by children themselves.

The programme offered possible starting points for developing requirements for the overt school curriculum, especially for reading, writing, listening, and speaking. From the very first activity of the programme, and with the central activity based on discussion, the main curriculum requirements addressed were speaking and listening. The programme offered possibilities for writing activities, but participating schools did not follow up. The focus group also commented that the programme fits well with PSHE requirements.

Whether the programme delivered on its ambition to find resonance with participants' own realities cannot be fully evaluated, with more evidence needed. There are indications that this might be the case, given the value that teachers' focus group saw in the programme for engaging and creating strong connections to children.

A noted deficiency was the lack of practical activities designed for the participants, a lack owed to shortage of time. Children mostly watched the play and discussed what they had seen in between the episodes. The focus groups regarded this structure as one of the weakest points of the programme.

Another weak point for the focus groups is that the programme seemed difficult or inappropriate for the specific age-group, with the discussion not managing to engage all children. Yet more hard evidence is needed to support this argument.

It does appear there is a mismatch between the programme's aims and methods and the demands and timetable of the current overt school curriculum. Teachers mentioned that the programme did not fit the curriculum demands, of which Big Brum needs to be more aware. Some teachers, as mentioned, wished to be better briefed, wanting to be fully aware of the programme's aims and methods before its application in their schools, so they would have adequate time to prepare the class and to plan how to incorporate it into their teaching.

A last point needs to be made in relation to how Big Brum's aims and method are communicated, explained, and shared with the teachers of the classes. The focus group has produced some conflictual feedback specially in relation to how the specific programme intends to connect with children's realities and their curriculum.

Recommendations

Better communication is needed between Big Brum and teachers in relation to the aims and methods of the company's programmes. This might take the form of more frequent informational meetings and workshops, or brochures that contain relevant information for the programmes' topic and the rationale of the approach.

An explanation of the crucible paradigm should be included in the information provided, while a more detailed description of the programmes and their rationale could be included on the company website.

All relevant information should be made available to teachers before a programme is applied.

It would be useful if Big Brum could propose indicative follow-up activities in a form of resource packs, which were used in the past by most TIE companies, including Big Brum. The resource pack can be of course in electronic form, downloadable from the company website and include activities elaborating the crucible paradigm.

Special presentations of the programmes could be organised for the teachers, offering firsthand experience before the application of the programmes in schools. Such a first-hand experience may offer a better understanding of the aims and method of the company.

The company could try to foster closer collaborations with schools by becoming more informed about topics and themes that teachers are addressing in their classes. It is not possible of course to connect to each one, but it could help to connect the programmes with possible teachers' interests and curriculum requirements. Teachers will also feel more included in this process and can further develop the company's work in their classes and provide feedback.

The company can benefit from learning from students as teachers in a critical pedagogy model. It would be profitable for Big Brum to ask schools to systematically share certain materials produced by students through follow-up activities. A systematic exploration of this material may provide the company with useful feedback from the students and help to evaluate programmes' impacts and success, and revise them where necessary (see page 168). Similarly, instituting some monitoring for the applications of the programmes might yield useful feedback.

The programme could include more practical activities or/and engage participants in role taking. As Gillham has mentioned, this is a prerequisite for the specific paradigm that Big Brum develops; but of course, that requires negotiating teachers' time constraints and spending more time with each class.

Bibliography

Apple, M.W. (2019). *Ideology and Curriculum*. New York & London: Routledge, Taylor and Francis Group.

Baral, K. C. (2015). 'Postcoloniality, Critical Pedagogy, and English Studies in India'. In Darder, A., Mayo, P. and Paraskeva J.M. (eds). *International Critical Pedagogy Reader*. New York; London: Routledge, Taylor & Francis Group.

Big Brum. (2011). [online] *Artistic Policy*. Available at: https://static1.squarespace.com/static/60d061bcd571dc3fb7554ef9/t/60da28adc343fd57d8339fd4/1624910001086/Big+Brum+Artistic+Policy.pdf. Accessed 13 December 2023.

Big Brum. (2019). [online] *Engaging, Exploring, Expressing: the case for Theatre in Education*. Available at: https://docs.google.com/document/d/1EBSkjdv4iehF6xW5Qjyt-R1Pm9KEb6WhTFw47vayHsg/edit. Accessed 13 December 2023.

Big Brum. (n.d. a). [online] *What we do*. Available at: https://bigbrum.org.uk/about, accessed 17 January 2023.

Big Brum. (n.d. c). [online] *Our Nine Principles of Working*. Available at: Big Brum I 9 Principles of Working. Accessed 12 December 2023.

Bond, E. (1992). 'The Dramatic Child'. *Drama Broadsheet*. Vol. 9, issue 3, December 1992, pp.40-46.

Bolton, G. (2010). 'Protection'. In Davis, D. (ed), *Gavin Bolton: Essential Writings*. Stoke on Trent.

Cohen, L., Manion, L and Morrison K. (2017). *Research Methods in Education*. 5th ed. London and New York: Routledge Falmer.

Cooper, C. (2019). *Minotaur*. [Unpublished play]

Cziboly, A. and Union, E. (2010). *Making a World of Difference: A Dice Resource for Practitioners on Educational Theatre and Drama*. DICE Consortium.

Darder, A. (2018). *The Student Guide to Freire's Pedagogy of the Oppressed*. London: Bloomsbury Academic.

Davis, D. (2014). *Imagining the Real: Towards a New Theory of Drama in Education*. Stoke-On-Trent: Trentham Books.

Department of Education. (2013). [online] *The National Curriculum in England Key stages 1 and 2 framework document*. Available at: https://assets.publishing.service.gov.uk/media/5a81a9abe5274a2e8ab55319/PRIMARY_national_curriculum.pdf. Accessed 21 September 2023.

Freire, P. (1970). *Pedagogy of the Oppressed*. New York: Continuum.

Freire, P. (1996). *Letters to Cristina Reflections on my Life and Work*. London/New York: Routledge.

Freire, P. (1998). *Pedagogy of the Heart*. London: Continuum.

Freire, P. (2000). *Pedagogy of the Oppressed 30th Anniversary Edition*. New York/London: Continuum.

Freire, P. (2018). *Pedagogy of the Oppressed: 50th Anniversary Edition*. Bloomsbury Publishing Plc.

Gillham, G. (1995). 'Notes on a Curriculum for Living'. *SCYPT Journal*, No 30, June 1995.

Heathcote, D. (1996). 'Key Address by Dorothy Heathcote'. In Byron, K. (ed), T*he Fight for Drama – The Fight for Education*. National Association for the Teaching of Drama.

Hill, D. & Kumar, R. (2015). 'Neoliberalism and Its Impacts'. In Darder, A., Mayo, P. and Paraskeva J.M. (eds). *International Critical Pedagogy Reader*. New York; London: Routledge, Taylor & Francis Group.

May, T. (1997). *Social Research*. 2nd ed. Buckingham: Open University Press.

Neelands, J. (1990). *Structuring Drama Work: A Handbook of Available Forms in Theatre and Drama*. Cambridge University Press.

Neelands, J. (2025). *Structuring Drama Work* (3rd ed.). Cambridge University Press.

Nelson, N. & Chen, J. (2023). *'Freire's Problem-posing Model: Critical Pedagogy and Young Learners'*. ELT Journal, Volume 77, Issue 2, April 2023, pp. 132–144.

Nieto, M. C. Á., Vahl, M. M. & Farrell, B. (2020). 'Critical Pedagogy, Dialogue and Tolerance: A Learning to Disagree Framework'. In Macrine, S. L. (ed), *Critical Pedagogy in Uncertain Times: Hope and Possibilities*. S.L.: Springer Nature.

Ross, E. W. (2015). 'Dr. Dewey, or: How I Learned to Stop Worrying about Where Ideas Come from and Love Critical Pedagogy: Authority, Hierarchy, and Me'. In Porfilio, B.J. & Ford, D. (eds). *Leaders in Critical Pedagogy: Narratives for Understanding and Solidarity.* Rotterdam, The Netherlands: Sense Publishers.

Shor, I. (2018). "A Luta Continua": Afterword to Pedagogy of the Oppressed. In Freire, P. *Pedagogy of the Oppressed: 50th Anniversary Edition*, Bloomsbury Publishing USA, 2018.

Vygotsky, L. (1986). *Thought and Language.* E. Kozulin, A. The MIT Press.

Yin, K. R. (2009). *Case Study Research: Design and Methods.* 4th ed. Thousand Oaks, CA: Sage.

The impact on young migrants

Balbir Sohal and Gilroy Brown

Executive Summary

This study examined the impact of drama on pupils who were new arrivals or migrants, as part of the 'Creating "Schools of Recovery"' model. The evaluators watched 21 performances in three primary schools over a period of two years. Most of these schools had a high proportion of children from migrant backgrounds in comparison with national averages, and this included a small number of children who had come to the UK within the previous two years.

Data collected included: observations of performances by researchers; listening to pupils' and teachers' views through the process of focus groups; one to one conversations and questionnaires. Despite trying, the researchers were challenged in gaining access to parents'/carers' perspectives, a shame as it was felt that would have enriched the information on the target group and their experience of the project.

Four strong themes emerged in our data analysis, related to the impact of the project on young migrant children:

- Empathy
- Belonging and relationships
- Sense of agency
- Resolving conflict situations

Our findings revealed that:

- Drama is a very effective tool as it offers new arrival and migrant pupils an opportunity to put their points of view across and be heard.

- These pupils were confident in exploring different and sometimes complex themes and more importantly found that their voice was being valued.

- Analysing and reflecting on the performances also allowed these pupils to work through personal issues, explore their emotions and their identities.

- The language and self-expression used was beneficial in terms of the pupils' personal development and wellbeing: giving time and space for young migrant pupils to talk and express their feelings does assist in understanding themselves and others in the world, which is so important in forging their own identities.

It was challenging to measure the impact on teachers when looking at their pedagogic approaches, due to a number of factors such as investment of time and prioritising the project.

Background and contextual information

New arrivals, migrants and refugees cannot be seen as one homogenous group as their backgrounds and life experiences are different. Refugees, for example, are among the most silenced and marginalised members of our community. The lens that we looked at within this project was how pupils from these groups engaged with the theatre they experienced from Big Brum and the impact of this within their learning.

The focus of the evaluation was the experience of those pupils who were either new arrivals, migrants, or refugees. We focused on three primary schools situated within the West Midlands region. Benson and Rookery Schools are both situated within Birmingham, Stoke Heath is situated in a neighbouring city, Coventry.

Birmingham is the second largest city in England and is home to over 1.1 million people ... and growing. Its rich history and culture are reflected in its varied neighbourhoods and environments. Birmingham suffers from high levels of deprivation, with 43% of the population living in the 10% most deprived neighbourhoods in England, making it rank as the seventh most deprived local authority in England. While there are pockets of deprivation in all parts of the city, deprivation is most heavily clustered in the area surrounding the city centre.

Today, 44% of the city's population have a migrant background, with around half of that number having been born abroad. The Indian community accounts for 7% of the working age population in Birmingham, compared to 3% in England: the city also has the second-largest Pakistani community in the United Kingdom. The 2021 Census recorded that there were 195,102 Pakistanis living in Birmingham, making up 17% of the city's total population. Black Caribbean, Black African and Black (other) people total 9% of the population.

Coventry is a diverse and cohesive city with a relatively young population. Over the past few decades, the city has become increasingly ethnically diverse, with 45% of the population identifying as being part of an ethnic minority[5] compared to 26% in England as a whole. A larger percentage of school children in the city come from an ethnic minority than the proportion of those from such minorities in the adult population. Migration now accounts for a growing portion of the city's expansion, with students attending the two major universities in the city contributing to this.

Coventry has a long history of providing safety to those fleeing conflict and persecution and has been recognised as a City of Sanctuary and International City of Peace and Reconciliation for many years. Coventry has taken part in the national Vulnerable Persons Resettlement Scheme (VPRS), Vulnerable Children Resettlement Scheme (VCRS), and the more recent UK Resettlement Scheme (UKRS). As of March 2022, there were 1,368 asylum seekers receiving support in Coventry. This is the fourth most of any local authority in England (with only Birmingham, Liverpool and Southwark supporting more). The true number of asylum seekers residing in Coventry is estimated to be 2,000 people – the highest proportion of asylum seekers per head of population in the West Midlands region. As of September 2022 the number of Ukrainians living in Coventry under one of the UK support schemes was approximately 200.

A series of unprecedented world events throughout 2022 and the lifting of restrictions following the coronavirus (COVID-19) pandemic led to record levels of international immigration to the UK. The main drivers of the increase were people coming to the UK from non-EU countries for work, study and for humanitarian purposes. There are significant inequalities across Coventry's neighbourhoods and the extent of that inequality is large compared to other areas nationally. As a Marmot city,[6] Coventry is working to address the inequalities by resourcing and delivering universal services.

---

[5] The term 'ethnic minorities' refer to all ethnic groups except the White British group. Ethnic minorities include white minorities, such as Gypsy, Roma, and Irish Traveller groups, as well as those who identity as White Irish and 'White Other' (often people who have moved to the UK from other European countries).

[6] A Marmot City involves taking a whole-systems, assets-based approach to adopting Marmot Review (2010) policy objectives related to health inequalities and related matters.

Schools' background

The three schools involved in this study are primary community schools that provide education and support for families within their respective schools and their surrounding areas.

Benson Community School is situated in West Birmingham, with a catchment that is primarily within the city centre. Rookery is situated just outside Birmingham city centre. Over 76% of the population in these areas consists of ethnic minorities. The largest minority groups are Asian, Asian British (38.6%), followed by Black, African Caribbean (25/9%), Mixed or multiple groups (5.1%) and other ethnic groups (7.1%).

The Benson School ward is amongst the more deprived wards in the city and has the sixth highest share of residents with no qualifications of the 69 wards in the city. Resident employment rates in the ward are much lower than the city average and claimant/unemployment proportions are well above the Birmingham average. Rookery School is mid ranking for deprivation as it contains some established inner city estates. Resident employment rates are slightly higher than for Birmingham as a whole and claimant/unemployment levels are below the city average.

The number on roll at Benson over the period of the study was 432, with an age range of 3 – 11 years. The gender of the pupils is mixed. Children entitled to Free School Meals (FSM) was 222, although more were entitled to this support. Pupils for whom English was not their first language were 283 (67.9%). 52 pupils (12%) were eligible for SEN support and 7 had an Education and Health Care Plan (ECHP).

At the time of the study, Rookery catered for 462 pupils between the years of 3 – 11. The gender of the pupils is mixed. The FSM number was 204 and pupils for whom English was not their first language numbered 264 (57%). 68 pupils (14%) were eligible for Special Educational Needs (SEN) support and 18 had a EHCP.

Stoke Heath is located on the outskirts of Coventry city centre. The largest minority group within the locality were Asian, Asian British (21.7%), followed by Black, African Caribbean (10%), Mixed or multiple groups (3.4%), and other ethnic groups (4.9%).

In this school, there were 510 pupils on roll at the time of writing: it is a mixed gender school of whom 172 pupils were eligible for FSM. Pupils for whom English was not their first language numbered 286 (43%). 114 pupils were eligible for SEN support and 6 had an EHCP.

The use of theatre/drama within an educational setting with reference to refugees, migrants and new arrivals

The groundbreaking Theatre in Education (TIE) movement was first pioneered by the Belgrade Theatre in Coventry in 1965 as a way to use drama and theatre to create a range of learning opportunities for young people. Certainly, a lot of the work was about raising difficult and sensitive topics and issues with children and young people. Certain topics that teachers had difficulties in exploring, such as nuclear disarmament, war, sexuality, often formed the content for these experiences. Undoubtedly, teachers perceived the approach in a positive light, citing the importance it had towards educational outcomes.

In essence 'theatre' means 'to gaze on' (implying the presence of spectators), whereas 'drama' is 'a thing done' or an event in which those present are not so much onlookers as active participants. Chris Cooper (2013, in Jackson & Vine, 2013) argues that TIE is 'theatre' in form but 'drama' in content.

Big Brum's distinctive approach to Theatre in Education, as set out in its Artistic Policy and 'Nine Principles of Working' (see page 9), differs from companies with a more issue-based or curriculum-orientated focus.[7]

The use of drama and in particular TIE and interactive drama within educational settings allows pupils to develop empathy, tolerance and social awareness, cooperation and collaboration. It also helps nurture key concepts of democracy, justice, rights and responsibilities, identities and diversity (Cziboly and Union, 2010). It offers a personal connection and engagement for viewers and pupils, unlike any other educational method.

---

[7] The following offers a TIE approach that differs from Big Brum's, but may be familar to some readers:

"It's important for you to remember the following characteristics that typify TIE:

- *There is a clear aim and educational objective running throughout.*
- *A small cast so actors must be versatile and often have to multi-role.*
- *A low budget so actors often play instruments too.*
- *The production must be portable so the design is simple and representational.*
- *They explore issues from various viewpoints, so we can see the effect of an action upon a range of people.*
- *There is some level of audience involvement.*
- *They are rarely wholly naturalistic because direct address or narration is used to engage the audience.*
- *The costumes are simple and representational, especially if actors have to multi-role.*
- *They may include facts and figures to educate the audience.*
- *They may have a strong message or moral running throughout."*

Children need to understand key processes and skills (critical thinking and enquiry, advocacy and representation, taking informed and responsible action). This is important for all children. However, children who are from a refugee/new arrival/migrant background have a different starting point. Their migration circumstances, processes of settling here and experiences of British society differ. Also, as a result of complex and shifting British immigration policies, they are in different legal relationships with the state in terms of rights and obligations. Different social locations, identifications and values in terms of ethnicity, gender, class, stage in the life cycle, also affect these groups' identities. At times there might be conflicts between constructions of self, community and society. Sometimes integrating into a new social environment leaves these children and their families with no space to reflect on their experiences.

> *"Drama is an ideal vehicle and can offer a safe and non-threatening environment for exploring issues such as identity, a sense of belonging, by the use of story children can engage creatively and imaginatively and bring in their individual experiences, elicit empathy and more importantly give children confidence to use their voice and be heard and encourage and empower children to investigate challenging situations."* [8]

It is important that all children develop a sense of agency in which they feel equipped to fulfil their role as informed citizens of the future. This is even more important for those pupils who are from a refugee or migrant background, as this group is often marginalised, invisible and disfranchised.

Findings, discussion points and impact
To help us navigate the impact of what this project had on the focus group of new arrivals and migrants, four strong themes emerged:

- **Empathy**
- **Belonging and relationships**
- **Sense of agency**
- **Resolving conflict situations**

---

[8] Solomon's Theatre Company, www.Solomontheatre.co.uk

Empathy

By being actively involved in the TIE programme, pupils can begin to understand life from another person's perspective. Pupils can gain new experiences and perceptions that enable them to shape their understanding of life and also enrich their confidence levels (Cziboly and Union, 2010). In particular, refugee children who have undergone forms of emotional turmoil can develop a positive outlook by engaging in activities that help them in coping with difficulties facing them. Drama, in these programmes and this project model, allows the creation of safe spaces for pupils to explore issues that matter to them.

The plays were able to elicit a sense of empathy from the pupils and resonate with their personal experiences. One example was the feeling of abandonment experienced by the Miller's daughter ('Rumpelstiltskin'). At Benson, a Nigerian boy (a relatively recent arrival) alluded to his father, when thinking about the Miller giving away his daughter. When asked how he felt, he spoke of experiencing anger and sadness. The pupils also made links with the character Oliver Twist who they were currently studying as part of their story project. They saw similarities between Fagin and the Miller in terms of their exploitative motives. One boy commented that *"the father indulged himself"*, and when asked to elaborate on this, he stated that the father was indulgent and driven by his own self-interest. The vocabulary and understanding of the words within the correct context was advanced, and demonstrates a rapid language acquisition within this stimulating and favourable dramatic environment.

The callousness of the father, giving his daughter away, also aroused a sense of indignation from the rest of the group. They alluded to the daughter being seen as a *"commodity"* and pondered on the question *"how can you give a human being away?"* This question, central to the story of 'Rumpelstiltskin', clearly also relates to the themes of belonging and ownership that we outline below.

Some young migrant pupils felt uneasy and made reference to feeling *"sick"*. They were upset that the girl in the story could not stay with her dad and that her mother had died. Interestingly, they felt sad in themselves and for the girl in the play at the same time. It is noteworthy that it was mainly the girls that expressed this.

A number of these pupils spoke of feeling fearful and slightly bewildered before the performance, when they observed the actor-teacher, who played the Miller's daughter, tearing a paper doll apart. There were gasps of surprise, and one child was visibly distressed and thought the doll had died. However, as the play progressed, they were able to see the circumstances that led to her actions, which deepened their understanding.

The performance of 'Minotaur' managed to capture the visceral thrill of the fighting between Theseus and the creature. There was a considerable level of theatrical authenticity (the weapons, bloody garments, severed head) that gripped the audience. The questioning that followed the performance explored the reason why the Minotaur did not appear to want to kill Theseus. As a result, with probing questions from the actor-teachers, the pupils began to see the Minotaur as a figure that was also a victim of circumstances and needed to be pitied. When questioning the pupils as to why the Minotaur did not attack Theseus, the initial response from the pupils was that they saw him as a lonely figure and many young migrant children could empathise with him.

Belonging and relationships

A sense of belonging involves feeling accepted and liked by the rest of the group, feeling connected to others, and feeling like a member of a community. Human beings in general have a desire for strong social ties and quality relationships. Many migrant pupils and recent arrivals face unique challenges, and they may have distinct social and emotional needs because of their differing backgrounds. Apart from their lived experience, these pupils are negotiating new roles and identities in an unfamiliar cultural context; this adjustment to a new environment can take a long time. Therefore, feeling a sense of belonging is particularly important for migrant pupils so that they can see themselves as belonging to the host community: part and parcel of this is being accepted by the school community.

These children were able to gain a deeper understanding of the concept of 'belonging' as a result of having to empathise with the daughter in 'Rumpelstiltskin', who had been abandoned by her father. This in turn led to deep conversations in the classroom about their own sense of belonging to a community, be it peers, family, classroom or some other group. The pupils saw the marriage of the daughter and the King as being one sided and transactional; purely for the King's benefit and personal pleasure. By not belonging to herself, the young migrant children recognised that the daughter had also lost her sense of identity and value.

The actor-teachers asked the question *"can you really belong to anyone?"* This elicited a number of responses from the pupils; some young migrant pupils stated that the daughter belonged to her dad and then she belonged to the King. They recognised, as children themselves, that they did belong to their parents but *"when you had no parents then you belonged to yourself and have control of yourself."* That was to say that when you are on your own you belong to yourself. Another pupil said, *"Belonging meant that something is yours, it's yours and nobody else's"*. And, as one such pupil aptly stated, *"to be a person is to be you, a child belongs to itself you can't really give it away"*. A further young migrant pupil commented *"the baby is alive, it's more precious than gold, you couldn't therefore put a price on anyone"*. A few of these pupils were also indignant, stating this was not how normal people should treat each other!

The different classes were very engrossed during this discussion and could relate this question to their own experience. Whether it was easy for the queen to give her baby away, the unanimous response was *"No!"* There was a deeper discussion from some young migrant children in that the queen was *"giving away the next generation of your family and therefore no longer part of your family"*.

The aspect of relationships aroused the same level of feeling as those that occurred when discussing 'belonging'. Conversations in the classroom enabled all pupils, including young migrants, to further explore their understanding of relationships within various communities (i.e. peers, family, classroom). These discussions took place during some of the schools' Personal, Social, Heath Education (PSHE) days.

Sense of agency

Once pupils have the right to express themselves and influence decisions that concern them, they may be said to have agency. When children have the opportunity to do this, they can develop the feeling of control over actions and their consequences, which can give them control over their own lives. To have a sense of self relates to the previous theme of belonging. Thus, framing agency is an aspect of learning. This is perhaps especially important for young migrants and recent arrivals.

> *"Agency propels developmental outcomes, especially self-identity, which is an agentic core of personality by which humans learn to increasingly differentiate and master themselves and the world. It gives meaning and purpose to life and perspective to human efforts. Through it, individuals come to situate themselves, for instance, as belonging to a distinct 'race', place, ethnicity, nationality, gender, or culture"* (Guo & Dalli, 2016: 6).

The young migrant pupils were highly engaged when given opportunity to interact with the actor-teachers during 'Rumpelstiltskin'. One pupil stated, *"I liked the part when I was asked to write on a piece of paper* [suggesting solutions for the Miller's daughter, who was distressed] *to fix it."*

Being reflective of what they had experienced was captured by the actor-teachers using the following rubric with the pupils:

I can't … … … I don't know how … … … and I need … … …

When engaging with the character of the Miller's daughter, these pupils said they could not imagine what it would be like to be alone or live without the King. Also, that she was struggling to take care of the baby on her own and she did not know whether she could have a life of her own. The latter seems particularly resonant in relation to the potentially precarious situation encountered by recent arrivals.

When presented with the phrase, *'I don't know how…'*, the young migrant pupils commented that they did not know how the Miller could give away his daughter and some were shocked by what he did. Others stated that maybe he needed to do that so that he and his daughter could survive; it was a matter of necessity. At times, the pupils put themselves in role as the characters of the play, such as the Queen when her husband died. They did not know how to look after the kingdom and the baby, and many of the pupils were offering solutions, such as asking friends, her father, the people in the kingdom. Some of the pupils alluded to the girls' future, in that she could find another husband.

When asked by the actor-teachers, mid performance, *"what did the girl need?"*, there were a number of suggestions. These included, *"help, support, a friend, a companion"*. Not only did this demonstrate the children's sense of agency, it also demonstrated empathy. Furthermore, these suggestions link to notions of relationships and belonging, as discussed above. The children suggested that the Miller's daughter needed people around her that might help her take care of her baby, *"she needed money, food and needed to protect the baby"*. A number of pupils were anxious that she also needed to know the lullaby so that the baby could sleep, and they wanted her to stop crying and to ask for help. Again, there seem to be particular resonances here in children's potential home and family circumstances as young migrants and recent arrivals.

Resolving conflict situations

Conflict is an inevitable part of life and being able to resolve conflict situations and improve relationships is essential for everyone. Problem solving skills, listening, communicating and using dialogue effectively empower pupils to handle conflict in a safe and productive way (Peacemakers, 2022). This is even more important for pupils from a migrant background who have to negotiate their way with fellow pupils, their school and the community in which they live. Environment plays an important role in developing conflict resolution skills amongst pupils. The use of thinking, offering suggestions, stating the consequences and relating it to real life situations can be effectively used within a drama setting. The ripple effect in this is that it enhances pupils' self-esteem, self-worth and their emotional intelligence.

The pupils were given the opportunity to engage in conflict resolution, notably in the second performance of 'Rumpelstiltskin'. Through the actor-teachers' consistent use of still images, and questions to assess the audience's level of engagement, the pupils were able to interact confidently with the actor-teachers on stage and assist with the development of the play. The best example of this was when selected children were asked to advise the Miller's daughter when she was in state of indecision. She was conflicted because she did not want to give her baby away and she did not know how to tell the baby she had thought about giving her away.

A range of solutions were offered by the children to the immediate problem and to possible issues that might arise later. Advice from young migrant children included "...to stay calm and take a deep breath and think about what she could do herself..." also "...to take a step back and she would make it alright in the end". One interesting observation was that while the pupils thought the Miller's daughter should tell her baby daughter the predicament she had been in, a majority of pupils in all the schools said it needed to be handled when the baby was older, so that she would understand. Some said they could write a letter now and give it to her baby daughter when she was older. Some stated that the Miller's daughter (now Queen) could also add that she "had made it right in the end". One of the young migrant pupils gave a rational explanation and stated that sometimes it is the "adult's fault and they do things wrong but they can make it right in the end". All these suggestions imply an emotional intelligence, a degree of resilience and an experience of the world that these children have been able to bring to the story.

Young migrant pupils' experience of the project
Overall, there was a genuine openness on behalf of the pupils. They really enjoyed the dramatic/theatrical experience and their reaction to the performances was very positive.

However, there were two pupils (at Rookery and Stoke Heath) for whom it was more challenging again, as both children had additional needs (identified as being on the Autistic spectrum). This resulted in the length of concentration needed being difficult for them to manage. In one of these schools there was a migrant child who was hearing impaired.

For all the pupils in the target group, English was their second language. Various strategies that the teachers deployed were used to support these groups of children in all the schools. What was also notable was the actor-teachers engagement with these pupils: time and space was given in order to include their comments in a whole class discussion

(see also section on the impacts on SEND children, page 96)

When gathering data after the performances, focus group discussions were deployed. A number of questions were asked (see Appendix 2, page 93).

The majority of the young migrant pupils really enjoyed the experience of 'Minotaur', with children commenting that it was *"a good play"*, they *"liked the play because it was three dimensional, made you think how the character thinks"*. One pupil said he *"retold it to his mother every night"*, although another pupil said he *"thought the play was too cute and didn't like the story"*. They found the set and the music/sound atmospheric and evocative.

All these pupils really liked the character of the Minotaur because he was big and strong. A number also stated it was a violent play, but they liked the blood which they knew was not real! One child said it was very extreme, eating people, but then went onto say that this used to happen a long time ago. A number liked the Minotaur because he liked blood and added that it was *"a shame he was judged for a crime he did not commit"*.

In 'Rumpelstiltskin,' most migrant children did not like the King because he was a *"gold digger"* and *"very greedy"*. When asked whether being greedy was good, the response was sometimes *"it can be"*, sometimes not. All liked the Daughter/Queen and thought she was a strong person in the end. A few liked the fact that she got mad and angry with Rumpelstiltskin.

The characters that these pupils identified within the play ranged from liking the fact that the Miller's daughter in the play became the Queen and also liking the fact that the King died. A few saw the Miller as strong because he had to make a hard decision. Even though Rumpelstiltskin was a villain, they liked him because he was clever and he became rich with all the gold. What was interesting was the rationale deployed as to why a particular character was the favourite: again, themes of status, wealth, strength and intelligence. It is interesting to set these values alongside the more intrinsic and empathetic values that we have identified above.

The young migrant pupils truly engaged as an audience when they were involved with the story; when the actor-teachers asked them for solutions and got them to think about different options within the fictional story. One pupil said this part was brilliant and a majority agreed with him.

One girl stated that, with 'Rumpelstiltskin', she felt sick when the girl could not stay with her father and sad that the girl's mother had died. The different plays, and the way in which they were used/framed/explored dramatically, raised a number of strong feelings amongst the pupils; feeling sick because of the story of the Minotaur, feeling good when the plays made them laugh. Generally, these children found the plays *"cool and fun"* and could relate to the characters easily.

In order to gauge the impact of how the pupils felt at the beginning and the end of the dramatic experience, there were a range of responses: some thought the plays were good and they liked the drama because it reminded them of English. A few said they were unsure what was happening in the beginning but then understood it later. For some, the plays were too long, while others said *"it was a lovely performance"* and that they liked the stories.

As to whether they thought drama was a good medium for learning, young migrant pupils' comments ranged from *"no"*, to *"it was ok"*, *"I'm not sure"* to *"definitely it was worth it"*. There is much to learn from these inconsistent comments, which might point towards the clarity of the question being asked. However, all in all, they really enjoyed the stories. The key words learnt and reinforcement of some concepts from the performances included; how important the law was, carnival, environment, serial killer, minotaur and myths, death and sadness.

Teachers' evaluation

Apart from discussions with the teachers, questionnaires were also deployed in order to gauge impact, the following performances were referred to; 'Ripped', 'Along the Silk Road', 'Rumpelstiltskin' and 'Minotaur'. Teachers confirmed that the use of drama was successful in encouraging the young migrant children to think about the characters' actions and motives through their understanding in a real-life context. They observed that by sharing ideas it aided thoughts for writing and therefore assisted pupils to understand texts and, more importantly, the feelings of the characters. The use of drama enabled the pupils to access and enjoy a form of cultural capital that they otherwise would most likely not experience.

What the teachers wanted for all their pupils, including young migrants and recent arrivals, was to be able to access the performances and enjoy them. One teacher in particular wanted the pupils to make links with work previously done in drama sessions and for the pupils to use the fiction of the drama to think about their own decisions in 'real-life' and how they could therefore influence their own futures. Another teacher wanted their pupils to engage with a text and to inspire creative writing, whilst a further teacher wanted the pupils to know and feel that they were deserving of such dramatic experiences.

As to what the young migrant pupils thought about the play afterwards, the teachers differed: one stated that the pupils had discussed the play and used it as an opportunity to reflect and consider motives; they found it enjoyable. Some found following the narrative challenging for their pupils, due to the language used. Two of the teachers said there was not really much of an impact and another said that *"I've not personally heard the kids speak about the play since – but then again this is the case for a lot of things"*. Some teachers knew how to follow the dramatic experience and integrate the pupils' learning by offering additional opportunities that the pupils could make use of when reflecting on their experience. However, others needed more guidance as to how best to follow up this approach to leaning, something might be addressed by the company more rigorously in future?

When asked whether anything surprised them in terms of the young migrant children's perceptions, one teacher stated that *"the children were very considerate of how the characters in the play felt and to understand why they made the decisions that they did"*. Another observed that *"It was nice to see the kids relax and enjoy themselves without feeling the pressure of a test, quiz, or worksheet."*

When asked about the impact of the performances on themselves, and what they felt, for one teacher it reminded them of when they had first read 'Rumpelstiltskin.' For another, it was interesting from an adults' perspective but they struggled to translate it to the classroom. In another instance, a child had experienced difficulty in accessing the performance and the teacher had spent most of the time during the performance reflecting outside with the pupil concerned.

In taking the learning forward for themselves as practitioners, the following ideas were raised:

*   applying the 'Rumpelstiltskin' play into a short writing activity for pupils to suggest a course of action for the girl identified in the drama;

*   another teacher tried to fit it into their English unit but found it did not quite fit;

*   for one teacher, it made them realise that they needed to be conscious of their pupils, particularly those with additional learning or language needs, in their desire to be involved.

This means that whilst the work was useful, teachers in this context were challenged to think creatively about how this might support, strengthen and/or supplement their pedagogical approach(es) in meeting the needs of all children, including young migrants and recent arrivals.

The performances explored a number of issues that really stretched the pupils' thinking capabilities. As to whether teachers thought that drama could explore difficult and complex issues, all agreed that a dramatic approach to this subject matter did indeed enable young migrant pupils to successfully *"depersonalise issues that the pupils may be surrounded by and use their knowledge to consider how to overcome challenges"*. One teacher stated that it *"offered another means of communication"*. Another teacher stated that she was *"blown away"* by the level of conversation that took place between the actor-teachers and the pupils and the responses from the children through skilful questioning. This demonstrates that the facilitation of the TIE programme that is integrated into the performance of a story is potentially a powerful approach.

Performances also differed in approach, depending on the actor-teachers involved, and therefore elicited different responses from the pupils. In Rookery, there were two performances of 'Rumpelstiltskin'. The first took place in the Summer Term 2023, with a Year 3 class towards the end of their academic year. The second performance was in Autumn 2023, with a Year 3 class a few weeks into the new academic year. The teacher commented that the first play was *"a challenge"*. When asked to elaborate she said *"the pitch was quite high … and some didn't get it"*. However, the second performance – with slightly younger children - was described as *"perfectly pitched"*.

Teachers in this school noted that the actor teachers were able to engage the children by being *"thoughtful about their responses and picking up on any misconceptions"*. The teachers added that the young migrant children felt that their opinions were valued by the actor-teachers. During the first performance in the Summer, the actor-teachers had asked a range of questions to assess the young peoples' level of engagement, whereas in the Autumn term the actor-teachers used more explorative strategies, such as pausing images, to specifically focus on key aspects of the play. The latter approach was seen to be more effective as this enabled all the pupils, regardless of ability, to move generally at the same pace, particularly those with additional needs.

The impact on the teachers was marked, with one stating that *"It has allowed me to consider and reflect how I can use strategies such as drama and role play within the classroom to explore other difficult scenarios such as in PSHE lessons"*. All the teachers wished to incorporate more drama in the curriculum: *"Generally, it has served as a reminder that I want the children I teach to have more enriching experiences in the classroom than the typical Maths and English, especially as I know most of them otherwise won't be able to experience them".*

The implications for their own teaching and learning, and how the dramatic experience has impacted on how teachers might deliver the curriculum, was also something a majority of teachers commented on, as demonstrated by comments such as *"It has an impact on how I can deliver certain lessons or approach challenging issues with my students to better them as individuals".* The last question asked of the teachers was for them to give words that described their own learning as a result of their own experience of the work. Words included the following: *"Motivated, reflection, continuous, values and respecting them, awareness, thought-provoking, empathetic."*

Big Brum's Nine Principles of Working
Evaluating the project against Big Brum's 'nine principles of working' (see page 9), the following conclusions were arrived at. These apply to work with all children in the schools, including young migrants.

Principle	Observation
1. Trust every child *Big Brum vows to treat young people not as undeveloped adults but as human beings in their own right, respecting their experiences and understandings, getting to the heart of what it is to be human.*	In the first performance of 'Rumpelstiltskin', Richard asked probing open questions at key points during the play. He explored the subject of belonging in great depth in an attempt to elicit greater empathy from the pupils. (This also links to *Theme 1- Empathy*, above). In the second performance of 'Rumpelstiltskin', Zoe freeze-framed the story when the King threatens the Miller's daughter. She emphasised that the character was distressed, had lost hope, was locked away and therefore had no control over her circumstances. This enabled the children to personalise the situation more acutely and deepen their sense of empathy, again linking to *Theme 1*. In the performance of 'Minotaur', Richard asked probing open questions about the Minotaur in an attempt to elicit empathy for him. He offered the pupils time to reflect and to imagine what it would have been like to be the Minotaur (alone , frightened, misunderstood).

2. High teacher-young people ratios *We facilitate small group work with up to 30 young people to ensure a high ratio of actor-teachers to young people, maximising participation and inclusion.*	The second performance of 'Rumpelstiltskin' maximised opportunities for participation and inclusion. Zoe used assessment for learning regularly by briefly pausing the performance and asking open and targeted questioning (also actively including the pupil with additional needs). She was also thoughtful about responses and addressed misconceptions. This clearly modelled and facilitated the conditions for *Theme 2 - Belonging and relationships* and to a lesser extent *Theme 3 - Conflict resolution*. Pupils were also asked to participate in the play and to determine the outcome of the story. This links to *Theme 3 - Sense of agency*.
3. Free for all audiences *A very important factor in breaking down the normal socio-economic factors that prevent young people from accessing the arts, especially theatre and drama.*	The in-depth discussions, study of characters / context and selected props in the classroom before the performance enabled the pupils to adopt the appropriate mindset required to appreciate the experience of theatre. This links to *Theme 3 - Sense of agency*.
4.Be crystal clear *We have clear and candid discussions with schools before we perform, identifying any special approaches that may be required.*	(See 5. Make art accessible)
5. Make art accessible *We're bringing art into a familiar space that young people already inhabit, breaking down a common barrier of arts engagement: attending arts venues and the 'alien' effect that has on young people.*	In all the performances the children were engaged and generally at ease as the audience. This generated a sense of 'belonging' (*Theme 2*). Some performances had a greater impact on young migrant children than others, but all the children enjoyed the experience.

6. Build safe spaces *We are carefully crafting every drama session so young people can place themselves into theatre and respond to reality at a safe distance from their own experience.*	This worked particularly well with most of the young migrant pupils. It was evidenced by the ease by which the children could describe the themes within the plays. Even though some themes resonated deeply, the pupils were able to detach themselves in order to articulate their answers. In this sense, the pupils were implicitly exploring a relationship to the theatrical experience (*Theme 1- Empathy*).
7. No wrong answers *Big Brum demonstrates that there are no wrong answers because we are interested not in what is 'correct', but in what young people think and the process by which they come to these conclusions.*	The actor-teachers in both productions ensured that all pupils' responses were valued and encouraged and the children engaged in reflection and conversations with talk partners to consider different points of view. (*Themes 1, 2, 3 & 4*).
8. Ask the big questions *We question effectively and are renowned for our ability to utilise poignant questioning with young people to open up imaginative responses and help them think in new ways.*	Please see comments above on the impact of the performances. It can also be said that the level of discussion that took place during and after the performances enabled some teachers to facilitate and develop more creative/critical thinking in subsequent classroom discussions.
9. Get lost in the moment *We work in the moment, entering sessions with the goal to respond to the ideas of the young people present as they process what they have seen and want to discuss with our people.*	This was especially noted when there was interaction with the pupils, asking them to problem solve and deploying at times the technique of freeze frame. The set (particularly in 'Minotaur') was very effective in engaging all the senses.

Methodology

Interaction between Big Brum and the schools started in January 2022 with a range of performances that were targeted at specific key stages; 'Ripped' (UKS2), 'Romeo and Juliet' (UKS2), 'The Silk Road'(UKS2), 'Rumpelstiltskin' (LKS2 – Year 3) and 'Minotaur' (LKS2 – Year 4). In depth analysis was carried out on the latter two TIE programmes in the three schools (see also timeline on page 4).

- 'Minotaur' – this story centred around the Minotaur, a Greek mythical creature, with the body of a man and a head of a bull. The Minotaur was placed in a labyrinth: he was dangerous and fed on human flesh. We noted that this TIE programme explored themes of heroes, sacrifice, choices, freedom, problem-solving and death.

- 'Rumpelstiltskin' – we noted that this TIE programme investigated the concepts of belonging, greed, sacrifice, anger, ownership, death, loneliness, strength of character, promises, and the basic drives and emotions which are shared by humans. The story explored the repercussions of a father 'giving' his daughter away to a king. This 'gift' was based on her supposed ability to make gold from straw.

The evaluators watched 21 performances in three primary schools over a period of two years. The performances were seen by approximately 620 pupils, ranging from Year 3 to Year 6. Among this number, there were several children who had come to the UK in the previous 2 years. At Stoke Heath, there were only 8 recent arrivals or migrants in the groups that we encountered. This was an unusually low number in comparison to previous years, and this was potentially an outcome of recent governmental immigration and settlement policies.

This evaluation was mainly concentrated on the two programmes; 'Rumpelstiltskin' and 'Minotaur'. Data was collated from the researchers' observations of the pupils' interactions with the performances, pupils' views and discussions in focus groups, questionnaires and one to one discussions with teachers. Views were sought from parents, but this proved challenging to organise (despite using strategies such as questionnaires being sent home and/or offers of coming to school sessions). One explanation for this might be that the English language was a barrier, or in the case of new migrants who had come to study in the UK, the pressure of time and availability. It is worth noting that migrant families are sometimes not sure as to how to support their children academically as they are not yet familiar with or fully aware of the education system of the country.

During the performances, we observed how the pupils interacted with the story, in particular focussing on those pupils that were new arrivals or recent migrants.

Observation was also made during the pre- and post- sessions that the teachers led within the classroom setting. Discussion with the pupils took place over the Summer of 2023 in focus groups, in order to uncover, discuss and understand commonly held perceptions and attitudes. Rather than attribute specific quotes to pupils and schools, we decided to incorporate them together so that the pupils could talk freely. This was especially useful because, for some pupils, English was their second language. The cohort of recent new arrivals in some of the schools was fairly small, so pupils from a range of ages were brought together as one focus group.

In order to evaluate what the teachers themselves thought of the impact of Big Brum's work, we designed questionnaires (Appendix 2). In some schools, this set of questions was adapted due to the nature of the conversations and the in-depth analysis of the participants. We did try to convene a teacher focus group, but time constraints of the schools did not allow this. Trying to get any feedback from parents/carers was also unsuccessful. It is worth noting that there was a high degree of interruptions and delays in delivering the programme due to staff illness and strike action – this was a very turbulent time for schools!

Conclusion

In our diverse schools today, migrant children have to negotiate new roles and identities in an often unfamiliar cultural context. Adjusting to this can at times be difficult. To ensure that migrant pupils not only adjust but thrive academically, socially and emotionally, school leaders, teachers and other educators can offer a variety of strategies and support to develop the students' skills. The use of Drama is one such pedagogical approach.

In the research, one could see that Big Brum being involved in the schools did influence the wellbeing of the young migrant pupils and the school culture. Young migrant pupils felt that they had a voice and more importantly that this was listened to. Time was dedicated to eliciting responses from these pupils and certainly it was found that the self-esteem of these pupils was raised, in that they were eager and willing to have a dialogue with the researchers. These quality conversations enabled the young migrant pupils to engage in critical thinking and also to articulate ideas and feelings.

The importance of dialogue was emphasised and the introduction of new vocabulary and understanding the context was also easily assimilated. When reflecting on their experience of the performance, particularly through being together in a small group, the young migrant pupils were able also to support each other: one example was of a young

Syrian girl translating for a Polish hearing-impaired pupil (as she had learned to sign), and offering us the boy's comments. The fostering of a positive spirit and encouraging others in the group to explain their answers to the question was also visibly noted. There was clear evidence of all four themes that we identified: empathy; belonging and relationships; sense of agency; resolving conflict situations

The teacher should, and does, play an essential role in the interaction they have with pupils, including young migrants. However, in terms of the project, the researchers found this was not the case with most teachers. Opportunities for facilitating the learning were lost during some of the programmes, particularly in relation to pupils who had additional needs. Those teachers who did engage with all pupils during the performance (including young migrants) were able to offer prompts to pupils to think critically and creatively.

In the future, when deploying TIE, any themes that arise from the performances need to be acknowledged and developed by teachers, by making time to explore and consolidate the learning within the classroom context (Fernezelyi & Varadi, 2010). This could be further enhanced by developing it in the following curriculum areas:

- Personal, Social, Health Education - exploring concepts of relationships, families, friendship, self esteem;

- Social, Moral, Spiritual, Cultural – pupils' senses are creatively engaged with the performance and they are willing to reflect and share their experience. They have an opportunity to understand consequences and differentiate right from wrong. Pupils can also gain positive awareness of their own and other cultures

- Cultural development - by engaging with the performance, appreciating different cultural perspectives and stories

Two of the schools did explore these themes within their curriculum in the short term. Long term, an important discussion for the schools is whether they need to further prioritise the arts. Potentially, and more importantly, Big Brum might need to consider navigating this context too. The impact of any intervention does take time and requires investment from schools. This project was also challenged by the other pressures upon schools, sickness and strike action.

A third of the teachers engaged in this project came away and reflected that this intervention was very useful and that the school should offer more opportunities like this. They also offered positive observations on their ability to support migrant pupils and it made them reflect on their own pedagogic approaches. However, for the remaining two thirds, there was not a marked impact that could be noted (see also page 122). For some schools, time was very much an issue, while a crowded curriculum, plus the issues of strike action and illness, made it difficult for these schools to manage the project.

In relation to young migrants' language acquisition and articulation through the medium of drama, the TIE programmes would have benefited if they had included more pupil interaction. It would have been useful to have included structured or scaffolding strategies that the teachers could deploy after the performance so that they could assist their pupils. A one-size-fits-all approach could be mitigated by offering advice on understanding the specific needs of children and how concentration levels can be scaled up.

It would have also assisted the teachers (and therefore all learners) if they had a resource pack with some techniques and strategies that they could use, so that Drama could begin to be embedded into the curriculum. The confidence of teachers does need to be boosted in the area of Drama: quite a few teachers were not confident and, if they had this support, could be creative in their approach to incorporating it (see also page 148).

Overall, there was a genuine engagement between the telling of the story and the pupils. The schools managed very well despite the number of issues they had to contend with. The young migrant pupils were able to understand difficult concepts, they were able to express themselves and to be creative: the performances touched them.

The use of Drama and stories is so powerful and all pupils – including young migrants and recent arrivals - need an inspirational environment that sometimes lies outside the ordinary. As Howard Gardner (2011) states, every child has a spark inside him and it's our responsibility as educators to ignite that spark.

"The use of drama enabled the pupils to access and enjoy a form of cultural capital that they otherwise would most likely not experience."

Appendix 1: Definitions

Asylum Seekers are people who have claimed asylum under the 1951 United Nations Convention on the Status of Refugees on the grounds that if they are returned to their country of origin they have a well-founded fear of persecution on account of race, religion, nationality, political belief or membership of a particular social group. They remain an asylum seeker during their application or an appeal against refusal of their application is pending. If their claims for asylum are successful, they are granted refugee status.

Unaccompanied Asylum Seeking Children (UASC) are children who enter the UK to claim asylum in their own right, and who are not accompanied by anyone who by law or custom would be responsible for their care. These children are accommodated by children's services as children in care

Refugees are people fleeing armed conflict or persecution. They are so recognised precisely because it is too dangerous for them to return home, and they need sanctuary elsewhere. Refugees are defined and protected in international law via the 1951 Refugee Convention and its 1967 Protocol as well as other legal texts, such as the 1969 OAU Refugee Convention. One of the most fundamental principles laid down in international law is that refugees should not be expelled or returned to situations where their life and freedom would be under threat.

In the UK, refugees are people whose asylum claims have been granted and therefore are legally entitled to remain in the UK for a defined or indefinite period of time, depending on their individual circumstances. They are also legally allowed to work, access welfare, housing and other public services.

Migrants are people who choose to move not because of a direct threat of persecution or death, but mainly to improve their lives by finding work, or in some cases for education, family reunion, or other reasons. Unlike refugees, who cannot safely return home, people who are migrants face no such impediment to return. If they choose to return home, they will continue to receive the protection of their government.

Appendix 2

The questionnaires/focused group questions shared with pupils, teachers and parents/carers were based around the following themes:

- Intent
- Implementation and
- Impact

The performances from which we obtained this data is largely focused on the following performances in the schools

- 'Ripped'
- 'Minotaur'
- 'Rumpelstiltskin'

Pupils

As the group of new arrivals, refugees and asylum seekers was small in the respective schools, it was decided to hold focus group discussions with the pupils. The questions were a guide and some groups did not complete all the questions as other issues were raised and we wished to enable the pupils to have a voice and speak freely.

Pupils:

- What do you think the play is about? (plot/character/relating it to themselves?)
- Was there anybody in the play that you liked/didn't' like and why?
- Which character/person would you like to be in the story and why?
- How did the play make you feel? Why did it make you feel like that?
- How did you feel at the beginning of the story? How did you feel at the end of the story?
- Do you like learning through drama/use of plays?
- What key words have you learnt today?

(A number of sub questions were also asked in order to enable the discussion to progress smoothly)

Teachers

Teachers completed a questionnaire and we also had formal discussions with them, Again, the following was a guide to enable us to capture the data we wanted.

- What does the use of drama enable the children to do?

- What would you hope the children get from this play?

- Have the children talked about the play? What did they think about it?

- Anything surprised you in terms of the children's perceptions?

- How did the play make you feel?

- How are you going to take the learning forward?

- Do you think that drama can explore difficult and complex issues with children?

- Have you noticed any change in the children from when they saw the production? (Over a period of time)

- What impact has this project had over you as a teacher?

- Can you give me three words that could best describe your own learning? (e.g. empathy etc)

- What are the implications for your own teaching and learning? Does it have an impact on how you might deliver the curriculum?

Parents/carers

Despite using a variety of strategies we were not successful in gaining any data from the parents. What was interesting is that the children did say that they spoke to their parents about the performances and some even recited the story to them. They noted that their parents were interested.

The following were the questions we tried to ask the parent/carers

- Has your child told you about the play they saw?

- What were the words they used to describe what they felt?

- Do you think it is powerful to use stories to explore things which happen in life?

- Do you use stories to explain and nurture your child?

Bibliography

Ballin, B. (2019) *Engaging, Exploring, Expressing – The Case for Theatre in Education*, Big Brum TIE, www.bigbrum.org.uk,

Cooper, C. (2013) 'The Imagination in Action - TIE and its relationship to Drama in Education Today', in Jackson, A. and Vine, C. (2013) *Learning through theatre: the changing face of theatre in education*. London: Routledge

Cziboly, A. and Union, E. (2010). *Making a World of Difference: A Dice Resource for Practitioners on Educational Theatre and Drama.* DICE Consortium.

Fernezelyi, B. and Varadi, L. (2010) *The Effects of the Theare in Education Programs of the Round Table Association on the Democratic Attitudes of Marginalised Young People,* United Democracy Fund

Gardner, H. (2011) *Frames of mind: The theory of multiple intelligences.* Hachette UK

Guo, K. and Dalli, C. (2016) 'Belonging as a force of agency: An exploration of immigrant children's everyday life in early childhood settings'. *Global Studies of childhood*, Vol 6 SAGE

Marmot, M. (2010) *Fair society, healthy lives: The Marmot Review: strategic review of health inequalities in England post-2010*. (2010) ISBN 9780956487001

Nsamenang, A.B. (2008) 'Constructing cultural identity in families'. In: Brooker L, Woodhead M (eds) *Developing Positive Identities: Diversity and Young Children*. Maidenhead: Open University Press

Peacemakers (2016). *Learning for Peace*. Birmingham: Peacemakers.

The impact on learners with Special Educational Needs and Disabilities

Dr Gill Brigg

Executive Summary

This report evaluates the impact of Big Brum's 'Creating "Schools of Recovery"' (SoR) Project model on learners with Special Educational Needs and Disabilities (SEND).

It draws on qualitative data within a phenomenological context, focusing on the lived experience of SEND children and their teachers. The data were gathered through in-person and virtual interviews with Big Brum and teachers from the schools involved in SoR, along with feedback sheets, emails, my own field notes, and tour reports.

- There were some generally positive responses from schools about the impact of aspects of the model on SEND children - resulting, for example, in raised levels of concentration and engagement. Particularly strong inclusive practice was the 'no wrong answer' philosophy as a way of valuing all ideas.

- However, there was a lack of pedagogical support, both before and after the performances, diminishing the impact of the model.

- In addition, there was a perceived lack of logistical security for schools, thus diminishing teacher confidence and increasing stress as performance dates were changed, or late to be confirmed, in some cases.

Major recommendations include:

  » involving a SENCO in the devising of specialist approaches to the model;

  » extensive Briefing Packs covering logistics and pedagogy;

  » the provision of specialist TIE programmes for SEND children.

The purpose of the recommendations is to develop the long-term empowerment and well-being of both staff and SEND children in the light of the Government SEND Code of Conduct (DfE, 2015).

There were limitations to the gathering of data for this report, largely in terms of quantity, due to the timing of the evaluation period.

Background

I was invited by Big Brum Theatre Company to evaluate the impact of the SoR project model on children with Special Educational Needs and Disabilities within six participating schools from January 2022 to the Summer of 2024. The schools, each situated within the West Midlands, were: Stoke Heath, Outwoods, Rookery, Fordbridge, Benson and John of Rolleston (see page 11). Each of these primary phase schools experienced the Big Brum project model and the performances around which the model focused were 'Rumpelstiltskin', 'The Giant's Embrace', 'Minotaur', 'Ripped' 'Romeo and Juliet' and 'Along the Silk Road'.

The SEND Context

Any young person with the label of SEND has arrived at that point after a great deal of bureaucracy, scrutiny, questioning and assessment. They may have an Education, Health and Care Plan (EHCP), a Personal Learning Plan (PLP - previously known as an Individual Education Plan), or they might be in the process of being assessed for a range of things that may impact on their learning, such as Attention Deficit Hyperactivity Disorder (ADHD), Autistic Spectrum Disorder (ASD) or Social, Emotional and Mental Health (SEMH) challenges. These children are likely to be on the school Special Educational Needs Register.

Almost 15% (14.4%) of the school population nationally has SEND. 2.8% will have their needs set out in an EHCP and the remaining 11.6% will be on some form of support such as a PLP (DfE, 2014). An EHCP outlines health, social care and educational support that is required to be provided to the child. It is a multi-agency document, drawn-up by the local authority, and stays with the child throughout their school life. Children with a PLP have a detailed plan, drawn up by the school, outlining how their disability impacts their learning. It will include teaching strategies and resources, including recommended external agencies whose role it is to support that child in school. The PLP can be amended or adapted. If a child is placed on a school's SEND register, they must have an EHCP or a PLP. Schools are not required to make their SEND register public.

Despite the raft of challenges experienced by a significant percentage of learners in primary schools, the Government Code of Practice suggests that almost all the needs of young people with SEND can be met within mainstream schools with specialist support (DfE, 2014). In 2023, 52.7% of all pupils with an EHCP were in mainstream, state-funded, primary or secondary schools (DfE, 2023). The reality of this means that classroom teachers, in collaboration with the Special Educational Needs Co-ordinator (SENCO) and Teaching Assistants (TAs), are required to plan for the significant pedagogical differentiation that this situation creates.

Using the social model of disability (Oliver, 1990), which suggests that it is the structures and systems of society itself that disable people, children with SEND may be educated within a mainstream system that is systemically unable to fully include them. Begum (2022: 37) states that: *"There is some degree of systemic tension between government legislation to educate SEND learners in mainstream schools without addressing the exclusionary nature of a disabling society"*. This is not to suggest that children in this situation are necessarily being failed, but this systemic issue may bring about some tension as teachers strive to provide a rich, equitable learning environment for children who may struggle with achievement through testing. This is especially highlighted when companies, such as Big Brum, visit schools with a vision of what can be achieved through a collective, negotiated and inclusive endeavour. This is in stark contrast to government legislation requiring schools to enforce standardised testing of their pupils based on a set of measurable, perceived norms created by a fundamentally disablist society.

The 'Creating Schools of Recovery' (SoR) Context
Big Brum's notion of 'recovery' comes from two distinct contexts:

- Post-Covid learning and teaching conditions within school populations.
- Working at a time of aggravated inequalities within communities as a result of socio-economic crises.

Consequently, this evaluation process is situated during a time of recovery within the context of continuing crises.
SoR is a development of Big Brum's cross-European project: 'To be or not be well', which ran from 2019 to 2022. The company stated: *"by working with teachers in affective,*

creative, and collaborative ways, the Company believes that they will be able to synthesise new forms of authentic educational practice that benefit all children." (Big Brum, 2019).

Having successfully tested a project model with one year group in one primary school, towards the end of the 2020-21 lockdowns, an upscaled version across multiple year groups in multiple schools in post-lockdown conditions was the ambition. The company's aim was, therefore, to carry forward the project model to develop this new, authentic, educational practice. In the words of the company itself:

> *"Schools of Recovery (SoR) substantially develops and extends a **model of work** that enables primary teachers to engage emotionally and intellectually with [the] Drama programmes' themes, so that they are able to offer sustained and inclusive support for all children, thereby maximising and prolonging (the) TIE programmes' benefits."* (Big Brum, 2019).

What is the model?

On the Big Brum website, the company states that all programmes within the SoR project have the following elements:

- Taster and follow-up sessions for teachers;
- Mentoring and planning support;
- Live theatre performances for children, except for 'The Giant's Embrace', which is a digital programme, accompanied by a set of storybooks.

Also offered are opportunities for testing and developing teaching materials and for teachers to work alongside specialist evaluators.

In this Evaluation Report, I begin with documenting feedback responses from teachers who experienced the model within SoR. I will then go on to reflect on these responses, positioning these reflections within some of the principles of Drama and Theatre in Education which are at the heart of Big Brum's work and some of the company's own Nine Principles of Working (see page 9).

I will then make a series of recommendations for the company to consider in order to increase the impact of the model on SEND learners and their teachers.

Gathering the Feedback

My reflective analysis was drawn from the following feedback responses gathered over a five-month period between September 2023 and January 2024.

- Feedback from Zoom recorded meetings from five schools following their involvement in the model.

- Face to face interviews with two teachers from one school on the day their children had seen a performance.

- Follow-up questionnaires from the same two teachers.

- Field notes from my observations at one school during two performances of the same programme.

- Zoom interviews with Big Brum's Lead actor-teacher and Big Brum's Educationalist at the conclusion of the model cycle.

- Written contemporaneous notes from Big Brum's daily tour reports from three different schools. These are internal reflections on sessions that have taken place and which Big Brum agreed to share for the purposes of this evaluation.

- Responses from teachers from a range of schools during a preparatory Zoom session, all of whom would be experiencing the same performance as part of the model.

- Email from a fellow evaluator recording her observations of an individual child during a performance.

- Informal conversations with Big Brum company members over three years about their approach to SEND pupils. These data are outside the specific remit of the SoR Evaluation Report brief.

Feedback Responses

The key feedback responses come from teachers reflecting on two questions:

- What was the impact of the Big Brum model on SEND learners?

- How might the Big Brum model have been more accessible to SEND learners?

What was the impact of the Big Brum model on SEND learners?

Teacher responses differed according to which performance their children experienced. At one school, 'Rumpelstiltskin' inspired the response that all children, including SEND, were *"very engaged"* and that teachers were not required to manage behaviour due to the children *"enjoying and participating"*. Additionally, *"it was the perfect length of time for SEND children who find it difficult to sit for long periods of time"*. The breaking up of the story of 'Ripped' into sections or 'chunks', with explanations in-between to guide thinking, was seen as being inclusive methodology to which SEND children responded well. There was very positive feedback from one school regarding the skill of the actor-teachers in ensuring that *"all kids connected with the live stuff in their own way and your staff could identify 'who needs more from me?' They were really natural at it."*

Another school noted that one of their SEND children, who was usually a passive learner, was *"surprisingly active"*. They attributed this reaction to: *"A different kind of context, different people, different kind of narrative, different approach"*. This was an example of a SEND learner being comfortable with a pedagogical approach unaligned to what they might usually experience, and out of that came unexpected engagement.

In the school that I visited, one teacher noticed that the minimal number of characters in 'Rumpelstiltskin' meant that it was not overwhelming and so it was easier for SEND children to focus. Additionally, *"a safe space was created whereby no answer was wrong. This encouraged pupils to offer their suggestions as they knew they would be acknowledged and appreciated regardless."* Positive feedback was given to the actor-teachers because they spent time before the performance chatting to the children. This was perceived as a way to gauge the children's capacity for attention and curiosity and thus be mindful of these audience characteristics during the performance.

Zoe Simon, Big Brum's lead actor-teacher recalls that, during 'Along the Silk Road', teachers noticed *"very thoughtful and very compassionate behaviour towards the actors on stage. Something happened to one of the characters in the play and (the SEND child) felt he had to get up and help because he was so drawn to what was happening."*

The teachers and a Big Brum team member whom I interviewed, along with a fellow evaluator, all recalled the moment in a performance of 'Rumpelstiltskin' when a SEND child chose to move into the performance space and sit in the box of gold. The child experienced the performance from his chosen vantage point. The evaluator observed his engagement and wrote: *"The student, although appearing distracted, responded to almost every question and his answers were not only accurate but demonstrated a deep level of understanding."* Crucially for that child, the actor-teacher enabled him to remain in the box, and modelled clearly to teachers that it was fine for him to stay within it. Zoe, who was actor-teacher during this specific performance, also commented on this child's behaviour: *"he came out with some very deep and meaningful things."* It would be interesting to further unpick this notion of deep meaning and analyse how observers knew that those comments were demonstrating understanding on a deep level and what was it about his vantage point that stimulated his reaction? It could be suggested that the child's decision to enter the fictional space of the actors was a means by which he felt less connected with the real world of the audience and more connected with the narrative and its issues, along with the characters inhabiting it.

Following a performance of 'Minotaur', the daily tour report from the company records that a teacher spoke to the whole room, which included three fellow evaluators looking at different impacts of the model, saying: *"We have never had anything like this before for our year group ... it was absolutely incredible."* However, the headteacher of the same school raised some concerns afterwards about how an autistic child had responded to some face-slaps within the story. Whether this was because there was a behaviour being modelled that the child could have emulated or whether the action could have triggered a trauma response is unclear in the tour report. However further clarification from Ben Ballin, Big Brum's educationalist (who was present at the conversation with the headteacher), confirms that the latter was the case, and it is clearly important that the tour report records this incident as concerning to the school.

In a similar vein, a school who observed their SEND children being *"glued to it and sat still"* in a live TIE programme, raised a concern that the concept of stealing, clearly an issue that belongs in the real world but which was part of the fictional narrative in 'The Giant's Embrace', may need more careful handling for those children who require the motives for such behaviour to be carefully deconstructed within the cultural construct of a performance.

A school, which hosted performances of 'Minotaur' for their Y4 children, fed back that it was *"too difficult for SEND. They did not follow it as the action kept stopping"* and that *"some SEND children struggled with the slower pace."* Feedback from the same school about 'Along the Silk Road' for Y5/6 stated that *"It was hard to access for SEND children. Some language and terminology and phrases were difficult to understand."*

One particularly memorable moment was recorded in the tour report, recounted by Ben, and mentioned by the school at the follow-up meeting. It concerned a child who attends the Autism Unit at the school and who tore up a dictionary during a 'Ripped' workshop as part of the theatrical experience. His teacher said: *"One of his issues was that he destroyed things at home and at school. We try and manage it with multiple layers of support and outlets."* The noting of this incident by three different sources, indicates that it was of significance, and I will return to it later in the report.

A teacher whom I interviewed after a performance of 'Rumpelstiltskin' commented that the SEND children were finding it difficult to understand the context of the story because it required a high level of receptive language skill. She noted that there was a deeper level of engagement when the performance moved beyond purely listening, specifically with the inclusion of more 'dramatic' elements. On further questioning, the teacher was referring to moments of bold physical action in the fictional space, such as the revealing of gold or the King leading the girl away. This enacted, visual representation of key narrative moments is an example of Big Brum's inclusive approach.

For one child I witnessed, the amount of language, combined with his requirement to move around the space to regulate his behaviour, was overwhelming, and he needed to leave and return to his classroom a third of the way into the performance.

Both teachers whom I interviewed after I had seen 'Rumpelstiltskin' in their school commented that there was a discrepancy of skills between the two actor-teachers: *"The lead was really vocal and animated which I thought was really engaging and inviting. The other one was too quiet, and the children couldn't hear her. This made it difficult to follow the story and the character."* This is relevant because SEND children may have a greater need for vocal volume and clarity to engage them in the fiction, especially if they have visual or auditory impairments. The contrast between silence and sound is a key factor in creating focus for audience members with SEND.

How might the Big Brum model have been more accessible to SEND Pupils?
All schools responded with a request for greater preparation for the content of the performances.

One school reported that they had to make their own visual materials to help SEND children understand the story of 'The Giant's Embrace'. Another suggested that a copy of a playscript in advance would have been useful to prepare children for the story they would witness. This same teacher felt that the *"very emotional/almost scary"* response felt by SEND children, could have been more regulated by knowing the story of 'Rumpelstiltskin' in advance. Again, another teacher suggested that a story outline of 'Along the Silk Road' would have been helpful.

A statement from a participating school articulates the need for preparatory work: *"I appreciate it's hard not knowing the children beforehand, but class teachers could have scaffolding in place and basic differentiation to take into account those children who would struggle to engage."*

Speaking about children who are socially awkward, a request from the same teacher asked if Big Brum could *"come up with a variety of roles that would suit them (the children). If teachers had those roles in advance, they could be allocated to specific children"*. This suggests a desire by the teacher to extend drama methodology into the classroom and shows an awareness of the capacity of role-play to support SEND children in their learning.

A different teacher from the same school asked: *"maybe some pre-teaching of the performance would have helped the children's understanding. There were scenes where it was difficult to understand what was happening for some of them"*. Similarly, from the same school: *"the theme behind it was quite difficult for them to grasp. They loved watching it, but some didn't grasp what was going on. Maybe someone could have paraphrased the scenes during the performance?"* There is certainly an emphasis on 'understanding' rather than 'experiencing something within' the performed moment implicit in this feedback. This may reflect the pressure on schools to adhere to the formalised testing of stories within the National Curriculum framework for Literacy. It could be that teachers are expecting their children to engage with the mercurial aspects of performance in the same way as readers might engage with the permanence of a written text. There is some pedagogical conflict here.

One school, with reference to 'Ripped', felt that the Shakespearean language was a barrier to accessing learning for SEND children. A film, provided for teachers by Big Brum, was divided into ten- minute 'chunks' which included a recap of the story with each 'chunk'. A teacher recounted that each of these sections, in effect, took forty minutes of teaching time due to the amount of explanation that the teacher felt was needed. Therefore, despite the care that Big Brum took in 'chunking' the text in order to make the language more inclusive, the reality of delivering that careful pedagogy was deemed unachievable by this teacher. Another school, speaking about the same performance, had the same reservation, suggesting that some drama interventions would have been helpful. The same school commented that there was *"quite a lot of listening"* and that their SEND children could have benefitted from kinaesthetic breaks, described by the teacher as needing *"more hands-on moments"*. It is interesting to note that this section of the 'Ripped' programme was designed to be led in the classroom by teachers who, in theory, could have differentiated their pedagogical approaches according to the needs of the

SEND children. This suggests a perceived lack of skill and a distinct lack of confidence.

Teachers at the school where I observed 'Rumpelstiltskin' suggested that more interactive opportunities would have aided engagement. This school also felt that the characters in the story needed to be more relatable to the SEND children and, in addition, *"the plot went over some pupils' heads"*. Interestingly, it was felt that the SEND children would have benefitted from knowing that much of the performance was purely a 'watching experience' as some of their children put their hands up to comment on action without being asked to contribute. Both teachers felt that all children had to sit down for too long, resulting in restlessness at times.

One school commented that 'Minotaur', which was created for Y4 children, might have been better suited to a Y6 group.

I also looked at the feedback responses from teachers when asked how the experience of the Big Brum model could be improved for learners generally. It is a given that SEND learners are a sub-set of the general population of learners and so these responses are of relevance.

A general theme across all schools was that information and logistics from the company arrived with the teachers too late to enable the model to be included in the curriculum: *"Knowing when it's going to be so it's not last minute – we could focus our curriculum – or if it's stand-alone, we need to be flexible"*. From the same school: *"(The performance) doesn't link with our curriculum at school so time is the biggest battle."* Another school: *"A clear purpose would give us more idea how to prepare"* and *"more collaboration with Big Brum would have made it easier."*

The enthusiasm for preparation and follow-up materials was evident despite a lack of confidence from one school: *"(We needed to know if) the follow-up work drew out the correct themes that Big Brum considered relevant"*. The same school suggested that Big Brum could share some best practice examples of written work from other schools involved in the model. It was also felt that, within a school, shared planning and speaking with colleagues who had already worked with Big Brum, would be of benefit (see page 148).

Zoe noted that one school, who had a long relationship with the company and its model *"has been really good and instigated a lot of the follow-up work themselves."* However, she recognised that this pedagogical confidence was not the norm and was very clear in her view that *"without the teachers being supported it doesn't trickle down."*

Reflections on the Responses

Different Types of SEND

Throughout the evaluation process, I chose not to ask teachers specific details about the needs of their SEND children. These support needs would likely encompass children with Physical Disabilities, Sensory Impairments, Social, Emotional and Mental Health Difficulties along with a range of neurodivergent conditions, including Autism. Some children may intersect two or more of these categories of need. I was wary of further pathologising these children by asking their teachers to use these labels as part of the reflective process. I was aware that Big Brum had previously worked with learners with Physical Disabilities in specialist settings on a project called 'The Needs and Wants of Learners with Physical Disabilities' (Ballin, 2018) and this had been evaluated as being successful by the commissioning funder, the schools, and the company. None of the feedback from schools informing the SoR evaluation overtly mentioned the specific physical, auditory, or visual needs of the children who took part. Without specific prompting from me, the feedback largely centred on the capacity of the SEND pupils to engage cognitively or socially with the learning opportunities offered by Big Brum. Therefore, I posit that the majority of my evaluation is in support of those learners with neurodivergence, including Autism.

Logistics

Much of the teacher feedback about improving accessibility for SEND pupils was linked to more efficient organisation. Teachers noted that they required time to find links to their fixed curriculum. Additionally, there was a request that greater notice would enable performance spaces to be booked with sufficient time for colleagues to be re-roomed without losing goodwill.

Big Brum has a long and respected history of working in schools and the company is fully aware of the lead times required to enable schools to prepare for their visit. According to Ben, dates and times were sent to members of the Senior Leadership Teams appropriately in advance. Much of the above feedback about the logistics of the model points to the information not reaching the class teachers early enough.

Zoe corroborates this and acknowledges that there was some confusion of booking dates and timings: *"Things weren't condensed. I can understand that would have unsettled teachers and made planning very difficult so that's something to work on for us."* When asking her to explain the word 'condensed' a little further, she talked about the multiple calls and emails resulting from logistical changes which would put pressure on busy teachers.

These may sound like purely logistical issues but, by implication, they hint at class teachers not currently feeling that the model offered by Big Brum is sufficiently streamlined into the complex DNA of their schools. This disconnection may not be the case for Senior Leaders who are the initial recipients of logistical information well in advance of the visit by the company. However, it is unlikely to be the responsibility of these Leaders to prepare SEND learners for the experience ahead of them. It may be that the complexities of communication within schools disrupts the flow of information towards the teachers who need sufficient lead-time to plan and prepare for the company's visit. This is something that Big Brum will need to address if their work is to be inclusive for SEND children.

Radical Inclusion

The Big Brum team has an eloquent theoretical educational philosophy and is ambitious about how its model impacts teachers, but the company's input is one of many external influences within a school, several of which will offer a very different set of expectations.

> *"The pressure and power applied by policies on schools and practitioners do not always support the Inclusion philosophy, particularly if the outcomes associated with Inclusion are not achieved. Since Inclusion is achieved in different ways in schools, it becomes an aspiration rather than a procedural implementation."*
> (Begum, 2022: 218).

A basic tenet of Big Brum's work is that of radical inclusion. Outlined in their 2019 Report 'More and Better: Engaging, Exploring, Expressing', evaluators stated:

> *"TIE is radically inclusive, providing time and space for young people's learning in a way that cuts through established ideas about 'ability' (and 'disability') and has value for all learners."*
> (Big Brum 2019).

This recognises that radical approaches are required in order to address systemic inequalities that exist in many of society's monoliths, such as schools, as suggested by Begum.

The company's ambition in this regard is irrefutable. In response to the question: 'have teachers asked the company to develop their SEND work?' Ben states:

> *"We're interested in finding out more about it because we're aware that we're keen to reach and engage those children most on the margins. There's a sense in which all children are displaced or marginalised in all sorts of ways through their experience of*

the world." (2023)

Speaking about working with Reception children during the same interview, he suggests that *"when we tune in, (some) may appear to be on the margins and if anything, we prioritise those children."*

This is an example of Big Brum ostensibly putting marginalised pupils, some of whom will be SEND children, at the core of their practice. Big Brum believes that by maintaining the philosophy that all children are marginalised, then its approach prioritises the needs of all children. However, I would suggest that some children are more on the margins than others, and that children are not equally unequal, as it were. So, it could be argued that, in terms of SEND needs, Big Brum's definition of radical inclusion could be perceived by teachers as too 'broad-brush' and somewhat at odds with the differentiated learning approach required within classrooms. Indeed, the Government's SEND Code of Practice is prescriptive in this regard, demanding that: *"Potential areas of difficulty should be identified and addressed at the outset. Lessons should be planned to address potential areas of difficulty and to remove barriers to pupil achievement."* (DfE, 2015).

Zoe alluded to the complexity of radical inclusion for SEND pupils when asked if schools provided information about those children in advance of the company's visit: *"We don't necessarily get pre-warned. It's difficult because those children do need extra support, but in terms of the way we operate, that support is from the teachers. We try and interact with (the children) as we would with any other child ... so sometimes it's not any more useful to know."* There is a recognition within Zoe's statement that, despite the company practising radical inclusion, extra support is needed from the teachers of SEND children throughout the performance and/or workshop activities. This, of course, is what teachers do much of the time for SEND learners because, in UK classrooms, these children are not at the centre of the process of whole class planning. Many teachers wanted there to be differentiated tasks, both preparatory and follow-up, provided by Big Brum, to lighten the workload a little, in recognition of the demands of the SEND Code of Practice as mentioned above.

In terms of inclusion in the narrative content of performances, some teachers expressed surprise that their SEND children were drawn into the action or engaged in dramatic moments. Surely this is a 'low bar' for schools to set? How refreshing it would be if there was no surprise at this being the case. I would encourage teachers and Big Brum to work together to co-create expectations of how SEND children can be connected to both the form and content of the performance. If Big Brum were to practise radical inclusion led by the needs of SEND learners, these marginalised children would drive the creative process and thus there would be a greater likelihood of engagement being less surprising.

Crucible Paradigm

There was a greater amount of feedback from teachers when asked to suggest how the model could be more accessible, in comparison to the question about the impact of the model as they received it. This suggests that they know the key to improving the model, and points to a degree of ambition regarding how Big Brum, teachers and SEND children could work together to explore the performances. This reflects Heathcote's Crucible Paradigm, which is not only at the heart of Big Brum's work, but also a fundamentally inclusive methodology, believing, as it does, that the actor/ teacher and the child work together to create meaning (Johnson and O'Neill,1984).

> *"In TIE, the Actor Teacher and the young people co-operate in learning. This is the means by which we explore in order to explain to ourselves. We refer to this as the 'crucible paradigm' where we stir our knowledge around together. This not only transforms the relationship between teacher and student, but it transforms the relationship between student and student, who become collaborators in their learning."* (Big Brum, 2011).

I feel that teachers could use extra support with this in the context of SEND. For some SEND children the triadic arrangement of child, actor and teacher may be a relationship outside their experience. Even if the SEND child operates independently in school, without adult support, the experience of an actor 'stirring knowledge' with them may be confusing. Some may have challenges forming relationships with new acquaintances whose language register and body language, often within a fictional context, are at odds with those usually encountered in school. The newly equitable relationship with adults as co-creators may differ from a traditional teacher/child relationship that has taken months or years to form. Indeed, somewhat ironically, the SEND child may need a very specific, didactic learning style to provide them with structure and routine to free up their creative selves. Teachers spoke about the need to have preparatory materials to support their SEND learners and to prepare them for the company's visit. Teachers recognised the pedagogical skills offered by Big Brum and saw the potential for the resultant learning, but the Crucible Paradigm requires an approach that lasts longer than the short amount of time that Big Brum spends with a school 'inside the crucible', so to speak. The company's aim to offer *"sustained and inclusive support"* to teachers surely requires that teachers have training in the specific dramaturgical, pedagogical, and self-reflective skills so that they can continue co-making meaning with learners in the classroom, stimulated by the performance.

In the Crucible Paradigm there is an expectation that learning is collaborative and emergent, but in the case of teachers who had to explain the narrative of stories and underlying ideas to their SEND pupils, transmissible knowledge travelled in one direction only. During the preparatory session for 'Rumpelstiltskin', Richard Holmes, Big Brum's Artistic Director, spoke about the central question for the children being 'who owns me?' Referring to the girl in the story he said:

> *"The girl is them. But more importantly the young people are exploring the world situation through the safety and distance of the drama of the play. The young people are taking ownership of themselves in the world by questioning the world that's in them. A world that views everything including all of us as both commodity and consumer."*

The company feels that children will experience these deep, subliminal meanings subconsciously and osmotically. This is hard to evaluate. But the primary symbolism in 'Rumpelstiltskin' of young people in danger and the adventures they have, requires good quality teaching materials which include the 'safety and distance' devices that teachers can use in preparation and follow-up.

The sharing of good quality materials that teachers could use either in an extant way or which could be differentiated according to the needs of their students would be of huge benefit. One school felt that drama interventions would have been helpful. This was clearly something that the teachers believed it was Big Brum's job to provide, feeling that they had neither the pedagogical skills, nor the time, to devise for themselves. It would have been an opportunity to strengthen the quality of the learning experience and bolster the Crucible Paradigm, whilst also providing a form of Continuing Professional Development (CPD).

Angle of Connection

In celebrating children's innate capacity to be experts in being 'them', Big Brum offers a basically inclusive philosophy. The challenge comes in how to relate that type of 'knowing' to the lives and dilemmas of others as presented within a performance. Richard Holmes, in his introductory talk to teachers who would be experiencing 'Rumpelstiltskin', explained:

> *"We'll be asking the children to bring their skill and expertise in being young people. It's what they're really brilliant at and at knowing stories and 'story' and at being experts at play. These are the things we're asking them to bring with them. So as to understand the actions and behaviour of a young girl who is about the same age as they are."*

This explains the power of creating a strong 'Angle of Connection' - so that the child can begin to understand others in relation to their own lives. This requires the child to be simultaneously both inside and outside the fiction during the performance, or, across all aspects of the model, through the provision of good quality drama-based learning materials. This state of metaxis as described by Davis (2014: 53) may not be easily attained by some SEND children who may need scaffolded, slowed-down pedagogy to enable it to happen. In addition, SEND children, particularly those on the Autism spectrum, may not be 'experts at play' in the same way as their neurotypical peers. SEND children's play development may be delayed according to the specific nature of their learning disability and, indeed, whether or not they have experienced play at home with guardians and/or siblings. Peter states that *"It is crucially important that children with SEND are supported to make links from those learning areas in the drama as they may not otherwise make the connection"* (Peter 2021). Practitioners using Process Drama as a learning medium, along with specialist theatre-makers, recognise the complexity of this state for some participants and deploy 'stopping and re-starting' strategies to support with reassurance as audience members are processing the metaxis as it unfolds: *"This enabled the actor to be both inside and outside the story at the same time. The 'availability' of the actor to reassure audience members was paramount ..."* (Brigg 2023).

Sometimes the Angle of Connection may make itself apparent. As mentioned earlier, the SEND child who ripped the pages during the 'Ripped' workshop was noted by observing adults. This piece of dramatic action was part of a structured activity with the ripped dictionary being a central object in the process drama. Retrospectively, the company was told that this type of destructive behaviour is something the child displays at home. The tour report extends the context of this by explaining that he came late to the session when the needs and wants of the character of Rosie (the dictionary-ripper in the story) had been explored. The report asks the question *"Would his experience of enacting Rosie have been different if he had been there from the beginning of the session?"*

This raises some interesting points. His absence from some of the session meant that he did not witness any of the nuances behind Rosie's behaviour, thus a learning opportunity was missed. It could be that he was not enacting the ripping within the dramatic frame, which would reinforce metaxis, but merely ripping the dictionary because it was a physical action with which he was familiar. He may have strong sensory connections with objects of different textures or weights and the destruction may have been a way of regulating or de-regulating his arousal. His emotional state could have been triggered by being elsewhere when his peers were already engaged in the drama. Whatever the reasons were, this was one example of how prior knowledge of that SEND student would have been beneficial. Ben called it a *"profound need"* to rip up the dictionary. It would be interesting to consider the word 'profound' when applied to a SEND child. That child may find profound meaning primarily in kinaesthetic engagement with the world rather than in an analysis of his place within that world. Ben continued: *"What they're playing out through the theatre, is something that is part of their lived experience of the world in a very direct and quite literal way. It gave them permission to do something and explore something."* I feel that this incident was somewhat left in the air for that student and his teacher. It could simply have reinforced behaviour that those who care for him are desperately trying to modify. Ben recognises challenges of this nature: *"there's something that we and the school need to learn in order to communicate with each other about the needs of that child and the group."*

Ben's response hints at the differentiation required to engage certain SEND children, who may fall outside of the range of engagement 'hooks' required by neurotypical audiences. In the spirit of radical inclusion, the writing and rehearsal process at Big Brum sees all children as being marginalised, thus creating work which is intended to reach everyone. However, it could be argued that there are still likely to be children who fall outside of this approach who need specific, differentiated strategies to draw them in. Without drawing them in, they cannot experience metaxis and, without experiencing metaxis, they will never be able to find an Angle of Connection. A specialist offer from Big Brum for these children could be a way of addressing this challenge.

No Such Thing as a Correct Answer
A very strong message put across by Big Brum is the idea that no answers are wrong ones in the context of what it means to be a human in this world. This liberates the children to contribute freely to discussion and to operate within both the Crucible Paradigm and Angle of Connection. This point came across clearly from the two company members with whom I spoke.

Ben stated in his Zoom interview with me:

> *"Children struggle if they've been conditioned to think there's a right or wrong answer to everything. They sometimes struggle with open exploration. We give children permission. There are no right or wrong answers when it comes to what it means to be you."*

Zoe spoke about how this approach enables confident dialogue between actor-teacher and SEND pupil *"because we never limit what they can say."* For SEND children, this is clearly a liberating concept, but it is predicated by a requirement for them to understand the question to which they are expected to respond. This may sound like a statement of the obvious but SEND children with neurodivergence, when working alongside their more neurotypical peers during a TIE visit, are processing a myriad of new and extra stimuli, which may form a barrier: new adults, acting, a change of spatial configuration, to name but three. Even whole class experiences may be anathema to them. So, the non-wrong answer strategy takes extremely careful interventions to stimulate authentic responses from SEND children. Peter suggests: *"By slowing down children's play it can challenge their thinking, often to resolve a problem in a situation of uncertainty, and where there may be no right or wrong answer"* (Peter, 2021). This notion of uncertainty, or indeed anxiety, for SEND students operates on two levels. The first is uncertainty about the question being asked, and the second is the unusual pedagogical environment in which they find themselves. A teacher commented with reference to SEND learners: *"Fear is your natural response if you don't know theatre."* So, the 'no wrong answer' challenge is about both the form and content of that which is being explored. We can imagine that this fear may well be felt more acutely by SEND children due to the numerous challenges they face within the education system. Maybe this is another pedagogical justification for the company putting SEND learners at the core of their radically inclusive approach.

I finish these reflections with reference to two of Big Brum's Nine Principles of Working.

Principle Number Two – High Teacher-Young People Ratios.

"We facilitate small group work with up to 30 young people to ensure a high ratio of actor teachers to young people, maximising participation and inclusion."

Some SEND children may require kinaesthetic breaks in the performances as a way of supporting them in their understanding of the fictional world, and to support the Angle of Connection. For some, it is a way of processing new ideas. However, this may precipitate the child leaving the space, especially if their supporting adult is unsure of Big Brum's expectations of behaviour. If a child leaves the performance, an adult needs to accompany them, which means there may be fewer adults in the space who have knowledge of any remaining SEND children. This is a shortfall on two counts: the child misses part of the performance and the adult, having left the space with the child, is not available to support them with whatever they might have missed. Of course, a class-size group is preferable to a full Key Stage, or more, attending a performance, but account needs to be taken of the impact on the SEND children remaining in the room if an adult leaves with an individual SEND child. In one of the performances I witnessed, it was the class teacher who left with a SEND child, thus leaving Teaching Assistants with the remainder. This fundamentally diminishes the impact of the model on SEND children.

Principle Number Four - Be Crystal Clear

"We have clear and candid discussions with schools before we perform, identifying any special approaches that may be required."

Responses from teachers, and the actor-teacher with whom I spoke, suggested that there were few, if any, special approaches identified as being required by their SEND learners. I have a strong sense that this is because many teachers are unsure about what they can request. The company is seen as being the expert and that somehow teachers feel it is their role to adapt accordingly and to defer. Put simply, teachers may not know what they do not have in terms of the potential of theatre to enrich learning for their SEND pupils. They react with positive comments because they may not know how impactful the work can be for SEND children. They may not have seen it in action. There is little in the way of CPD for this work and few companies offer specialist approaches. Of course, this somewhat bold stance is based on my experience with companies and schools beyond the remit of this evaluation, but I believe that teacher responses to the Big Brum model support these stark generalisations.

To some degree, this lack of confidence explains why teachers may try to control verbal or physical behaviour by SEND children during a company visit. However, this very idiosyncratic communication is often interpreted by Big Brum as willingness to engage in the form and content of the piece. Zoe recounts observing a teacher who was working one to one with a SEND child whilst also overseeing the whole class: *"I think she was trying to hold him back at times because he would suddenly become quite vocal, but we gave him space to say what he was going to say and there were some quite profound things he came out with."* Placing this anecdote within a broader context, she adds: *"I don't know whether they're always given the space to speak, and if they do, it's not quite in keeping with what's going on in the situation, in the moment. They can be overlooked or moved-past."* I believe this is because teachers want to make the visit from the company as disruption-free as possible and may be unaware of the ability of the actor-teachers to handle such idiosyncratic behaviour. Big Brum's philosophy is always to give the child space to speak, even within a system that sometimes finds that option too time-consuming in the context of class size and teacher to child ratio.

Therefore, clarity should also extend to a dialogue about what the model can achieve if Big Brum were to work in greater partnership with schools to improve access for SEND pupils. Some teachers commented that *"we didn't quite know what was expected of us."* This may be further evidence of communication issues between Senior Leaders and class teachers, the former having been included in discussions with Big Brum about expectations.

General Conclusions

I am aware that my conclusions are drawn from a limited set of teacher responses (see Data Collection, below) but there are some clear common threads which emerged. My face-to-face conversations with teachers were focused on 'Rumpelstiltskin' and it may be that other performances using the model provided materials and support for teachers of which I was not aware.

From the wider data set gathered through feedback discussions, the teachers gave generally positive responses about what Big Brum contributes to the education of their children. There were a few examples of excellent engagement from SEND children and some examples where SEND children were overwhelmed or disengaged.

The teachers seemed to be unaware that SoR was predicated on *they themselves* being engaged emotionally and intellectually, in order to offer sustained and inclusive support to their SEND children.

The teachers required a greater level of logistical and expectational clarity from the leadership team in their school prior to the performance and for the model as a whole. All schools requested that high quality, curriculum-linked, preparatory materials (including drama tasks) be provided. Ideally these would be already differentiated for SEND learners. If this is not the case, sufficient time needs to be allowed for teachers to create differentiated tasks for their specific SEND learners preferably in partnership with Big Brum.

All teachers recognised that there were many potential learning opportunities for their SEND learners if Big Brum could do this work in greater partnership with them.

The company provided taster and follow-up sessions for teachers. However, from the evidence I saw, neither of these sessions provided pedagogical materials which would have impacted SEND learners in the classroom. Therefore, there was no pedagogical scaffolding for such children. This may have been different for schools which experienced 'The Giant's Embrace', which was accompanied by a set of storybooks.

I saw no evidence of SEND mentoring or planning support for teachers and, indeed, this was something which teachers requested in their feedback.

I conclude with a quote from Zoe. When I asked how she felt SEND children could be more included her response was:

"It has to do with the communication with the teachers. What I'd like is for teachers to trust us and trust the process. I'd like them to feel more comfortable to include more children with SEND. We might create special sessions for SEND. It's allowing teachers to know what it (the drama) can do."

Methodology

This Evaluation Report draws on qualitative data within a phenomenological context, focusing on the lived experience of SEND children and their teachers.

Data Collection

Despite the appearance of the Evaluative Report being based on a relatively broad data set (see page 100), the actual relevant data I was able to apply to specific SEND evaluation was extremely limited.

Why were there limited responses from teachers?

My data-gathering visits to the schools, originally planned for the Summer Term 2023, were pushed into the Autumn of the same year due to demands on hall space. The performances spanned two academic years, meaning that staff who had experienced an introductory Zoom meeting were not, in some cases, the staff who saw the performance. Therefore, the handing-over of logistics and preparatory issues to a new staff team was fractured and inconsistent. I feel that this caused teachers to feel underconfident with any questions I might ask them about the model. There were many changes of date and changes of timings when I was trying to set up visits and interviews. A teacher, whom I had heard talk enthusiastically about the benefits of the model to SEND children on a Zoom evaluation with Big Brum, did not reply to my request for a follow-up individual Zoom conversation. Therefore, those data do not appear here. The face-to-face interviews that I had arranged with one school via the headteacher were met with confusion from the staff team. During the hastily convened chat, one teacher had to leave after 15 minutes and the other after half an hour. There was a clash with staff meetings on this occasion and these took priority. I was only able to visit one school to see the performance as the cycle was coming to an end and opportunities to experience a live performance, and talk about it with teachers, were running out. The cycle had been running for over a year at the point when I visited the school. The difficulty in my talking to teachers indicates that some schools, despite being great supporters of the work of Big Brum, did not feel particularly invested in the development of the model. A couple of schools referred to the performance as 'a treat' or a 'one off', indicating that the model was not viewed as a coherent entity. It did not help that I lived some distance from the West Midlands and had no previous relationship with the schools.

Some teachers commented that they had been informed of the dates of the performances very late, thus making planning a challenge. I suspect that some teachers will have felt some degree of overwhelm at having to respond to my questions, feeling professionally compromised that they were unprepared to do so.

Due to the logistical challenges which I outline above, my work with teachers came at the end of the data-gathering cycle for the project as whole, and other evaluator colleagues had already visited and spoken with them. This was simply a case of unfortunate timing.

At the outset of SoR, I was reflecting optimistically on the level of in-depth teacher feedback following the 'To Be' project from which SoR had stemmed. However, in retrospect, the focus on teacher well-being, and teachers' responses to the question: 'Images of myself during lockdown' which characterised the beginning of 'To Be' meant that teachers were in a different place of priority: they had all faced the collective trauma of successive lockdowns and Big Brum served a huge need at that specific time. SoR did not have the same impact on unlocking the feeling-states of teachers. Zoe reflected on the well-being of teachers during the timescale of this evaluation process: *"Some of the feelings I got from teachers and the atmosphere within the school – I think we're in a time where teachers need so much support. We can't do this model without supporting the teachers."*

This lack of teacher focus on their own well-being was echoed by the minimal response to the question 'What did you notice in yourself?' put to teachers to during SoR feedback sessions. Their 'human-selves' were subsumed under the pressing, externally driven demands on their 'teacher-selves'. With SoR, in contrast to the 'human-self' focus of 'To Be', there was a sense of teaching having reverted to being driven by external factors, such as assessment and planning. There was much less emphasis on Big Brum starting with teachers reflecting on their well-being, and this may have impacted how they prioritised scrutinising the model. The addition of several specialist evaluators visiting schools may have impacted negatively on teachers' desire to commit time and energy to self-reflection. Thus, the main aim of SoR was compromised in its mission to enable primary teachers to engage emotionally and intellectually with the themes of the programme.

Why did I not gather evidence directly from children who experienced the model?
It seems counter-intuitive that, despite best practice for researchers working in the field of SEND education requiring input from the children themselves, the child's voice in its direct form, up to now, is absent from this report.

The Evaluation is focused on pedagogy spread across a number of component parts and, given that I would only be able to visit a single school once, I felt it best to work with teachers who were, in effect, gatekeepers to the learning process for SEND children. When interviewing Ben, we spoke about the individual needs of learners:

> *"There is a question for me about the relationship we need to have with teachers in a school. We may have to work with them for a while – before we can frankly discuss the needs of individual children. I don't think it's possible if you walk into a school for the first time."*

This was precisely the position I was in as an evaluator, and I was aware from the outset that measuring impact on an individual child of a specific performance, let alone the project model, was fraught with the risk of misinterpretation. I had no prior knowledge of the child, but the teachers did. Thus, I made the uncomfortable decision to reflect on the experience of these SEND children through the lens of the teachers and teaching assistants.

Recommendations

The following recommendations, drawn from my data and positioned within my reflections, will offer some suggestions as to how Big Brum's model could have greater impact on SEND learners.

There are three sets of 'voices' in the recommendations.

The first are my recommendations, the second is the voice of the teacher and the third is that of the child. They all carry equal status. The child voice reflects that data set gathered during this process focusing on the needs of neurodivergent children.

My Voice

- Invite an experienced SEND teacher or SENCO to work with you to revisit your definition of radical inclusion and re-position SEND learners at the centre of your creative process. This is likely to benefit all learners.

- Create Briefing Packs on your website and in hard copy form. The content of these packs will cover logistics and teaching ideas as suggested in the Teacher Voice and Pupil Voice recommendations below.

- Consider creating work specifically for neurodivergent children in order to best serve teachers in their adherence to the SEND Code of Practice.

- Develop CPD for teachers with regard to using Drama pedagogy to engage SEND children before, during and after Big Brum's visits.

Teacher Voice

- We enjoy hearing your philosophy and approach when we meet before you come into school with the performance, but this can never be my priority. Logistics are my priority because without 'when' 'where' and 'how' we do not feel in control, and this can cause stress. Tell us what you need well in advance.

- Make it easier for my Senior Leadership Team to disseminate information from you. For example, this could be a Briefing Pack in hard copy or on your website. These could include: story breakdowns, scripts if appropriate, and some drama activities so that we can strengthen the Big Brum model. This would give our SEND learners the opportunity to practise 'playing' with the ideas. I will never have time to devise these for myself, but I absolutely recognise the benefits of using them.

- Send us Social Stories to prepare our SEND children for your visit. This will help to minimise anxiety. You can find some examples here: https://www.theautismpage. com/social-stories/

- Expect there to be some contradictions within our cohort of SEND children. Some may need action slowed down, whilst some children might respond best to faster delivery. Their needs will be idiosyncratic so ask me lots of questions.

- Let me know exactly what you expect of me, especially if we are the focus of long-term development of Big Brum's relationship with our school.

- If possible, cross-reference your work to my work. Have a conversation about how we can merge our teaching and learning. This will enable me to support SEND learners in a more targeted way.

- If our SEND learners are going to access stories and ideas, send us the best performers you can find. We need the best performers for our children.

- Invite our SENCO to attend planning sessions but do not expect them to do anything specific. Their job is an almost impossible one but, by including them, it will help them to feel supported.

- Speak to our full KS team, including TAs, and reassure us that you expect some SEND learners to move around the space to make sense of both the real world and imaginary world and that you are prepared for it and will not judge us because of it. It would be even better if there were built-in opportunities for all of our children to move around the room during performances sometimes so they can get a cognitive break.

- Continue to chunk your performances so that our SEND learners have a chance to process, catch-up and have adult intervention if they need it.

Child Voice

- Move me from my classroom to the hall as gently as possible as I can get overwhelmed with corridors and too much excitement.

- Do not shock me with loud noises or sudden bright lights when the story is being told. I will learn more if I know there will not be any shocks.

- Encourage me to visit the room where the story will be told before everyone else arrives.

- I might find it hard to sit still so expect me to move around. I might even go into areas that belong to the actors, but I may need to do this for reassurance. It is helpful if all areas of the space are kept as clear from distractions as possible.

- Help me to move in and out of the pretend world by using my name, if you think that would help, and remind me when we are going back into the story.

- Use fewer words, or can you sometimes communicate with us without using words? This helps with the 'white noise feeling' that I sometimes find hard to process.

- Give me lots of time to think about things.

- Don't be afraid to say things like: 'this is only a story' or 'we're going to play that game again' or 'remember... I'm pretending to be a king'. This will help me practise how to play the theatre game.

- Only take me out of the story space if I get overwhelmed but provide me with a resource box so I can explore things about the story back in the classroom. Visit me before you leave so I can say goodbye and give you the box back.

References

Ballin, B. (2018) *The needs and wants of learners with physical disabilities.* Leicester: PDnet. www.bigbrum.org.uk/projects/learners-with-physical-disabilities [Accessed 23 May 2024]

Ballin, B. (2023) Schools of Recovery Evaluations. [Zoom Recording. Restricted Access] [Accessed between 5 and 26 February 2024].

Ballin, B. (2023) interview with Gill Brigg. 31 January. [Zoom Recording. Restricted Access].

Begum, S. (2022) *Practitioners' Perceptions and Attitudes Towards Inclusion of Children with Special Educational Needs and/or Disabilities [SEND] in a Primary Mainstream School.* Doctor of Education (EdD). Birmingham City University. https://www.open-access.bcu.ac.uk/14247 [Accessed 5 February 2024]. Unpublished thesis. p37 p218.

Big Brum (2011) Artistic Policy. *The 'Crucible Paradigm'.* Available at https://static1.squarespace.com/static/60d061bcd571dc3fb7554ef9/t/60da28adc343fd57d8339fd4/1624910001086/Big+Brum+Artistic+Policy.pdf

Big Brum (2019) Project Learning Resources. *'To Be', or not be well? Drama and Theatre in Education.* Available at https://bigbrum.org.uk/projects/to-be [Accessed 9 February 2024].

Big Brum (2019) *More and Better: Engaging, Exploring, Expressing.* Available at https://static1.squarespace.com/static/60d061bcd571dc3fb7554ef9/t/63c6adddbc1f6451ff469035/1673965030252/Engaging%2C+Exploring%2C+Expressing.pdf [Accessed 1 April 2024].

Big Brum (date unknown) Project Learning Resources. *Creating "Schools of Recovery".* Available at https://bigbrum.org.uk/new-page [Accessed 9 February 2024].

Big Brum (2023) Tour Report. Unpublished.

Brigg, G. (2023) 'Under Stjänorna (Under the Stars): Teachers as Careful Actors and Actors as Careful Teachers', in *National Drama Magazine*, 30.1, pp. 25-28.

Davis, D. (2014) *Imagining the Real: Towards a new theory of drama in education.* London: Trentham.

Department for Education (2014) *SEND code of practice: 0 to 25 years.* Available at https://www.gov.uk/government/publications/send-code-of-practice-0-to-25 [Accessed 19 February 2024].

Department for Education (2015) *SEND Code of Practice: 0-25 years.* Available at https://assets.publishing.service.gov.uk/media/5a7dcb85ed915d2ac884d995/SEND_Code_of_Practice_January_2015.pdf [Accessed 1 April 2024]

Department for Education (2023) *Special educational needs in England.* Available at https://explore-education-statistics.service.gov.uk/find-statistics/special-educational-needs-in-england [Accessed 19 February 2024].

Johnson, L., and O'Neill, C., eds (1984) *Collected Writings on Education and Drama – Dorothy Heathcote*, London: Hutchinson.

Oliver, M. (1990) *The Politics of Disablement*, London: Palgrave Macmillan.

Peter, M. (2021) 'Professional development in drama with learners with special educational needs and disabilities (SEND)' in *NASEN Support for Learning*, 36. 3, 424

The impact on teacher development

Rebecca Taylor and Emma Davis

Executive Summary

The evaluation considers the Big Brum 'Schools of Recovery' project model through the lens of 'teacher development' in non-lockdown conditions. Continuous professional development is an important aspect for both employers and employees in any given career. In this case, the evaluation examines to what extent the model, as realised through this project, provides opportunity for teacher development, whether its potential is reached and the impact of this, if any, on teaching practice.

Data was gathered from a variety of platforms throughout the project, which included evaluators' observations of live drama sessions in schools, feedback meetings (both face to face and online) with teachers from several schools and anonymous questionnaires sent out to teachers involved across the project.

The findings highlighted several themes within the context of teacher development. These were: priority and value given to the project; teacher workload; the environment and teacher reflection.

» **Priority and value given to the project.** Engagement and participation were limited across all elements of data collection, suggesting the project was not given priority by teachers involved in the project over other work-related tasks. There was clear evidence throughout that teachers felt pressure to continue with other aspects of their teaching role such as planning and marking. This supports the contemporary issue within the education sector of **teacher workload** being too high.

» Alongside this, **the environments** provided were not always conducive to effective learning and development through drama. This again highlights the low priority given to the project by schools as well as highlighting the importance of implementing effective environmental characteristics in order for the project to reach its full potential.

» The last key theme was **teacher reflection**. Interestingly, many teachers highlighted positives within the live drama sessions, particularly referring to the engagement of children and there being less need to manage behaviour. However, on the whole, during feedback conducted, teachers then said following the project, that they had not implemented any strategies seen nor had they changed their practice. There was little evidence of teachers acknowledging altering their practice following the project. This suggests there was minimal reflective practice and adaptive teaching following the project. However, some of the feedback on this is contradictory.

The evaluation also acknowledges that, in light of the pockets of deprivation in which the children live, opportunities to access live drama would often be limited and therefore the 'Schools of Recovery' project model offers opportunities to enhance cultural capital.

Overall, participation, engagement and priority have been found to be a real challenge throughout the project in which it is felt the project did not meet its full potential for teacher development. Considering that the aspect of 'teacher development' was just one angle to be addressed across a complex project, this could have meant each element became diluted and that teachers were not fully aware of all the aims of the project model. The scope of the project aims therefore could be deemed as too ambitious and therefore individual aspects lost rigor.

Several recommendations have been made to support the project model meeting its goal. In summary, these cover factors including:

» A need for tools to be implemented to ensure communication of expectations;

» 'Buy in' from schools, leaders and teachers;

» Appropriate environment, conducive of learning for children and teachers;

» Active participation to encourage teacher engagement.

Background and Contextual Information
In order to give context to this evaluation, it is important to start by defining what is meant by professional development. The UK Government (2024) suggests that different terms can be used when discussing teacher development, such as:

- *"professional learning"*;
- *"continuing professional development"*;
- *"continuing professional development and learning"*;
- *"joint practice development"*;
- *"in-service training"* (INSET).

They go on to suggest that *"training activities can be formal and structured (staff meetings and training sessions), or informal, unstructured and collaborative (informal conversations and the sharing of advice)."* Hendricks (2021) considers classroom observation as a tool for teachers' professional development and despite some pitfalls, observations can be a highly effective means to improving practice. This supports the finding that, although Big Brum's project model did not explicitly deliver 'teacher training', there were however opportunities for professional development for teachers through observation, reflection and critical discussion (see page 148).

Teachers involved in this study had the opportunity to observe a drama session and consider factors such as student engagement, adult and child interaction, questioning techniques, drama as a pedagogical approach and links to teaching. Although their observations might not necessarily have provided teachers with the teaching of specific skills that they could adopt in their classrooms, it could have allowed for a reflection on their own teaching and effectiveness of their current strategies and in this sense, the project and input from Big Brum was a form of Professional Development.

A focus on teacher development is important, as suggested by Somantri and Iskandar (2020), who note that it is crucial in ensuring that teaching and learning standards are upheld and improved in the school setting.

Reflective practice is a fundamental aspect of professional development for teachers, and its impact on classroom effectiveness and personal growth cannot be overstated. Kramer (2018:211) states that *"reflective practice is supposed to positively affect teachers' agency, expanding their scope of action and opening up perspectives for professional development"*. This is echoed by Suphasri and Chinokul (2021:3), who suggest the value in reflection is that *"when teachers reflect on their teaching practices, their awareness of their teaching increases, and they can then unlearn the ineffective teaching methods which may have undesirable effects on students' learning experience."* Engagement in reflection on their own skills and the effectiveness of strategies used by the actor-teachers in this programme could have led to improved teaching strategies by the teachers involved.

124

This could be achieved as teachers analysed their practice as part of the data collection process. As a result of reflection, teachers can develop their practice, which leads to the enhancement of children's learning in the classroom.

It was therefore envisaged in the project that teachers would reflect on strategies used, their own techniques in the classroom and consider how these connect, perhaps prompting an increased level of self-awareness. The project also had an initial goal of teachers 'tuning in' to the children's responses to the story/drama and the needs that these demonstrate. Nesbit (2007) highlights the connection, suggesting that self-awareness is an indication of the quality of reflective practice. It was therefore envisaged that this insight into their teaching practices could lead to an adaptation of some of the techniques used in the programme. In summary, it was expected that teachers' involvement in this study would contribute to personal growth and positive outcomes for both teachers and children.

The professional development opportunity offered as part of the 'Schools of Recovery' programme was aimed at enabling teachers to reflect on the use of dramatic approaches and techniques to inspire children's learning and development. Part of this involved the teachers reflecting on how the dramatic experience/Theatre in Education approach impacted on their teaching, if at all. This process of reflection is important as *"being a professional involves the need for you to review your practice in an ongoing way in order to keep your knowledge up to date and to continue to develop your professional skills. Professional practice is constantly changing and never static"* (Bassot, 2016:2).

Additionally, professional development is an important focus in relation to the project's focus on 'recovery', with Ofsted (2023) noting that *"the pandemic increased the pressure on teachers' time, which reduced their ability to access development opportunities. And where they were able to access any, the training was very often delivered remotely, and many teachers thought it was lower in quality."* In their review of teachers' experiences of training, Ofsted found that *"many teachers want more time dedicated to professional development, but that workload pressures prevent this."* However, a consideration here needs to be not just how the training is delivered and whether that is online or face to face, but also how often training takes place. For instance, Sims and Fletcher-Wood (2020:4) reflect that *"it takes time for teachers to assimilate new knowledge"*. They go on to suggest that training, which takes place as a one-off event may not be effective as it needs to be *"sustained over time"* (Sims & Fletcher-Wood, 2020:4). This could provide a barrier to the potential of the project model being realised if teachers are not provided with appropriate time and space. This could be due to the limited time available for schools to engage in such projects due to other demands and attainment pressures.

Alongside this is the notion that the academic subjects in primary schools are impacting on the opportunities for creativity. Cremin and Barnes (2018:430) state that *"creativity is not seen as an event or a product (although it may involve either or both), but a process or a state of mind involving the serious play of ideas and possibilities."* This programme involved children being exposed to drama-based experiences, which had the potential to extend thought, play with ideas, and develop a creative approach to the curriculum.

Cremin and Barnes go on to consider the ways in which children have opportunities to *"possibility think"* and which ...

> *"will involve you in immersing the class in an issue or subject and helping them ask questions, be imaginative and playfully explore options, as well as innovate. At the core of such creative endeavour is the child's identity. Their sense of self-determination and agency and their understanding of themselves as unique thinkers able to solve life's problems are essential ingredients of their success, resilience and general health"* (p.430).

The live Theatre in Education approach offered children the opportunities to have a free space in which to engage and become immersed in the performance, subverting more didactic approaches to education potentially seen in schools. Questions that were asked of the children enabled the sharing of ideas without a right or wrong answer. Kenyon (2019) considers the benefits of Drama in primary schools, noting that it is the area of the curriculum which is most about the process of learning rather than the product. As Drama, therefore, can play a key role in learning and development, it was important to consider how teachers viewed Drama prior to the study. Some commented that their school promoted drama through Christmas performances and class assemblies. This reveals a potential lack of understanding about the potential of Drama in Education and/ or Theatre in Education as a pedagogical approach to teaching and learning. One teacher commented that Drama ...*"is key. Children need to live a story/concept before they can talk about it and then write about it."*

The Continuous Professional Development (CPD) opportunities for teachers taking part in the project consisted of support and planning as well as encouraging them to reflect on their own learning. This may have differed across schools in relation to particular programmes. For example, five schools had more 'formal' CPD based around 'The Giant's Embrace' storybook and film: in one school, this was for the whole staff; in another for EYFS and KS1; and in the others, for single year groups. This would have taken the remit of the research beyond experiences for children. By way of initial support to ensure the success of the project model, all teachers were invited to a pre-session for programmes such as 'Rumpelstiltskin', which set out the aims of the research. As this was recorded, teachers unable to attend could watch it back and therefore still feel prepared for the 'Schools of Recovery' project.

Breakdown of the Schools Involved in Data Collection

Data on teacher development was primarily collected from three of the six project schools (see page 11).

Schools	Programme
Fordbridge Community Primary School, North Solihull	Fordbridge is a primary school in North Solihull, accepting children between the ages of 2 and 11 years with 548 children on roll at the time of the project. 61.2% were eligible for free school meals. The school is part of the Prosper Together Multi Academy Trust, having converted to an academy in February 2023. Prior to conversion, the school was graded by Ofsted as 'Good'.
John of Rolleston Primary School, Burton-on-Trent	A primary school near Burton-on-Trent, accepting children between the ages of 5 and 11 years. At the time of the project, there were 364 children on roll. 10.7% of children are eligible for free school meals. It is part of the Central Cooperative Learning Trust. Prior to conversion, the school was rated as 'Good' by Ofsted.
Outwoods Primary School, Burton-on-Trent	Located in Burton-on-Trent, accepting children from 5-11 years. At the time of the project, there were 456 children on roll. 20% of children are eligible for free school meals. It is part of the Central Cooperative Learning Trust. This school has a 'Good' Ofsted rating.

Findings and Discussion Points

This section will discuss the data collected throughout the study from various means and what this tells us about teacher development. Data for this study came from questionnaires, mind maps, feedback meetings and observations. This was collated both during the time frame when the live performances were taking place as well as afterwards as part of a process of reflection with the teachers.

Data was collected as follows:

Questionnaire	Sent to all schools who participated in the research in order to forward on to relevant teachers.
Feedback Meetings	These took place face to face and online with teachers who participated in the study across four schools.
Observation	The two evaluators observed two performances of 'Rumpelstiltskin' at Fordbridge Primary School
Mind maps	These were collated as part of the face-to-face meeting with one school.

Observations:

The researchers observed two performances of 'Rumpelstiltskin', which took place at Fordbridge Primary School with Year 3 children..

It was noted that children engaged well and one particular child (later identified as having SEND) especially interacted in the performance (see pages 101-102). However, there were some interesting points noted from the observation in terms of factors that could have impacted on potential teacher development as a result of the session.

Teacher Consistency and Engagement. During one performance (Session 1), there were two adults present for parts of the session. One was in the class initially but appeared to be working one to one with a particular child. Another came in towards the end of the session, relieving the other. However, there was little engagement with the session or children as she was working on her laptop. This leads us to question why the same adult was not present for the entire session, to what extent did the class teacher value the experience and what external pressure were they facing? There is an element of choice to be considered here. Were staff choosing to take the time out for other activities or had the school allowed them to not be present? Perhaps being present for sessions should have been a non-negotiable within the project.

However, were individual teachers given the choice to take part in the project or was this forced upon them? Patall, Sylvester and Hans (2014) highlight that there's a clear link between choice and willingness to engage. Perhaps teachers were not given the choice to take part in the project and therefore hindered engagement and participation. It could be suggested that staff didn't understand the potential value of the project for their own professional development, or perhaps they did but felt other tasks held more importance and needed to take priority. Input being delivered by another practitioner could have provided staff with an opportunity to 'get things done'. On the other hand, could it have been that staff felt underqualified and inexperienced in drama as a pedagogical approach and therefore 'left it to the experts', consequently withdrawing themselves from involvement? Perhaps if the model had incorporated a more active role for teachers, this barrier could have been lessened.

During another performance (Session 2), the class teacher was present for the entire performance, both in the classroom and the hall. However, it was observed during the initial performance in the classroom, that the class teacher was sat marking books at their desk. This would suggest that the full potential for teacher development through the project model may not have been reached due to a lack of teacher engagement. It does need to be noted that 'teacher workload' is a contemporary area for discussion within the education sector and consideration needs to be given to the potential volumes of work the class teacher may have been facing and therefore finding themselves unable to dedicate their entire attention to the session. Ofsted (2023) elaborate on this point and explain that both teachers and leaders feel the need for more time to be dedicated to continual professional development (CPD), but this is often prevented by other workload pressures. It was also mentioned by Ofsted (2023), that even when time in schools has been set aside for development activities, other responsibilities often intervene. This could very well be the case in this situation. Despite this opportunity for CPD to take place through the project, we question the priorities of other workload pressures. Adler (2002) raises an interesting point relating to this by suggesting that distance from a place of work or practice provides a vantage point for development. Being immersed in the day-to-day job can provide challenges in terms of professional development as day-to-day duties and challenges of the school and or classroom are still very present. It could be suggested that teacher development could have potentially been enhanced through the project if sessions took place away from the school in which teachers worked. This is further supported by Sellen (2016) who states that 60% of teachers feel that their high workload is a significant barrier to accessing development opportunities. This heightens the fact that teacher workload is not only detrimental to teachers' health and wellbeing but also to the uptake of CPD and therefore high-quality practices. This observation has put into practice what the Teacher Workload Survey (2019) outlined, where most participants said they felt they spent too much time on general administrative work including marking and planning.

It is also worthwhile here to consider the impact of neoliberalism on the landscape of education in a current context. Neoliberalism can be defined as the marketisation of education with an increased focus on assessment, measurable outcomes and progress, which put the parent in the role of consumer, choosing schools based on their potential for academic achievement (Moss & Robert-Holmes, 2022). The impact of this can be seen on an increasingly pressurised working environment in which teachers and headteachers are forced to comply with surveillance agendas such as Ofsted inspections and moderations (Fairchild, 2018). McDowall Clark (2022:5) considers how this increased accountability can be seen to be in conflict with the nature and ethos of the profession. She goes on to assert that accountability is visible in education through the 'legislated curriculum'. Echoing this is Roberts-Holmes (2020) suggesting that literacy and numeracy progress needs to be evidenced through data collection in schools. This could be a factor in the increased focus on academic subjects over a more creative curriculum (see page 148). The impact of neoliberalism in relation to this study could also link to the workload pressures and accountability and limited prioritisation of professional development opportunities.

The Environment. The programme that the evaluators observed took place in both a classroom and the main school hall, which was already set up in preparation for the children to come. Although the session was meant to start in the classroom, one class was led by an adult into the hall. This was disappointing as the children (Year 3, age 7-8) saw the scenery before the scene had been set in the classroom. This was a shame as the initial 'wow factor' and engagement hook of the children seeing the set for the first time had been lost. We could question why the adult was not aware that the session started in the classroom and would then transition into the hall. This again raises questions about the extent that teachers were made aware of the project model and what their expectation was of it.

Approximately twenty minutes before the end of the observed session, staff entered the hall and began setting up for lunch. This was extremely noisy and therefore distracting to the children, the actor-teachers and the observers. It was difficult for the evaluators to hear the actor-teachers over the noise and, despite moving closer to the children, it was still not possible to clearly hear. As a result, children became distracted, evident through fidgeting, turning around to watch the lunch set up and talking between each other, which had not been the case during the rest of the performance. Children then began entering the hall for lunch, which created further noise. The class teacher then had to step back to try to ensure there were no children from lunch coming close to the performance. This distraction however, hindered the class teacher from having the full opportunity to develop in terms of their own professional judgement and also hindered children from potentially getting the most out of the project from the performance. Again, this led the researchers to question why school staff came in to set up, when the hall was clearly being used for a performance and why there was a crossover between the performance and children beginning to eat lunch. It was noted that there was a hall divider, which could have been used that would have limited the noise and visual distraction, but this was not utilised. Perhaps this could have been planned for in advance. This again raises questions about the priority given to the project and the responsibilities of various stakeholders including the company, school leaders and teachers in the planning and preparation of the project.

Feedback Sessions with Teachers

Several feedback sessions took place that involved some of the schools that took part in the project. One particular feedback session took place at a school in Burton on Trent over the period of 1 ½ hours with evaluators and teachers, another feedback session took place in meeting space at a school in Birmingham over the period of 45 minutes. A further school in Birmingham opted for a 20-minute face-to-face session. Finally, one took place online over the period of 1 hour with another school in Burton. Admittedly, there are some inconsistencies with the structure of each feedback meeting to be considered including time, model (face-to-face or online) and structure (each meeting took on a slightly different format). It could be questioned whether the feedback meetings were intended to be a part of the project model or if this was an addition to give feedback to the model itself. Either way, it is possible some further consistency here would have been beneficial: but again, perhaps would have relied on this being communicated as a clear expectation of the project with outlines, timing etc. Teachers from all year groups who took part in the project were present for the meetings and this was the first opportunity for teachers to formally hear from each other's experiences. Evaluators attended 75% of the feedback sessions - details can be found in Appendix 1.

These sessions offered a chance for researchers and teachers to come together to discuss aspects related to the 'Schools of Recovery' programme. This included teacher reflections on their own experiences and how they perceived the children's engagement and the impact this had. Unfortunately, these sessions were limited because of time constraints within the schools, impacting on the data collection. This led us to question why schools were limiting the time teachers were available to spend contributing to the feedback. This experience is potentially evidence of the impact of neoliberalism, as described above: the increased accountability on schools and teachers and the commoditisation of their time clearly influencing their ability to engage. Interestingly, Skerritt (2020:5) notes that *"relative to other schools in England, academies come under increased scrutiny and face intensified accountability."* As Fordbridge, Outwoods and John of Rolleston are all academies, we could assume that this sense of scrutiny and pressure is felt by their teachers, which has then impacted on their full engagement with the study.

Feedback brought to light some interesting perspectives, which could have impacted on the performances and therefore the opportunities for teacher development. It was noted that some teachers were not in the performance sessions but had to teach the follow up sessions, which was noted by the teachers as *"quite tricky"*. This was also noted by the evaluators, who observed some inconsistencies with the performance of 'Rumpelstiltskin'. It was not clear at the beginning of the session whether the teacher or teaching assistant was in the class at the time. Much time was spent supporting an individual child rather than the whole class, hence the confusion. This confusion was exacerbated when about ten minutes before the end of the performance, another adult entered the hall and the other left. The adult who had just joined the session sat working on her laptop until the end of the performance. Although this was surprising, it presented some interesting questions for the evaluators around communication and prioritisation:

- Was the aim of the SoR project and its model clearly communicated to schools?
- What was prioritised which meant that the usual teacher was not present for the majority of the session?

In terms of the teacher entering towards the end of the performance and spending time on her laptop, this could link to the ongoing concern over teacher workloads. This could also be a reason why the teacher at the start of the second performance, whilst in the classroom, was marking books rather than observing how her class engaged. The issue of teacher workload is becoming increasingly relevant with increased media coverage related to teacher strikes and the recruitment crisis. This also aligns with the efforts of the UK government in tackling teacher workload and with their resources for addressing this ongoing challenge. Allen et al (2021:658) note that workload has become *"a topic of intense policy interest because research with in-service and former teachers has concluded that workload, in particular the overly-bureaucratic requirements for planning, marking and data entry, are driving teachers out of the profession."* This is echoed in a study by Brady and Wilson (2022:208) who consider from the results of data collected on teacher workload that *"most consider workload to be a 'very serious or 'fairly serious' problem."* Additionally, a study by John Jerrim (UCL Social Research Institute), Sam Sims (UCL CEPEO) and Rebecca Allen (2020) found that one of the biggest causes of stress for teachers was administrative tasks.

It could, perhaps, be considered here that the involvement of teachers in the 'Schools of Recovery' project could have impacted further on workloads and stress. The Education Endowment Foundation (EEF) (2021:9) proposed that professional development opportunities should be carefully considered, and that those implementing professional development should *"Recognise the time constraints faced by teachers and adapt professional development accordingly. Those designing and selecting professional development should critically assess how a professional development programme will fit in with the school routine."*

Additionally, feedback indicated that some teachers did not know which performance they were watching until the day. This suggested poor communication to the class teachers. This can be an issue as it leaves teachers feeling unprepared and unable to engage in prior discussion with the children about the performance. Other teachers commented that they would have liked more information ahead of the performances. For example, knowing the story beforehand and/or crib sheets to support teaching and learning. This would have been beneficial in helping the teachers feel prepared, and this would perhaps have impacted on professional development as well as their engagement in the project (see also pages 96 and 148).

However, it would be reasonable to note here that teachers did have the opportunity to attend a 'pre-session' as part of the project model. Unfortunately, this was not fully attended and despite the recording being available, there is no clear way of knowing to what extent this was accessed afterwards. Also, with some settings changing teachers for different aspects of the project, this could suggest that this could have contributed to teachers feeling unprepared. This suggests that teachers needed to have experienced the whole project model to be best positioned for successful engagement and for full project potential to be realised.

The subject of pedagogical approaches was also discussed as part of these feedback meetings. The project model itself is built upon Big Brums 'Nine Principles of Working' relating to pedagogical approaches when working with children and young people (see page 9). The pedagogical approach taken by Big Brum in the 'Schools of Recovery' model aligns with other work by Big Brum and is acknowledged through the 'Human Spaces' report (Bolton, 2018), an evaluative study that discusses successful factors in Big Brum's approach including: *"co-creation, imagination as a teaching tool, being present and fiction to reduce vulnerability."* These elements resonate with the 'Schools of Recovery' model, having been evident within observations and within teacher feedback.

There were some positive comments, with some teachers feeling that 'chunking' the drama into smaller sections worked really well and made the performance accessible to children. There was also some agreement that 'prompting' questions supported engagement and really helped with *"getting children into the scene"*. Interestingly, teachers noted that across the performances there was notable engagement from the children and that there was very little need to manage behaviour during the sessions. Although this point is not necessarily explicitly related to teacher development, it is still worth considering in more depth. It shows us the benefit of live drama, particularly in the fallout from Covid. This is a point made by Arts Council England (2022:2) who note that *"throughout lockdown, pupils faced huge upheavals in their day to day lives. But we also saw the positive power of creativity in supporting their learning, mental health and resilience."*

It was interesting to consider the observations of teachers as this demonstrates their ability to reflect and consider their own perspectives on children's engagement and interaction with a live theatre performance. Particularly interesting was the observation that children liked to pretend to be a character and to answer questions through the lens of different characters when talking about the project. Rather than saying *"I think the girl was sad ..."* they preferred stepping into the girl's shoes saying, *"I'm sad ..."*.

Additionally, the nature of the performances was related by some to the Philosophy for Children (P4C) initiative[9] in that teachers felt the project highlighted how to ask open ended questions and that you do not always need to expect a specific answer, that sometimes posing a question and just considering this is enough to provoke higher level thinking skills.

---

[9] For more on Philosophy for Children, see: https://p4c.com/about-p4c/

Questionnaires

Questionnaires were rolled out to all schools, that could be filled in anonymously. They consisted of 5 questions which teachers could complete online in their own time. A summary of the feedback can be found below (Fig 1).

Fig 1: Summarised feedback from questionnaires (n = 7)

57% attended the pre session or watched the recording
71% highlighted that children were engaged/enjoyed the performance
43% gave examples of how they had adapted their practice following the project **57%** said that there were no adaptions to practice made
86% gave examples of skills the project helped them to develop **14%** said that the project did not support the development of any skills
71% of teacher respondents said they had not been able to use any techniques that they observed in the project in lessons **29%** said that they had

To summarise, 86% of the teacher participant responses gave examples of skills the project helped them to develop, which included:

• **Acknowledging feelings and emotions**

• **Prompting student voice**

• **Questions for empathy**

• **Student engagement**

• **Visual writing**

However, 14% said that the project did not support the development of any skills.

71% of teacher responses said they were able to identify that the children enjoyed the performance and were engaged. Nonetheless, 71% of respondents also said they had not used or implemented the techniques they observed in lessons (even though the majority had said that the project had helped them develop the skills outlined above).

Firstly, we wanted to establish how many teachers involved had either attended the pre-session recording in person or caught up by watching the recording prior to the TIE performances. Unfortunately, only 57.1% of teachers attended or watched and this, therefore, could have impacted on their understanding of the purpose of the school's engagement with the Big Brum project and the expectations (Fig. 2). Had they engaged beforehand, they would have been aware of their crucial role in making the project model workable. This could have impacted on their involvement during the performance as well as in the feedback meetings. It leads us as evaluators to question whether teachers were asked if they wanted to participate in the project and had an option to participate or not. This could have impacted motivation, engagement and the overall value teachers gave to the project.

Fig 2: Teacher attendance at pre-sessions.

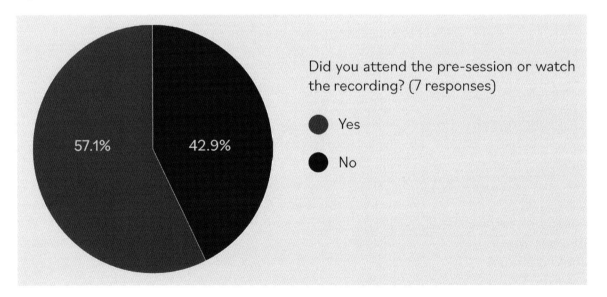

It should be questioned why 42.9% of respondents did not attend. Could this have been because of the school not prioritising the project? As suggested earlier, it might also be considered that time constraints and work pressures could have influenced the non-attendance. Research by Brady and Wilson (2021, p.48) suggests that *"teachers in England have been found to work more hours each week compared to most other jurisdictions."* This suggests that when analysing our data, we should be reflecting on how workload stress and pressure might impact on engagement with the study.

Next, we wanted to establish what, if anything, the teachers got from observing the children take part in the Big Brum programmes. The strongest element coming through here was the children's engagement, noted by the teachers, with 71% of responses highlighting that children were engaged/enjoyed the performance. Comments on the questionnaires included:

> *"The children were so engaged and shared their ideas clearly during and after the production."*

> *"Most children were very engaged and loved the live theatre element."*

> *"The children engaged well with the performance and participated well in the group discussions, even though the themes of the play were a little hard for all of the children to understand. They did enjoy it, but I would say only the most able children really understood the underlying themes."*

This links to the researchers' own session observations. It was noted that children engaged well, which was evident in the workshop observed by the researchers. It was particularly pleasing to note that one teacher noted the way the child's voice was considered as part of the performance. They state that *"Children's voice was key. All lines of enquiry considered and POV [Points of View] valued."* This is supported by (UNCRC, 1989) on the value of listening to the voice of the child and enabling their formal Children's Rights, especially Article 13: *"the child shall have the right to freedom of expression."*

Question 3 asked teachers to consider whether they had adapted their practice in any way and, if so, how. Unfortunately, there were only 3 positive responses to this, with others stating *"no"* or *"not really"*, making it difficult to draw any useful conclusions based on teacher responses. However, some conclusions can be drawn from the lack of response itself. The reduction in engagement for this particular question could suggest some discomfort with the question and a feeling of inability to answer it. This would be a reasonable assumption as there was no time limit given to the questionnaire or individual questions and this question appears part way through the questionnaire. It could be queried as to whether teachers knew that an element of the project would focus on teacher development. This again goes back to the need for teachers to experience the whole project model. Also querying if they knew how to adapt their practice to use drama as a pedagogical approach.

Would the project model have benefitted from a more interactive workshop with teachers to support the element of teacher development? Although responses suggested that there was not an impact on teaching practice, others were more positive, with 43% giving examples of how they had adapted their practice following the project. One teacher stated *"In class we linked our learning to what the children had watched. The children were able to connect similar character traits from their class text, Oliver Twist, and 'Rumpelstiltskin'."* Two other teacher responses were concerned with the benefits of using visuals as part of their teaching, including *"I talk a lot about drawing a picture in your mind when choosing vocabulary"*. This idea is supported by Arts Council England (2022:5) who suggest that high quality Drama education should be *"embedded in the curriculum, both in the delivery of English and as a subject in its own right."*

Question 4 asked teachers to reflect on any skills they may have learned through the project. Although two respondents did not feel their skills had progressed as a result of their involvement, one of these stated *"Not really. although I did like the idea of watching the drama and stopping at various points to draw the children in"*. This suggests that although they might not have seen a direct impact on their own skills, they were able to acknowledge good practice. This is interesting and perhaps highlights the valuable position Big Brum possesses in the way they are able to operate. Unlike the teachers, Big Brum does not face the restrictions of frameworks and day-to-day demands of school life, allowing for a unique approach. As well as teachers perhaps not having the flexibility or time to use Drama as a pedagogical approach to the extent that Big Brum can, there may also be barriers in terms of staff expertise, vision and creativity. It seems this has been appreciated by the teachers, despite perhaps not being able to implement this as an approach themselves. Future considerations could be given to the project model on how Big Brum can develop a model that supports teacher development which takes into consideration the full demands on a class teacher.

Two responses were linked to emotions:

> *"As a school we were embarking on a journey of acknowledging feelings and emotions and this helped reinforce this."*

> *"Questioning for empathy."*

These points are supported by Smith (2014, p.60) who describes the benefits of Drama experiences as being linked to not just an effective teaching and learning strategy but also a way to *"engage children emotionally."*

Furthermore, a teacher commented *"We've included more Drama during our lessons, which has been useful to 'hook' the children before we begin a topic"*. This could be useful when considering the way Drama can be used from the perspective of inclusion. For instance, Arts Council England (2022:3) reflect on how the Ofsted inspection framework *"places strong emphasis on the need for pupils to develop the cultural capital required to succeed in life"*. When we consider that not all children will have opportunities to be exposed to live Drama and theatre outside of school, it becomes apparent that engagement in the project model has potential to impact on cultural capital.

Another teacher suggested that a skill they had learned was *"promoting student voice"*, which links to Question 2 (when we asked teachers to reflect on what they gained from observing). This also links to previous research on Big Brum's pedagogical approach as evidenced in the 'Human Spaces' report (Bolton, 2019 : see also pages 56 and 78 of this report).

The final question asked whether teachers had been able to use any techniques observed during the project in other lessons/situations? 71% said they have not been able to use any techniques that they observed in the project in lessons. Four teachers answered *"no"* or *"not yet."* However, there were two interesting responses here. One stated *"not as yet, but hope to. Relate issues in literature to more relevant / immediate context for the children to build empathy and understanding of each other."* This draws attention to the project model's potential to develop other aspects of the child such as emotional literacy (see page 76).

Another respondent added that, *"I have used this technique when teaching road safety - watching a video, pausing and asking children to re-enact a situation and then explore what was happening and use the experience to summarise and make generalisations"*. This technique was observed by the researchers during the performance of 'Rumpelstiltskin'. The actor-teachers delivered part of the performance, which was scripted, and then paused at points to encourage the children to react and join in. This notion of slowing-time in a fictional context was observed to be beneficial in enabling children to process their thoughts and feelings prior to communicating these verbally (see page 113).

As only seven teachers responded to the questionnaire, broad conclusions cannot be drawn. In retrospect, it would have been useful for the teachers using the questionnaire to have noted which performance they watched. This would have allowed for a deeper understanding of which programme had the greatest impact on the experiences of teachers and to draw conclusions as to why this might have been the case. Nevertheless, this evaluation has revealed that it is clear that at least some teachers have been able to describe approaches they have subsequently taken as a consequence of the project model. However, due to limited data, it is unclear how the project model has impacted teacher development in its entirety.

Potential Recommendations for the Project

There are several aspects to consider in terms of recommendations in order for the project model, in future, to be given the best opportunity to reach its full potential regarding teacher development.

Firstly, there needs to be a consistent 'buy in', a firm value and priority given to the project; not just from schools, but from the individual teachers involved. As part of this 'buy in', teachers could be involved in evaluating their own development as learners. It appears that potentially schools agreed to take part in the project, but individual teachers may not have been given the choice to participate. This involvement, voluntary or not, might not have been clearly communicated and/or the rationale for the project may not have been made clear. One recommendation could be to give individual teachers a choice to take part in the project, therefore giving a personal investment and commitment, which should enhance participation. However, it needs to be considered that this may prevent the project model being realised if there is an over-reliance on individual class teacher commitment. An alternative to support this further is that Big Brum could supply school leads with the tools needed to ensure clear expectation of the model is communicated with all staff regarding necessary involvement and a rationale for the project.

Secondly, it is clear that teachers prioritised other duties such as marking, planning etc. during this time. There is a need for teachers to be relieved of the pressures of other duties to be able to be fully immersed within the project and achieve its full potential in terms of CPD. However, teacher workload is a much larger issue that needs to be addressed across the sector. Yet, one suggestion would be to conduct sessions off site. This would remove teachers from the environment of their roles and from being preoccupied with the day-to-day tasks. It would give teachers the space and time to dedicate their full attention to the sessions, allowing for them to be able to take more from the project. There are of course logistical considerations with this approach, such as transport to location, payment of location, appropriate space, which may impact schools being able to engage with such a project, however, from a teacher development perspective this would be a more conducive strategy.

As well providing teachers with appropriate space from other tasks, a neutral location would also support the creation of an effective environment for children and actor-teachers. It is clear from the data collected that the characteristics of the environment had an impact on the delivery of sessions, the engagement of teachers and children and therefore also the potential development of teachers and children. A protected space away from the school would allow Big Brum to control the characteristics of the environment in its entirety. This would protect the sessions from distractions and the continuation of the running of normal school activities that could be detrimental to the impact of such a project (for example, school halls being set up for lunch). School environments are often multi-purpose and therefore the use of a selected environment, solely for the use of the project, could have been beneficial to all participants through providing characteristics that support full engagement and participation from all.

Finally, our data shows that despite teachers identifying positives in the pedagogical approach through the dramatic experience, there was a lack of teachers feeling that it had impacted their personal practice or teachers that were able to implement strategies into lessons. One recommendation here is to clearly set out the expectations for teachers initially. Many teachers felt they did not have enough information prior to the sessions. If teachers were given clear expectations of the project with a specific brief to reflect on the impact of their development and alteration to their practice, perhaps this would have given them a focus point before, during and after the sessions. With an aim to develop strategies to embed drama as a pedagogical approach and stimulus into their teaching practice, teachers may have been more proactive in implementing techniques and more able to reflect on the impact of these through the lens of personal development. However, further clarity would have been beneficial into whose responsibility this was. It could be argued that teachers, at some points, were not fully prepared for what was expected during the project. Although project leads were in each school who may have supported and encouraged teachers to engage and reflect throughout, there remains a question of how the project leads could have been best supported. With clear expectations provided, a more active role for teachers could have been planned into the project model, offering a more immersive professional development experience. Active participation from teachers could have driven a need for commitment, dedication and engagement.

In addition to the recommendations for this particular project, a need for a specific teacher development programme has emerged. Big Brum could consider the development of a teacher training programme to support teachers in developing and practising specific skills, creativity and expertise to implement Drama as a pedagogical approach whist managing restrictions to teacher workload.

Methodology

The purpose of this section is to set out the design of the study and justification of the data collection tools used. Additionally, ethical considerations will be discussed.

It was initially decided to utilise a competency wheel to collect data for this study. The aim was to collate teacher's perceptions of their strengths prior to the performances by Big Brum in order to use this as a baseline of teacher's skills. Following the performances, the teachers would then reflect on their development and make adjustments to the competency wheel accordingly. However, engagement with the competency wheel was poor and none of them were returned completed. Instead, a questionnaire was chosen as an alternative form of data collection. It was felt that the questionnaire, unlike the competency wheels, would not require staff to complete, safe keep, revisit and return the document. This was done in hopes of maximising participation.

The questionnaire was created and shared online using Google Forms. It was hoped that this would be a more popular means of teachers sharing their experiences on their professional development. Informed consent was sought from all participants by including a short explanation of the purpose of the questionnaire in order for them to choose whether to engage or not. This part of the process is important as Cohen et al (2017:123) assert that gaining informed consent from participants *"is a cornerstone of ethical behaviour, as it respects the right of individuals to exert control over their lives and to take decisions for themselves".* However, it should be remembered that issues of power could be in play here as Cohen et al (2017:136) remind us that *"the researcher is often seen to be, or is, in an asymmetric position of power with regard to the participants; the former may have more power than the latter, be this by status, position, knowledge, role or whatever."* This could have impacted on the data collection, including engagement with the questionnaire and responses in feedback meetings.

As the form was completed online, rather than in person, participants could remain anonymous, potentially encouraging further participation. An online questionnaire is also advantageous in that it does not require returning or revisiting. However, there was still a disappointing response rate which brings into question why this was not a priority given that schools had access to this live theatre workshop experience. Denscombe (2021:217) considers the success of questionnaire as a data collection method, noting that *"in terms of achieving a reasonable response rate [it] generally depends on getting potential respondents motivated to put in the time and effort to answer the questions."*

The link for the questionnaire was sent to Big Brum, who forwarded it to the schools taking part. This meant that the evaluators at University College Birmingham did not have to request access to teacher's emails, helping to ensure confidentiality and privacy.

Completion of the questionnaire was mentioned in face to face and online follow up meetings with teachers. Big Brum also encouraged teachers to complete it during email contact with them and this was followed up several times. However, participation was low with only seven responses received from approximately 80 teachers (less than 10%).

Additionally, it was decided to collect data through evaluators' observations of performances, feedback meetings with school staff and completed mind maps during feedback meetings. Attending feedback sessions generated data from the teachers as they reflected on their experiences of being a part of the programme and also considered the children's engagement.

Ethical considerations. The evaluators were reliant on Big Brum having considered the ethical impact of carrying out research in schools with teachers and children. Therefore, Rebecca Taylor and Emma Davis were only required to consider their own engagements with teachers and children, ensuring professionalism and adherence to school policy, such as signing in as visitors. Any data collected on teacher professional development has remained confidential throughout and has only been shared with Rebecca and Emma as representatives of UCB and with the rest of the evaluators involved in the project. Individual teachers or children have not been named in order to protect the confidentiality and anonymity of participants. All data has remained on password protected laptops and any meetings have been held privately where conversations could not be overheard.

Limitations and recommendations on the evaluation process. Although data was collected through a variety of mediums that provided several valuable reference points for the evaluators, there were challenges in collecting this data extensively. Due to evaluators' time and work commitments, as well as the sheer number of performances conducted across the period of time, there were a limited number of sessions evaluators were able to attend and therefore observations could not represent all sessions.

However, observation themes were consolidated by teacher feedback sessions. Yet, teacher feedback sessions were not taken up by all schools and therefore this limited the evaluation slightly. There were also some inconsistencies with teacher feedback sessions and schools could only commit to certain criteria. Some schools could commit to longer periods of time in face-to-face sessions whereas some schools could only commit to a short period of time conducted online. This meant that feedback sessions and data collection methods needed to be adapted to suit the model of each feedback session. This does lead to question the richness of data collected in the shorter sessions. Finally, the questionnaires, although providing value, added further detail to the feedback sessions, had a low uptake and therefore could not represent the entirety of teachers involved within the project.

It is difficult to draw clear conclusions and recommendations from this study due to many factors which may have impacted on the data collected and how this can be ethically and rigorously examined to ensure it is valid and credible. As our focus was on teacher development, it would have been valuable to ascertain a baseline of teacher's skills prior to participation in the study (e.g. using the proposed competency wheel). Additionally, factors including age, teaching experience, prior professional development opportunities, time qualified and gender could have influenced the experiences of teachers.

Overall, across the project and during evaluation, participation and engagement has been a challenge which has impacted on both the evaluation and the project as a whole.

References

Adler, J. and Reed, Y. (2002) *Challenges of Teacher Development*. Hatfield: Van Schaik Publishers.

Arts Council England. (2022) *Drama: a guide for governing boards - providing high quality drama education in schools.*

Allen, R., Benhenda, A., Jerrim, J. & Sims, S. (2021) 'New evidence on teachers' working hours in England. An empirical analysis of four datasets', *Research Papers in Education*, 36:6, 657-681, DOI: 10.1080/02671522.2020.1736616

Bassot, B. (2016) *The reflective practice guide: an interdisciplinary approach to critical reflection*. London: Routledge.

Bolton, C.(2018) *Human Spaces - An evaluative Case study. Creating spaces for young people to explore what it means to be human*. Birmingham City University Report.

Brady, J. and Wilson, E. (2022) 'Comparing sources of stress for state and private school teachers in England', *Improving schools,* 25(2), pp. 205-220.

Cremin, T. and Burnett, C. (2018) *Learning to teach in the primary school*. Fourth edition. London: Routledge.

DfE. (2019) *Teacher workload survey 2019*. Available at: https://files.eric.ed.gov/fulltext/ED601913.pdf (Accessed: February 13th 2024)

Education Endowment Foundation. (2021) *Effective Professional Development.* Available at: https://d2tic4wvo1iusb.cloudfront.net/production/eef-guidance-reports/effective-professional-development/EEF-Effective-Professional-Development-Guidance-Report.pdf?v=1709823080 (Accessed: February 15th 2024)

Ewens, T. and Cammack, P. A. (2019) *Reflective primary teaching: meeting the teachers' standards throughout your professional career*, 2nd edition. St. Albans: Critical Publishing.

Hendricks, S. (2021) *Classroom Observation as a tool for professional development*. Available at: https://www.linkedin.com/pulse/classroom-observation-tool-professional-development-stuart-hendricks (Accessed 8th March 2014)

Jerrim, J., Sims, S. and Allen, R. (2020) *"The Mental Health and Wellbeing of Teachers in England."* Nuffield Foundation.

Kenyon, G. (2019) *The arts in primary education: breathing life, colour and culture into the curriculum*. London: Bloomsbury Education.

Kramer, M. (2018) 'Promoting teachers' agency: reflective practice as transformative disposition', *Reflective practice*, 19(2), pp. 211–224.

Moss, P. and Roberts-Holmes, G. (2022). 'Now is the time! Confronting neo-liberalism in early childhood'. *Contemporary Issues in Early Childhood,* 23(1), 96–99.

Nisbet, P. (2007) *Self-awareness, Self-reflection and Self-regulation: An Integrated Model of Managerial Self-Development.* Available at: https://www.anzam.org/wp-content/uploads/pdf-manager/1947_NESBITPAUL_144.PDF (Accessed 1st March 2024)

Ofsted. (2023) *Independent review of teachers' professional development in schools: phase 1 findings.* Available at: https://www.gov.uk/government/publications/teachers-professional-development-in-schools-phase-1-findings/independent-review-of-teachers-professional-development-in-schools-phase-1-findings#:~:text=Consequently%2C%20teachers%20and%20leaders%20want,but%20other%20school%20responsibilities%20intervened (Accessed: February 6th 2024)

Patall, E. A., Sylvester, B. J., & Han, C. W. (2014). 'The role of competence in the effects of choice on motivation.' *Journal of Experimental Social Psychology*, 50, pp. 27-44.

Roberts–Holmes, G. (2020) 'Transforming Early Childhood in England Towards a Democratic Education', in: Cameron, C. and Moss, P. (eds.) *Transforming Early Childhood in England: Towards a Democratic Education*. London: UCL Press.

Sellen, P. (2016) *Teacher workload and professional development in England's secondary schools: insights from TALIS,* Education Policy Institute. Available at: https://www.teachertoolkit.co.uk/wp-content/uploads/2016/10/TeacherWorkload_EPI.pdf (Accessed: 8th February 2024)

Somantri, C., Iskandar, H. (2020) *The Impact of CPD in Teaching, and the Role of Principal in Promoting CPD: A Literature Review.*

Suphasri, P. (2021) *Reflective Practice in Teacher Education: Issues, Challenges, and Considerations, PASAA,* 62, pp.236-264.

Skerritt, C. (2023) 'School autonomy and the surveillance of teachers'. *International Journal of Leadership in Education*, 26(4), pp.553-580.

Smith, P. and Dawes, L. (2014) *Subject teaching in primary education*. Los Angeles: SAGE.

Appendix 1 – School Feedback Meeting Notes

School A (25/10/2023): A feedback session took place in a classroom at a school in Burton on Trent over the period of 1 ½ hours. Feedback has been arranged into appropriate categories.

Feedback on the performances:

- Teachers in the room agreed that the start of 'Rumpelstiltskin' was quite emotional with the 'ripping' of the paper doll at the start.

- Year 4 staff feedback that the year 4 children found 'Minotaur' quite scary and felt this would be better suited to a year 6 cohort.

- Teachers agreed that 'the hook' in 'Minotaur' was really good and captured children's attention brilliantly.

Feedback on the organisation:

- Some teachers were not in the performance sessions but had to teach the follow up sessions which was *"quite tricky"*.

- Some teachers said that they didn't know which performance they were watching until the day and that this suggested poor communication.

- Teachers would have liked more information ahead of the performances, e.g. story beforehand, crib sheets etc.

Feedback on pedagogical approaches:

Teachers felt that 'chunking' the drama into smaller sections worked really well and made the performance accessible to children. Year 4 teachers would have liked to have watched the whole play first and then rewatched with the small sections and interactions with the children.

- Agreement that 'prompting' questions supported engagement and really helped with 'getting children into the scene'.

- Teacher agreed across the performances that there was notable engagement from the children and that there was very little need to manage behaviour during the sessions.

- It was noticed that children liked to participate in the performance and enjoyed interacting with the characters during the drama.

- Teachers noticed that children liked to pretend to be a character and to answer questions through the lens of different characters when talking about the project. Rather than saying *"I think the girl was sad..."* they preferred stepping into the girl's shoes saying, *"I'm sad..."*

- Teachers felt the project highlighted how to ask open ended questions and that you don't always need to expect an answer. Felt like it reflected the previous P4C (Philosophy for Children) initiative. One member of staff said that they have *"tried to use that in PSHE."*

- Staff felt the sessions demonstrated how wider connections can be made in planned activities where there are elements beyond the here and now that can be incorporated.

Following the initial discussion, staff were asked to complete several 'mind maps' to focus responses.

School B (15/11/2023): A feedback session took place in meeting space at a school in Birmingham over the period of 45 minutes. This feedback session took place in the form of a whole group discussion. Feedback has been arranged into appropriate categories.

Feedback on performance:
- Staff felt that students were engaged from the beginning.

Feedback on organisation:
- For 'Rumpelstiltskin', staff said that different groups had different experiences and different delivery approaches.

Feedback on pedagogical approaches:
- Staff said that they *"wouldn't say teaching has changed as a result."*

- However, they also said the project made them more aware of children's participation in the classroom.

- Teachers felt they were able to use *"stepping into drama"* in sessions more readily.

- Sessions brought to light what is needed to be thought about, particularly around giving children more opportunities.

- Could see the benefit of stepping away from just *"delivering information."*

- The school uses the approach 'Talk for Writing' and staff agreed that this lends itself to the use of Drama really well and that they need to make more use of that.

- Staff agreed that the project reminded them of something they are not doing enough of.

147

Informal mentoring

Rebecca Patterson and Alison Ramsay

Executive Summary

This section draws on literature about mentoring to review actual and potential mentoring practices in the project, 'Creating "Schools of Recovery" (SoR) and to propose an informal, generative approach to ongoing and future mentoring in relation to Big Brum's work with schools. Discussion is organised around the following themes:

- modelling provided and desired;
- curriculum connections;
- acknowledging teacher hesitancy/uncertainty;
- towards a model of informal mentoring.

The report offers indicative pointers towards such a model and offers several recommendations about what this informal mentoring process might look like.

*"Informal mentoring as an attending to teachers' personal experience and engagement with the **how** and the **why** of the drama, can thus become supportive of a teacher social imaginary bringing disruptive drama pedagogies, and pedagogies that make use of drama as a stimulus, productively into view alongside established classroom practices."*

Literature review

A literature review is, in essence, a critical evaluation of the material that is already in existence, here in the form of a brief synopsis or the key areas relevant to the SoR project. It will look at content relating to existing research, theories, and evidence in the field of mentoring in and between schools. It will also provide a critical evaluation and discussion of this content.

The purpose of including a literature review in this section of the report is to build an argument for the mentoring process as part of the bigger project aims and outcomes. The inclusion of relevant reading, and a critical analysis of the material will help us to refine our thoughts on the mentoring process, especially with regards to the inter-school discussions, and the school-to-school mentoring relationships that it is hoped will become established as a result of the project so that formative working practices will be developed both with the input from Big Brum, and also independently from them.

By establishing a familiarity with and understanding of current thoughts and research around the purpose and actions of mentoring we hope to have a better understanding of what research has already discovered and be better able to identify what might be useful to explore within the remit of this area of the report. Mentoring, by and from Big Brum themselves, is very much part of the project's aims and intended outcomes. However, there is a separate strand of evaluation that focuses on Teacher Development (see page 122) and therefore we will try not to overlap too much in this area.

It is evident that education professionals are increasingly being expected to look to research to support decision making in the classroom, and in making informed decisions about how to make the most of their time, resources, and expertise. However, there is an increasing amount of educational research evidence available, as well as materials and products that make claims said to be 'based on research'. It can be difficult and time-consuming to make judgements about the reliability and usefulness of the material that is available. It is therefore important to critically consider what research evidence is useful and how it might then be integrated with professional expertise and insights in order to enhance practice and experience. Knowing where to look is often difficult and time consuming, and therefore schools are often reliant on, and accepting of, whatever the trend or zeitgeist in educational policy has to offer.

In contrast, however, Harper-Hill et al (2022) suggest that individual teachers are more likely to consider professional input or training as a possible enhancement to their practice when it is instigated by the teacher as a learner. In other words, teachers who have a strong sense of agency are more likely to initiate personal transformations. This may be an important consideration in the context of the potential mentoring process that we hope will be a legacy of this project. Mentoring is described by Denmark and Posden as a sustained relationship between novice and an expert (2013:10). However, in the context of this project, it is perhaps better framed as a relationship between the mentor and mentee designed to build confidence in an unfamiliar area of expertise. In other words, how Big Brum operate and the intentions around the mentoring programme in this project, are two-fold.

The first is the mentoring process that Big Brum have provided the schools and teachers in the form of ongoing teacher development or CPD (e.g. through teacher sessions around 'The Giant's Embrace'). The mentoring that we are looking at here is separate from this and focuses more on the building of networks of mentoring between teachers within the schools Big Brum have been working with, and between schools both in localised areas, and more generally in terms of all schools that have worked with Big Brum during the 'Creating "Schools of Recovery"' project. Already, this suggests a greater sense of agency for the participating teachers, and the initiatives taking place in partnership schools in East Staffordshire and North Solihull may well provide Big Brum with further insights in this area.

Remembering that the focus of the project is creating schools of recovery, it is interesting to note that Mullen, et al (2021), as guest editors, published a collection of papers in which they aimed to reimagine mentoring and coaching, educational interactions, processes, and models considering dramatic changes and human needs in what they describe as *"disrupted world contexts in education."* The work is very much a reaction to the consequential changes brought about by the Covid-19 pandemic, and they discuss testing the capacity development, effectiveness, adaptability, or resilience of people within dramatically changing educational settings. This is relevant in that it is, to some extent, the place where this project emerged from. Mullen, et al (ibid) concluded that the most fruitful mentoring is that which has notably supported teachers' well-being, which is also very much at the heart of the SoR project and worthy of note in terms of the ways in which the mentoring process might develop in the future.

Big Brum's intentions in terms of the support they offer teachers is about exploring teachers' perceptions of alternative methods of engagement through Theatre in Education as a way to transcend traditional schooling and inform education (Adams, 2013 in Jackson and Vine, 2013) and to create spaces for young people to explore what it means to be human (Bolton, 2018). With this in mind, it is worth considering what is understood by the term 'mentoring' in more depth.

Denmark and Podsen (2016) write about mentoring with student teachers and early career teachers, now referred to in England as ECT.[10] They suggest that teachers tend to work in isolation in the privacy of a single classroom environment, and in these spaces a sense of self-governance emerges. However, they also note that the culture of teaching does not tend to encourage distinctions (ibid:10). In the present climate in England

---

[10] Early Career Framework ECF requires any school inducting new teachers to offer a two-year package of high-quality professional development – an increase on the previous one-year induction period, 2019

there appears to be an even greater deterrent towards teacher individuality as the Initial Teacher Training Core Content Framework (ITT CCF 2016) supports trainees to succeed in the classroom whilst eventually being assessed against the Teachers' Standards. Mentoring and support from 'expert colleagues' now forms a key-element of this multi-year entitlement but within a very prescriptive framework, and from September 2024 the mentoring process will intensify even further with the introduction of the Intensive Training and Practice (ITAP).[11] This leaves little room for schools to offer alternative mentoring opportunities outside of the CCF recommendations.

This could result in the 'mentoring' work that we are advocating between teachers and between schools around the SoR project, being either confused with the governmental directives on mentoring or lost under the burden of expectations elsewhere. Conversely, however, Daichendt et al (2014) look at the history of mentoring specifically in the field of visual art and allude to the classical era of Medieval Guilds, and the role of the Master Artists in the process of instruction for students and to the artisan environments, which favoured small hubs of creativity where skills and traits were honed through a mentorship-like atmosphere (Daichendt, 2010).

The mentoring that is envisaged in the SoR project is more akin to the latter model as it is intended to encourage participating teachers to engage with Big Brum's wider artistic policies, and in doing so, to find their own way of using the experiences and the materials that often accompany the TIE programmes in a nonprescriptive manner. In this, we are aware that the nature of what is prescribed by current English teacher education policy directives may itself be transient given the impending UK General Election. This approach to the mentoring process does not require individual teachers to change their practice but rather it offers assistance in charting a course whereby participating teachers can develop their own ways of responding to and making use of drama. This type of mentoring is about nurturing and encouraging professional pedagogical growth, which may or may not involve a process of observation and feedback, but it is certainly not a stipulation.

Drama as an art form is often conceptual, and although there are a variety of techniques, such as those modelled in the performances and the classroom interactions between the actor-teachers and pupils that can be taught, the point of the mentoring in this context is also about teachers helping each other to understand and value the experiences that they observe their pupils having and to perhaps make use of some of the approaches they have experienced in their own classrooms. In other words, there is a confidence to the self-

---

[11] https://www.gov.uk/government/publications/intensive-training-and-practice/intensive-training-and-practice-itap

governance that offers a wider notion of a model for learning. As a closing remark, perhaps we should reframe the term mentoring in this context and call it 'informal mentoring' in order to make a clear distinction.

Analysis and findings

As part of our role as evaluators of the proposed mentoring process between participating teachers and between the different participating schools, we are reflecting on some of the ideas that have been generated by the project to date. We recognise that the original plan to create and structure a more formal mentoring process between teachers and between schools may not have been possible due to various constraints. We have therefore landed upon the idea of an informal, generative mentoring process that exists in the in-between spaces, and which is fuelled by ongoing communications between all parties and participants. The informal mentoring process, it is hoped, will echo the findings of Harper-Hill et al (2022) and be largely initiated by the teachers themselves and driven by their own requirements.

The essence of the SoR project is to give every teacher and child an experience that responds to the contemporary moment/pressures, thus enabling a reengagement with each other as human beings via the medium of Drama. At the time of writing, we remain in a period of 'recovery' from one crisis, but we are also in the midst of other continuing and intense crises. It is Big Brum's contention that in educational theatre and drama it is possible to tackle any subject matter with young people following Heathcote's notion of the 'crucible paradigm' (in Bolton, 1998). In other words, the carefully chosen content of all of the plays within this project are designed to allow the pupils to 'stumble' upon knowledge as they engage with the material, and perhaps more importantly, consciously recognise that which directly and individually affects their lives. Echoing this is the Durham Commission on Creativity and Education report which argues that...

> "our current, knowledge-based system only goes part of the way towards equipping young people with the skills that will give them the confidence and resilience to shape their own path through life. They need to make the most of our human capacity for imagination and critical judgment, especially with our ever-greater dependency on technology and artificial intelligence. They need to exercise creativity"
> (Durham Commission, 2019: 5).

The role of Theatre in Education then, as suggested in the third of Big Brum's nine principles (page 9) is about 'breaking down the normal socio-economic factors that *prevent young people from accessing the arts, especially theatre and drama',* in order for the pupils to be able to access the material, at whatever level works for them. The company, and specifically the actor-teachers, can then consider the most appropriate form of intervention in the context of every performance. This kind of mediation follows Vygotsky's theory of *"the zone of proximal development"* (1978) by creating a forum for energetic engagement, which Vygotsky referred to as *"the wind that puts the clouds in motion"* (Vygotsky, 1987: 282).

As teacher educators ourselves, we are acutely aware of the day-to-day pressures placed upon classroom teachers as well as school leaders under the auspices of the neoliberal practices, which dominate the present educational landscape. The scope of this project is huge in terms of the potential for further reflection on the use of drama as a pedagogical practice in primary education, but that is beyond the remit of this section of the evaluation (see however page 28). We will therefore focus on the responses we have collated from the participating teachers by analysing a small amount of data shared by various members of the evaluation team and by Big Brum with the permission of the schools.

Our evaluation of the process of mentoring between teachers, and between schools has to some extent been thwarted by events beyond the control of all of us, including time and geography. However, we have engaged with a great deal of commentary from the online evaluation sessions between the Big Brum team and participating teachers as well as our observations and conversations in school when sharing in the performances and interactions with pupils and staff. The response has been overwhelmingly positive, and it has been a privilege to observe and to be a small part of the project.

The following analysis now draws upon data gathered during meetings with teachers at two schools participating in the SoR project, hereafter referred to as School A and School B. Audio recordings of these meetings are used to identify emerging themes around the notion of 'mentoring' framed in the preceding literature review. In respect of School B, there are three audio recordings referenced and these are identified as Recording 1, 2 and 3. Mind mapping outcomes from activities undertaken during the meeting in School B are also drawn upon to support the analysis.

In the literature review, we addressed how mentoring in the context of the SoR project might be conceptualised differently from understandings and ensuing approaches in teacher education and development at this time. This acknowledges that current mentoring practices in teaching are very much bound in England to teacher competency/ assessment frameworks, such as the Teacher Training Core Content Framework (2019) and the Early Career Teacher framework (2019). In these frameworks, the notion of an 'expert colleague' who is there to guide and to evaluate developing professional practices against existing criteria looms large.

In contrast, what informs this analysis is mentoring understood as an informal, generative activity with the aim of building teacher confidence in an unfamiliar area of expertise, in this case Drama education and pedagogy. We are also interested in the extent to which this notion of mentoring might be fostered between teachers in schools and across school networks. The discussion is organised around the following themes provoked by the data; modelling provided and desired; curriculum connections; acknowledging teacher hesitancy/uncertainty; towards a model of informal mentoring.

Modelling provided and desired

Bolton (2018:3) identifies the key principles associated with Big Brum's approach to creating democratic classrooms through drama pedagogy. Notably, attention is drawn to how Big Brum actor-teachers facilitate engagement through a process of inviting participation on children's own terms, and explicitly valuing contributions in a manner that elevates what children have to offer in response to the drama. Questioning is equally recognised as a defining feature of Big Brum's dramatic pedagogy, with questions used to clarify meaning, provoke curiosity, encourage thinking and discussion, and to challenge preconceived ideas.

Data taken from audio recordings and mind-mapping activities reveal how observing Big Brum actor-teachers' work was received by teachers. In school A, a number of teachers stated they already used drama approaches and did not feel that watching the performances would influence their practice in any particular way. However, one teacher did suggest it was useful to see ways of *"provoking children to think through questioning"*. A similar point was made by a teacher in school B, who observed *"... children's responses were often completely different to what you might have expected as a teacher... what you were gathering were very individualised responses"*. The teacher elaborates on this:

> *"... there was never any judgement, it was always well received ... what do we think about that ... It was almost P4C[12] in how wide the questions and responses were ... but that was really powerful."*

---

[12] Philosophy for Children (P4C) is a pedagogical approach widely used in primary schools, centred on community building through the fostering of children's critical and creative thinking – see https://p4c.com

Data here suggests that Big Brum's pedagogical approach did register with some teachers as offering a potentially different mode of working with children in the classroom. In the context of the informal model of mentoring we are exploring in this analysis, Big Brum actor-teacher modelling might be conceived as creating an opening into 'unfamiliar' pedagogical territory, namely drama-based practices. The teacher goes on to reference a colleague who did try to apply something of what had been observed in their own teaching of Personal, Social and Health Education (PSHE). Although there are no details relating to what the outcome of this experimentation was, we might emphasise the teacher's willingness have a go as a generative consequence of experiencing Big Brum actor-teachers at work. Actor-teacher modelling in this instance might be understood as a form of mentoring in its own right.[13] This has some resonance with Daichendt et al's (2014) understanding of mentoring as occurring through the sharing of knowledge and skills within a creative community or hub rather than an overly prescriptive endeavour.

School B audio recording 3, however, also drew attention to how teachers' concern for children's behaviour and engagement limited their capacity to be fully 'mindful' of the pedagogical choices and strategies underpinning the performance. In response, experiencing the performance prior to watching it with the children was identified as potentially helpful in enabling teachers to make the most of the development opportunities presented:

> *"It would be lovely if you could perform for just us … So that we are not responsible for the children at the same time … we can actually appreciate the drama and watch the skill … and the structure of how you are producing it."*

It was noted that even access to video recordings of the different pieces ahead of Big Brum coming into school, could help teachers to attune to the pedagogical principles shaping the performances, or serve as guidance as to what to teachers should look out for. We propose the desire for pre-performance input detailed here, is consistent with the model of informal mentoring outlined above.[14] Specifically, we wish to emphasise how facilitating teachers' exposure to Big Brum's method of working, separate to their role as classroom teacher, might nurture professional curiosity in support of developing and extending knowledge and understanding of drama pedagogy and its potential. This a process that might be bolstered by providing a rationale for the pedagogical decision making behind the artistry and entering into dialogue with teachers about this. In keeping with the project aims, informal mentoring here becomes a mechanism for creating a

---

[13] See recommendation i

[14] See recommendation ii

conversation about what a recovery curriculum might include and enable, in response to the many challenges faced by children and teachers in the contemporary moment.

Nicholson's (2009) appropriation of Ricoeur's social imaginary in respect of theatre in education is pertinent here. As Nicholson explains, for Ricoeur the imagination functions to both preserve the status quo and to disrupt it by imagining the world can be different. Change is made possible when these dual functions come together, so that *'the utopian imagination that looks forward to create the future is in dialogue with the ideological symbols of the past'* (2009:50). It is Theatre in Education's capacity to explicitly provoke questions about what exists in support of new possibilities, that Nicholson aligns with the social imaginary as theorised by Ricoeur. We suggest that informal mentoring as an attending to teachers' personal experience and engagement with the how and the why of the drama, can thus become supportive of a teacher social imaginary bringing disruptive drama pedagogies, and pedagogies that make use of drama as a stimulus, productively into view alongside established classroom practices. While potentially generative in respect of shaping teacher practices, it remains that existing educational structures and discourses do present real barriers to the taking up of drama pedagogies. Not least the recognised demands of the curriculum, to which we now turn.

Curriculum connections

Audio recordings and mind-maps capture teachers' comments on the extent to which learning opportunities emerging out of Big Brum's performances, might be linked to existing school curricula. In School A one teacher observes in respect of 'Rumpelstiltskin' that *"there was a lot of discussion afterwards with the children ... but no, we didn't really take anything further forward with that"*. The fact that the production took place at the end of term is suggested as one reason for this, but the teacher also makes the point that *"it didn't really lead into anything that we were doing ..."* Although there was no expectation from Big Brum that the work would be developed or continued, a similar observation is made by another teacher on 'Romeo and Juliet':

> *"It was just interesting showing the children some Shakespeare really and getting them to kinda view that and discuss the themes that we'd talked about. But there wasn't anything specific that we took forward to an actual ... unit of work."*

Conversely, 'Along the Silk Road' is identified by another teacher as creating generative links with PSHE, and specifically discussions of value stimulated by the scroll resource.

"We did refer back to the story … getting across the idea that something is of value, doesn't necessarily mean monetary value. And we had quite a nice session where children were talking about special things that they had … And also that general respect for elders … A lot of our children do live in multigenerational families, so they were able to refer to their Grandparents and say … the respect that the boy in the story showed his uncle … that did mean something to them."

In School B audio recording 1, a teacher also refers to 'Along the Silk Road' as generating similar links to school values and related themes of responsibility, power and influence, impact of actions beyond the here and now, and peer pressure. The teacher, however, prefaces this by making the point that knowing the content of performances in advance would have enabled even more developed learning links.

"If we had been able to contextualise that a little more … it might have been quite a nice thing to talk about with the children beforehand. A quick skeleton overview of what was going to be in the sessions would have been really useful I think for us."

A related point is made in the School A recording, where not having enough time to plan for links to the school curriculum is identified as a barrier to teachers making more use of performance content in class teaching. Whereas knowing more about the production in advance of the performance, would create opportunities to amalgamate themes with school curricula, or to plan for additional learning activities to take place.[15]

"Forward thinking it would be about … knowing when it is, what we are doing, so it's not kinda last minute. Obviously then you can look at the curriculum and look to see where obviously weaves in within something that we are doing … Or whether it needs to be standalone … and then that would be something then we would then try to be flexible with, I think."

Glazzard and Stones make the case for an approach to curriculum design that responds to statutory requirements, but which is also flexible in meeting the diverse needs of children and emerging 21st Century challenges (2021:117). The importance of meeting curriculum requirements is very evident in the teacher reflections detailed above. Equally, there is an openness to finding space to plan for the rich learning opportunities Big Brum programmes foster. While this would suggest even closer collaboration between schools and Big Brum as desirable, the time for teachers to work together in response

---

[15] See recommendation iii

to performances also materialises as important in teacher reflections. This is captured in School B recording 3, when one teacher describes what future collaborative work might look like:

> *"Communicating with other staff around the trust. Sharing ideas, sharing planning if that was what people … felt would be beneficial. Taking photographs of wagolls[16] … Building up photographs of best practice examples of work … whether it's oral … outcomes, or whether it's art … classroom questioning."*

We propose the peer collaboration envisaged above aligns with the model of informal mentoring we are exploring in respect of the SoR programme. To borrow from the parlance of teacher education policy documents, we might imagine teachers becoming 'expert colleagues' in the Big Brum method and mentoring as a process of sharing accumulated knowledge and experience with less experienced colleagues.[17] As indicated in the reference to *"communicating with other staff around the trust"*, this is a process that has the potential to be of value both within schools and across school networks.

In the same recording, however, teacher observations also draw attention to scheduling and continuity of staffing as barriers to teachers developing their Big Brum knowledge and expertise.

> *"The big learning point that links into that … now we all have more of an understanding of the project, the importance of the scheduling. So that we have the same teaching team doing the online session … it is just a case of scheduling it in in the right way to make sure that there is that follow up. The way it landed, that happened in the summer term and then the performance was in the autumn term, so we had a different team of teachers. And it was a wonderful experience, but you are not going to be able to do as much."*

Teacher to teacher mentoring and collaboration within schools and across schools remains an important ambition of the SoR project. Data discussed here indicates that teachers recognise the possible benefits of this to their own practice and to children's learning. Following Glazzard and Stones (ibid: 2), we might consider the facilitation of informal teacher mentoring in the context of Big Brum's work, as supportive of an ambitious approach to the curriculum. This is an approach that is encouraging of teachers working together to enrich children's learning beyond what is prescribed by existing

---

[16] An abbreviation for 'what a good one looks like' (wagoll) widely used to refer to exemplars of work.

[17] See recommendation iv

school curricula and the National Curriculum (2014) itself. Increased communication on performance content between teachers and Big Brum is identified within the data as one way in which teacher mentoring within and across schools might be developed. In addition, to ensure continuity of staffing, the scheduling of the work is also recognised as significant.[18] This will enable teachers to develop the knowledge and confidence to integrate learning into curriculum planning, and to share their learning with colleagues in support of future innovation.

Teacher hesitancy/uncertainty

"Of course we need to teach the arts in school, but not instead of something else. The arts may be fun, but we've got real work to do in the school day".

"The arts, like athletics, are great extracurricular activities, but they don't belong in the required curriculum".

"The arts should be taught to kids who have talent. For the rest of us, they're simply a waste of time".

"With all the time spent preparing our children for so many important tests, there are no hours or minutes left to squander on the arts".

(Hoffman Davis, 2008, p 1)

These are examples of comments made by teachers in US elementary schools and are being used here to highlight Biesta's (2009) commentary on the USA reauthorisation in 2001 of the Elementary and Secondary Education Act ("No Child Left Behind"). This Act resulted in federal research funding being reserved for projects that engaged with a particular methodology promulgating the idea that education should be an 'evidence-based profession'. The methodology relied on large-scale studies that utilised the randomised controlled field trial being the 'gold standard' with 'careful measurement' of the correlation between input and output in order to generate scientific knowledge about 'what works' (ibid). The ever-increasing culture of measurement in education has had a profound impact upon the performative mechanisms which control teacher education and their ongoing professional development. The benefit for the policy makers is that accountability has shifted towards the individual teacher taking responsibility for each of their pupil's progress. In return, the pupils' output (measurable progress) provides

---

[18] See recommendation v

evidence from an ever-narrowing field of that which is deemed measurable. The question is whether we are measuring what we value, or whether we are just measuring what we can easily measure and thus end up valuing what we (can) measure (ibid).

Could this be a rationale for teacher hesitancy and sense of uncertainty around the inclusion of projects such as this one in the academic year? It seems that time constraints are perceived as the biggest barrier for most teachers we interviewed, and when asked when the preferred time of year might be for them to host the project, their response was, *"in the summer term after SATs when we are kind of open to any suggestions of things to keep them occupied and nice things to do with them."* I think we can all sympathise with this viewpoint. The time constraints were a consistent theme during one evaluation meeting in which it was mentioned several times such as the following examples.

> Teacher A: *"Just to kind of save a bit of time would have been really useful, you know maybe differentiated slightly as well so we've got a choice, erm, for a range of abilities would be really helpful."*
>
> Interviewer: *"I mean time is one thing that keeps coming up again and again, this is a perennial problem isn't it?"*
>
> Teacher A: *"I think time is always going to be one of those that is the battle. Erm, then I think obviously because they're not, they don't necessarily link to what we're doing at school, or books, or texts, or the curriculum that we are following, so that's additional time. So I suppose that is the additional time, that's the biggest battle we've got."*

Clearly there are other issues that are mentioned in the extracts above as well, such as potential and direct links to existing curriculum themes and topics. However, in this process of informal mentoring that appears to be emerging we are trying not to make assumptions that the same issues we allude to about are the only reason for a potential hesitancy to embrace the any of the ideas, content or approaches that have been shared by Big Brum. Although we are fully cognisant that there is still a struggle for the arts to be included in primary education in the UK, there is no doubt that there is an evidence base for a correlation between Drama and active learning along with all the synonyms associated with the word to 'activate', such as stimulate, galvanise, motivate, and accelerate (Anderson, 2013, p xvii), and therefore, it seems possible that whichever hurdles appear to be in the way for the participating teachers[19] to clear, they are not insurmountable.

---

[19] See recommendation vi

We think this is about careful listening, not just to what is being said, as we have a hunch that the policy drivers mentioned above have begun to condition us and frame our language communication into 'education speak'. We are interested in how things are said, the hesitations between answers and the processing of thoughts. When we listen more carefully to what the teachers say and the intonation in the voices it seems to be saying something richer altogether, that of course is difficult to harness and impossible to define.

However, perhaps there is a gap between those two things which relates to the statement above about the culture of accountability. Is there a sense in which the teachers may be feeling that they should be doing something more concrete (and measurable) with the stuff that the project is bringing up for their pupils as well as for themselves? What we are finding interesting is this sense of hesitancy that seems to be in conflict with their instinct to do something different. This perhaps reveals the tension between discourses we are introducing here in terms of the generative potential of drama, and the pull towards the delivery of existing curriculum content. It feels like a fast train careering towards the next academic year when it will start all over again. So, a question might be, how do we get back on the slow train which allows teachers to stop off at the station called 'maybe this would be interesting to explore'?

Recommendations

Towards a model of informal mentoring

As we have already mentioned, Big Brum acknowledges the fact that due to various circumstances such as timing, staffing, and other unforeseen events, the teacher mentoring process that was very much part of the early vision for the schools of recovery project did not take place. Consequently, the data that we have drawn upon for this section of the evaluation process is sparse in terms of any direct mentoring experience received by the teachers themselves either from Big Brum, or perhaps more pertinently, from each other. Despite this omission, in the process of analysing the data we have been able to gather, alongside that of other members of the evaluation team, particularly those who have been focusing on teacher development, we have noticed a willingness on the part of the participating teachers to do 'something' by way of mentoring in the future. As we noted earlier, the hesitancy in knowing what that might be has in some instances resulted in a sort of teacher paralysis. We are therefore presenting our reflections as a more formative proposal for the future rather than a summative statement.

By adopting a dialectical approach to the evaluation process with regards to the mentoring we aim to highlight points for future exploration in the project's next phase, rather than offering a set of fixed recommendations. We hope that the ongoing discussions will foster growth and evolution in the partnership between teachers, schools and Big Brum. This will be useful to Big Brum in that it can provide them with information, and potentially advice as to what participating teachers' needs might be, both in the short term, which include the remainder of this academic year, and the future, by looking towards models and ideas about how these elements of the wider project might look, which will inevitably be informed by what has gone before.

What might an informal mentoring process look like?

Recommendations for an 'Informal Mentoring' process.
(The following recommendations correlate with the themes we have drawn from data. The numbering below is highlighted earlier in the text through the use of footnotes).

i.   Modelling: Big Brum might consider creating resources that demonstrate Big Brum Actor-teacher modelling such as short video clips.

ii. Teacher taster sessions/preview of shows. Using a specific focus on the pedagogical choices underpinning the style of presentation/artistic approach.

iii. Signpost the Big Brum Artistic Policy document directly to participating teachers as possible pedagogical guidance to help inform their planning in response to the performances.

iv. Big Brum might consider offering an additional bespoke workshops exploring themes from the Big Brum artistic policy, such as 'the world is knowable', 'trusting the child', and 'the crucible paradigm', to teachers who would like to gain a deeper understanding beyond the taster/preview events. We might envisage these teachers acting as 'expert colleagues' and disseminating their learning to school colleagues.

v.   In order to address the potential discontinuity in staffing, and subsequent gaps in knowledge and understanding of the project's aims and intentions with regards to the teachers' input, we recommend further facilitation of conversations. This might take the form of a Big Brum 'expert colleague' (see above) providing further insights and guidance within schools and across partnerships.

vi. Consider how Big Brum's concept of 'key/central question' might respond to teacher uncertainty. By sharing this in the context of a workshop or demonstration, teachers will be given insight into the far-reaching nature of big questions in the context of artistic exploration. Unlike formal mentoring, we are trying to steer teachers minds

162

away from so as not to fall into the trap of 'we must', the company can re-iterate the 'no expectation' rule that is so important to the teachers who are already feeling under intense pressure to get it right.

Methodology

This evaluation made use of thematic analysis (Braun and Clarke, 2022), as a tool for working with the data to identify themes pertinent to mentoring within the context of the 'SoR Recovery' project. Our roles as teacher educators meant we approached this task with an established understanding of mentoring as an aspect of professional development integral to initial teacher education practices (DfE, 2019). However, we also wanted to remain open to how the SoR project might create different perspectives on mentoring to those prescribed in teacher education policy documents: an endeavour inevitably shaped by our experiences of watching performances in school and observing Big Brum practitioners at work, alongside teacher and pupil responses. To this end, the analysis we undertook was a hybrid approach involving both deductive and inductive encounters with data (Xu and Zammit, 2020). In other words, it drew upon existing frameworks associated with mentoring, while remaining open to new conceptualisations that might develop out of the data.

As previously noted, the data set that forms the basis of this analysis might be considered small. However, this should not detract from the interesting insights it yields on teacher experiences of the project, and what we have come to conceptualise as informal, generative mentoring. The data set comprised of an audio recording of a Zoom meeting conducted with teachers from one school (School A). In addition, a series of recordings taken from an in-person meeting with teachers in another school (School B), were also analysed. Mind-maps produced as part of the School B teacher meeting were drawn upon in support of the analysis. In respect of School B, the following questions served as provocations for both mind mapping activities and subsequent teacher discussions:

Do you think the project has helped you to develop any skills? If so, what and how?

Have you any previous experience working through drama? What is your knowledge/ understanding of drama as a pedagogy?

Following the project, have you adapted your practice in any way?

What would be useful before, during or after the performance to help you make the most of learning?

Looking forward, is there any support that could be put in place to facilitate teachers supporting each other in making the most of the learning opportunities presented?

Were there any specific barriers that hindered you in making [the] most of the learning opportunities?

Following Braun and Clarke (2022), we began the process of analysing the data with a period of familiarisation. This involved listening closely to the recordings and scrutinising School B teacher responses detailed on the mind-maps. From this we collaboratively generated (ibid, p.9) the following codes to describe segments of data that we identified as having some resonance with mentoring as applicable to the project:

- Acknowledging the resources provided, including Big Brum practitioner modelling
- Time pressures and timing restrictions
- Links to the curriculum
- The need to know more in advance
- Teacher insecurity/uncertainty around expected learning outcomes
- Continuity of staffing

These codes were then used to create data clusters, or themes, that we recognised as having potentially interesting stories to tell of how mentoring might be understood within the 'SoR project. The generation of themes was productive of rich discussions on mentoring as a professional development activity, both in our field of Drama education and teacher education more generally. Thus, our process became not one of searching for already existent themes within the data, but rather an active process of theme development (Braun and Clarke, 2022, p. 35). Our discussions were a vital element in enabling us as researchers to reflexively interrogate assumptions and ideas about what was being yielded by the data (ibid, p.9) and how this was informing our shared understandings of how mentoring was being enacted within the project. Finally, we refined our themes to settle on the following key ideas as the basis for conceptualising mentoring in respect of Big Brum's work, and how this might develop in the future:

- Modelling provided and desired
- Curriculum connections
- Acknowledging teacher hesitancy/uncertainty
- Towards a model of informal mentoring.

Conclusion: In summary of findings

From the analysis of the data, we have gained an impression that many of the participating schools, and individual teachers have entered the SoR project with a belief on their part that some form of work/output would be expected. Whether there is also an assumption that outcomes would in some way connect to either the National Curriculum, the individual school curriculum, or a specific key stage is unclear but there appears to be a desire for resources that would in some way assist in this area. Although Big Brum have never stated such requirements, and maintain a clear artistic policy in this regard, the assumptions may still have been construed from the initial conversations and it is an understandable misunderstanding given teachers' continual professional development obligations.

Harper-Hill et al's (2022) study of teacher attitudes towards professional training mechanisms suggests that there is clearly a need for both formal and informal professional learning but that it is not a straightforward process of delivering information to recipients and their passive reception. Therefore, the informal nature of the mentoring we envisage going forward should be perceived as dynamic and generative rather than instructional. Where possible content should be negotiated between Big Brum and the participating schools.

References

Anderson, M., & Dunn, J. eds. (2013). *How Drama Activates Learning.* Contemporary Research and Practice. Bloomsbury

Biesta, G. (2009). *Good Education In An Age Of Measurement: On The Need To Reconnect With The Question Of Purpose In Education.* The Stirling Institute of Education. University of Stirling [accessed online, 13/03/24]

Bolton, C. (2018) *Human Spaces - An evaluative Case study - Creating spaces for young people to explore what it means to be human.* Birmingham City University Report.

Braun, V. and Clarke, V. (2022) *Thematic analysis: a practical guide.* London: SAGE.

Daichendt, G. J. (2010), *Artist-Teacher: A Philosophy for Creating and Teaching,* Bristol, UK: Intellect.

Daichendt, G.J., Funk. C., and Swift, J (2014). 'Mentoring the contemporary arts student in the university. Visual Inquiry.' *Learning and Teaching Art,* Vol 3 Issue 3 [accessed online 6/04/24]

Denmark, V., and Podsen, I. (2016). *Coaching and Mentoring First-Year and Student Teachers.* 2nd ed. Hoboken : Taylor and Francis.

Department of Education (DfE). (2019) *ITT Core Content framework.* Unknown place of publication: Department for Education. [Online] [Accessed on 7th January 2022] https://assets.publishing.service.gov.uk/government/uploads/system/uploads/attachment_data/file/974307/ITT_core_content_framework_.pdf

Glazzard, J. and Stones, S. (2021). *An Ambitious Primary School Curriculum*. St Albans: Critical Publishing Limited

Harper-Hill, K., Beamish, W., Hay, S., Whelan, M., Kerr, J., Zelenko, O., & Villalba, C. (2022). 'Teacher engagement in professional learning: what makes the difference to teacher practice?' *Studies in Continuing Education*, 44(1), 105–118. https://doi.org/10.1080/0158037X.2020.1781611

Hoffmann Davis, J. (2008). *Why Our Schools Need The Arts*. Teachers College Press.

Jackson, A and Vine, C. (2013, 3rd edn) *Learning through Theatre*. London, Routledge.

Mullen, C., Hobson, A., and Searby, L. (2021) 'Mentoring in Times of Crises, Pandemics, and Social Distancing'. *International Journal of Mentoring and Coaching in Education* (IJMCE). Emerald Publishing Limited

Nicholson, H. (2009) *Theatre and Education*. Basingstoke: Palgrave Macmillan

UK Government. *Early Career Framework*. https://www.gov.uk/government/publications/early-career-framework [accessed online 6/03/24]

Xu, W. & Zammit, K. (2020) 'Applying Thematic Analysis to Education: A Hybrid Approach to Interpreting Data in Practitioner Research.' *International Journal of Qualitative Methods*, 19 pp. 1-9.

Beyond the school gates

Miranda Ballin and Ian McAndrew

Executive Summary

'Beyond the School Gates' is an observational study focused on a series of children's letters from Rookery Community Primary School and Outwoods Primary School. The letters were in response to Big Brum's Theatre in Education Programme 'Ripped,' which featured a filmed version of their performance of 'Romeo and Juliet'. The letters were part of a task set for the children where they were invited to write to Rosie's headteacher, a fictional character in the play, offering advice and support to him as to how he could best support Rosie … a child who has ripped a dictionary and left it outside his office.

Through this 'fictional lens' we have explored what the letters reveal about how we best support children both in school and 'beyond the school gates' as parents, educators, health workers, artists and practitioners. We have worked collaboratively, recording and later transcribing an interview, where we shared our analysis and responses to the letters.

The study explores four key areas of interest and outlines the findings and key discussion points related to these.

- Firstly, a comparison of the way the schools approached the task and how this impacted on the children's response.

- Secondly, the way the children characterised Rosie's problems and how they communicated this to adults.

- Thirdly, the nature of the interventions suggested by the children.

- Finally, the role of Big Brum in both setting the task but also how they best respond to the 'expert' advice offered by the children in their future work … and where this work is best placed.

It sets out the methodology that was employed to evaluate the work and offers a series of recommendations as a result of the study.

The report offers indicative pointers towards such a model and offers several recommendations about what this informal mentoring process might look like.

"Rosie's Mum and Dad need to help Rosie believe they will listen to her. I think you, Rosie's parents and Rosie should meet together"

Year 6 pupil, Rookery Community Primary School

Background and Contextual Information

What We Set Out to Achieve

We had initially hoped to do a comparative study with teachers which explored both the creative approach of teachers but also looked at how the work of Big Brum impacted beyond the school gates. In the event, we had insufficient data to achieve this work in the detail required, particularly as it wasn't possible to revisit the schools, so the findings, and therefore the conclusions, would have been incomplete.

We have reported on this process, as it could prove to be a valuable framework for future use ... and it was still important to note the teachers' responses. From our perspective, this value is particularly in relation to their observations about how children were more likely to share and respond to such work with parents when they are engaged and excited about an experience. However, we were unable to bring this aspect to a meaningful conclusion.

With that in mind we wanted to know if there was a way we could more usefully contribute to the evaluation process. We decided to review the sources of data available to us, accumulated by the whole group of evaluators. We began to look in detail at two sets of letters produced by Year 5 Pupils from Outwoods Primary School and Year 6 pupils from Rookery Community Primary School in response to Big Brum's Theatre in Education programme 'Ripped,' which incorporated filmed material from their 'Romeo and Juliet' performance. These letters were written in a fictional context to a headteacher in the school.

In the Theatre in Education programme 'Ripped' the children encountered the lead character 'Rosie'. The children were set a task where they were invited to offer advice to the schools, and in particular the headteacher, as to how they can best support Rosie. Rosie is presented as a character/young person who is really struggling, so the stakes are high regarding the need to help her. In the letters the children explored Rosie's dilemma and the reasons why she needed support.

One child heads up their letter *"Help humankind...!"* and then describes Rosie's distress: *"She put all her anger and grief into the dictionary ... she left it at the headteacher's office so no-one would know it's hers"* (Fig 1).

Heip human kind...!

I am writing to you to give u advice to try help Rosie

I thik that Rosie feels worthless because in Romeo and Juliet when Juliet found out Romeo went AWAY and Juliet felt hopeless and when ~~Juliet~~ Romeo found out that Juliet died (faked her death to be with Romeo) and he didn't know and Rosie could have lost a best friend or broke up with some one so she put all her anger and greif into the dictionary and must of regretted it after she did it and she didnt want to ten anyone so she left it out the headteachers office so no-one would know its hers. But let people know about

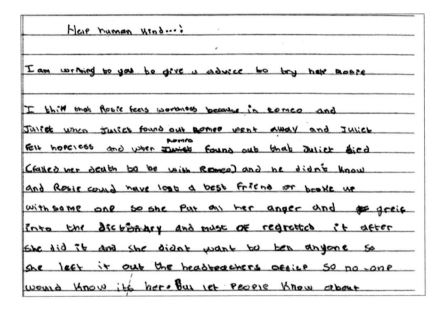

Fig 1: Letter from Rookery child.

Many of the children refer in their written response to a quote that Rosie has ripped out of the dictionary which says *"my face does not belong to me"*. They draw comparisons with the play they have previously seen and Juliet's distress, in particular Juliet's concern over her relationship with her parents. As another pupil describes it, *"Rosie's reactions are similar to that of Juliet, because she is frustrated by her parents not allowing her an opinion to marry Romeo"* (Fig 2).

~~Thank you~~ Rosie's reactions are similar to that of Juliet because she is frustrated by her parents not allowing ~~A~~ her an opinion to marry Romeo. Instead, they want her ~~Paris~~ ~~Sincerely~~ to marry, who they consider to be ~~Rosie's~~ ~~mother~~ the more suitable husband.

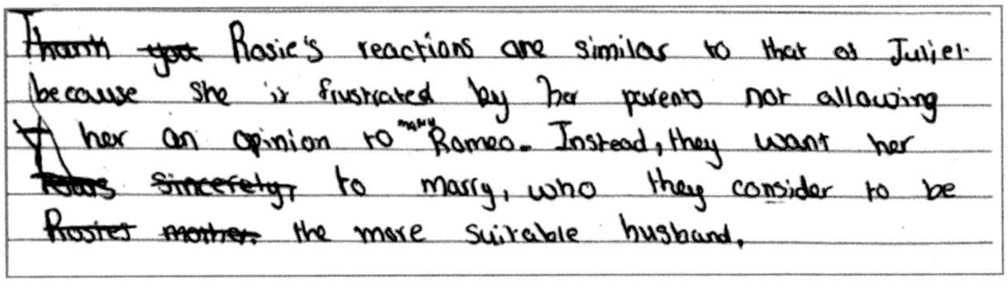

Fig 2: Letter from Rookery child.

They make suggestions in the letters as to who is best placed to help Rosie, or if there are ways in which she can better support herself.

The Process

We read the letters in detail. Neither of us had seen the Theatre In Education programme or witnessed the children's responses at first hand: we were therefore solely responding to the task and the letters they had chosen to write and we remained within the discipline of this.

We held a loosely structured conversation together that enabled us to develop our own thinking about the nature and significance of the children's responses and their suggested interventions on behalf of Rosie. The teacher from Rookery School describes in her accompanying letter how *"the children were very engaged in the story and the links to Rosie's difficulties"* (Fig 3).

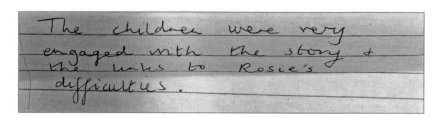

Fig 3: Letter from Rookery teacher.

The letters opened up a rich discussion for us as practitioners who usually operate 'outside of the school gate'. The fictional nature of the letters, in our view, allowed for a freedom of expression and a safety in the way the children responded. At times they responded directly by describing their own experience of trauma, *"I think I can understand why she did it, I have had traumatising experiences"* (Fig 4).

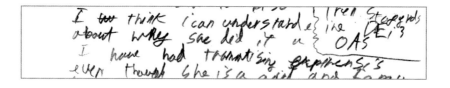

Fig 4: Child's letter from Outwoods.

At other times they 'stepped into the shoes' of the character and viewed the world from their perspective (e.g. *"Rosie could have lost a best friend or broke up with someone"*).

The letters encouraged an imaginative response, something that sits at the centre of Big

Brum's practice as a company and offers a chance to open up experiences to children, encapsulating both their lived experience and the chance to go beyond this. As described in Big Brum's Artistic Policy, they consider that *"art is social imagination which functions through a synthesis of feeling and thought with implications for future action in life"* (Artistic Policy, January 2011).

The children's considered responses offered an opportunity for learning for Big Brum, teachers, schools and a wider audience about how children perceive they can be better supported within an educational setting and who should be involved in this process. It allowed us to continue our interest with the inter-relationship between school, home and the wider community: to explore through these letters how Big Brum might facilitate a more effective relationship, triangulating between the three settings in their work, and how schools could engage with this. This felt especially useful in the context of 'Creating "Schools of Recovery" (SoR) and the move in the next phase of Big Brum's work to 'Communities for Recovery', where the different settings most powerfully intersect.

The local context for Rookery and Outwoods Primary Schools
Rookery Community Primary School is located in central Birmingham. The school has a high proportion of children receiving Free School Meals and who have English as an Additional Language. The school joined the SoR project in 2022-23, but has worked regularly with Big Brum in the past. (For more details, see page 73).

Outwoods Primary School is located in Burton-on-Trent, part of the East Staffordshire Levelling Up area. About 20% of children at the school receive Free School Meals or have English as an Additional Language, broadly in line with national averages. The school joined the SoR project in 2022-23: this was the first time that it had worked with Big Brum. (For more details, see page 127).

The local context for North Solihull - 'Communities of Recovery' will be situated here
Following the SoR project, in the next phase of its work, Big Brum has chosen to work in North Solihull, a highly disadvantaged area. In a 2018 'Locality Profile' shared with evaluators, Big Brum describe that 40% of the population is under thirty years of age, 58% of children are classed as being in need and children from the area are more likely to have a long term illness or disability. A high proportion of children are eligible for school meals and there are issues related to low levels of literacy, numeracy and retention at school, alongside disproportionate levels of crimes and domestic violence (SoR Commission

Launch, 2022).

In a more recent government study into Children and Young People which encompassed the whole of Solihull, there is a detailed analysis of the challenges that many children face regarding public health indicators, education, the levels of children in care and experiencing homelessness. This acknowledges that *"up to a quarter of children in several wards in the North of the borough are living in low income families"*. Here the report writers acknowledge the impact of Adverse Childhood Experiences (ACE) but also indicate how this is mitigated when children form trusted relationships with adults. *"When protected by supportive relationships with adults, a child is better placed to learn how to cope with everyday challenges. Adults who could provide a supportive relationship include parents, grandparents or members of the extended family but equally could be a teacher, support worker or other role model in the wider community."* They also point to the importance of peer to peer relationships and friendships for children with ACEs: *"Young people who have a reliable circle of friends have been found to be less badly affected should they have multiple adverse childhood experiences"* (Children and Young People in Solihull, 2022).

This background information informed our discussions as we considered how Big Brum moves from 'Schools of Recovery', including taking the SoR model into North Solihull and connecting it to the next phase of their work, 'Communities of Recovery'… which takes them into a community setting.

Key Areas of Exploration

We focused on four key areas of exploration:

A comparison between the way the children and teachers in Rookery and Outwoods Community School approached the task. Here we made a set of assumptions about how the teacher had led the task, as we didn't directly witness this process. Working on these assumptions, we explored the possibilities behind the different approaches taken by the teachers and the potential effect of this on the children's responses and eventual outcomes in the letters.

We investigated the way the children characterised the problems/issues that Rosie was experiencing and how they approached this. We were interested in their concerns, their ability to empathise and how they identified the problems Rosie was encountering. We catalogued the suggested interventions from the children as to how to help Rosie:

173

who in their view was best placed to support her. We considered the implications of their responses. We were interested in the repeated suggestions for more collaborative approaches between parents, teachers and outside agencies. We discussed what their responses revealed for us as practitioners, whether as teachers, parents, therapists, or Theatre in Education workers? We asked, are we listening sufficiently to the needs of children and their desire for us to communicate more effectively together?

We interrogated the role of Big Brum Theatre in Education in supporting schools and community interventions and whether they had a part to play in fostering more effective relationships, in particular with parents and teachers? Whether they were best placed to work within a school setting, supporting teachers to work more effectively with parents and other agencies? Or if they should work 'outside of the school gates', independently developing community interventions as suggested in their 'Communities of Recovery' plan (where they intend to develop hands-on creative opportunities and organise *"opportunities to experience high quality culture beyond the work of Big Brum"*, such as visits to cultural institutions). They suggest that this work is supported by Community Facilitators and will culminate in the children sharing creative work with others in the community (Slide 17, Schools of Recovery, Big Brum Theatre in Education, 2022). How does this way of working and approach impact on their Theatre in Education practice and their role in schools ... and do these inter-relate? Do they envisage this work supporting more collaborative relationships between home, school and the community?

We considered the role of a 'trusted adult' in the lives of children and how this could be strengthened through collaborative work, in particular for children who need additional support in order to build resilience and thrive at school, home and in their community. We were aware of the role of 'recovery' in Big Brum's plans and we considered what role Big Brum might play in this process of recovery in children's lives. We returned to the very nature of the task that the company had presented to the children and teachers: how it was this precise stimulus that had prompted our debate and drawn such a strong response from the children. We explored the significance of this. In the following section we outline some of the findings and discussion points in more detail to see what could be learned from this exploration.

Findings and Discussion Points

We analysed 28 letters from Outwoods Primary school and 32 from Rookery Primary School, 60 in total. The letters helped us to analyse anecdotal evidence in relation to these fictional letter/s that had been completed by the learners. This enabled us to identify how the learners were responding to the needs of the fictional character Rosie, and through this fictional 'lens' to understand more fully the needs and wants of pupils in their school.

How the school approached the task

We began by exploring the different approaches between the two schools in the way that the teachers introduced the task. As stated in the introduction, these were based on our assumptions. Ian's concern as an overall observation of the letters written by the Outwoods pupils was that they had been strongly guided by the teacher. His rationale for this was the recurring themes that infiltrated the majority of the letters, in particular the occurrence in twenty of the letters that Rosie has *"strong feelings"*.

In Outwoods, the children's responses were heavily influenced by the implementation in their school of the 'Zones of Regulation' programme, described quite accurately by one pupil as a *"tool kit."* On their website, 'Zones of Regulation' is introduced as *"A Simple Approach to Developing Self -Regulation"*. It was designed by Founder and CEO Leah Kuypers, a trained occupational therapist and specialist in autism in the U.S. It is described by Kuypers as a *"digital curriculum"* intended to *"address sensory regulation differences"* through *"emotional regulation, social cognition, executive functioning, and impulse control."* It categorises feelings into four different colour zones related to the emotions and the response differs depending on your mood. There are different strategies that the children are encouraged to use, related to the zones to support their emotional regulation (Kuypers, 2023).

In Outwoods School, the children are conversant with this way of exploring their feelings and therefore nineteen of them suggested this method as a way of supporting Rosie. Attached to this were different strategies that she could employ to manage her feelings. Ian's concern was that he suspected the children had been strongly directed to the framework of the 'Zones Of Regulation' by the teacher. Whilst he felt that. in itself, it was a useful tool for the children, he didn't think it was helpful when it was presented as potentially the only option for exploration. This in his view limited learning and understanding, particularly the pupils' ability to think imaginatively and creatively. He described how the children who were able to set aside the Zones of Regulation and contribute their own views were able to respond with more depth: *"what was written on the board potentially was pushed to one side and somebody truly wrote what was within."*

Miranda agreed with this analysis. Her concern lay in how the children moved straight to more practical strategies that could be employed to support Rosie, for example the use of stress toys, taking a walk. However, they were less able to write in depth about how Rosie was feeling. Everything was included under the banner of Rosie *"not knowing how to control her feelings."* The children struggled to further describe the nature of these feelings: *"once we band everything under 'strong feelings' which need to be controlled, are we helping those children identify the nature of those strong feelings, it becomes a catch all".* Whilst both Miranda and Ian recognised that the 'Zones of Regulation' framework was there to identify different feelings, this did not translate in the letters the children chose to write.

In contrast, Miranda returned to the letter written by a child who had directly experienced trauma and was therefore concerned that Rosie may be experiencing this herself. Perhaps because of their lived experience, they were more able to identify how Rosie was feeling, they empathised that Rosie may feel differently from them as they are a boy, they expressed concern that Rosie may have been bullied or suffered abuse, and described how *"she might not trust us, so let her open up slowly, let her back in ... and tell everyone to be kind to her"* (Fig 5).

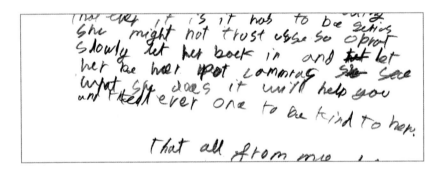

Fig 5: Child's letter from Outwoods.

With Rookery School, we know that the task was approached by enabling children to firstly work in groups and discuss their ideas and then write individually. It is possible that the teacher also contributed to the discussions or gave suggestions. Miranda pointed to the children's consideration, raised on a number of occasions, that Rosie was potentially suffering from insomnia phobia, *"an intense fear of sleep"* and this is why she described that "my face does not belong to me" (Ripped, 2023). It is possible that this was raised independently by the children but may also have been an explanation from a teacher.

However, with the children from Rookery School, Miranda and Ian felt that the children were given more licence to explore their feelings and offer solutions. Miranda felt that as the process was more open and exploratory, the children could write more creatively and freely. Therefore there was more 'congruence' in the way they responded to Rosie's feelings. Ian agreed with this and described how *"I felt that there were a lot of variants, a lot of thought, a lot of one's thinking that directly goes into the letters."* Ian's considerations, even from a curriculum or literacy perspective, were that he felt that a lot more autonomy was granted in Rookery by the teacher and this translated into a more imaginative and richer response.

In discussing the task that Big Brum had set the schools/children, we explored their intention behind the task. Miranda felt sure that the Company wanted to empower the children, to place them in the role of experts. Here, they were not placed in a fictional role as experts but rather the task honoured their knowledge and experience as children and their ability to empathise with and understand Rosie's dilemma. Miranda commented, *"I associate this with people like Dorothy Heathcote, they were the advice givers, they could speak from experience and they could speak from a position of knowledge."*

How the children characterised the problem

The children in Outwoods School referred twenty two times to their concern that Rosie didn't know how to control her feelings, but they were less able to identify the nature of these feelings (as we have described previously). However, some children clearly empathised with Rosie's situation and were keen to describe the nature of the problem. One child described how *"she needs to be listened to, and is insecure and sad, she needs to be taken care of"* (Fig 6).

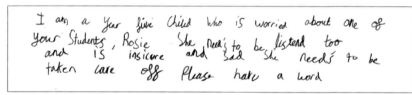

Fig 6: *"She needs to be listened to"* - Outwoods child.

Another child described how *"maybe you could find her a safe space"*. The children all expressed their concern for Rosie and some children recognised the seriousness of Rosie's dilemma (*"I am worried because she is desperate for help"*). One of the children identified where they thought her emotions lay within the framework of the Zones of Regulation: *"I think she is in a red zone, an angry zone, furious and out of control."* Another child also refers to the different emotions in the 'colour zones' and explains the need to listen to her: *"You should listen to her and not scream"* (Fig 7).

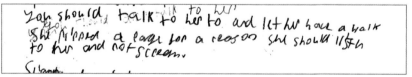

Fig 7: *"You should listen to her and not scream"* - Outwoods child.

The children in Rookery School referred in more detail to the context of the story, they made references to the 'Romeo and Juliet' film they had encountered and drew comparisons in more detail between Rosie's situation and that of Juliet: *"Rosie's reactions are similar to that of Juliet. Because she is frustrated by her parents not allowing her an opinion".* They made comparisons with the way Juliet is controlled by her parents, the fact that she isn't allowed to marry Romeo and how it is possible that Rosie is in a similar situation. One child suggests, *"Rosie's parents have sort of disavowed her, and some bullies might have taken advantage of Rosie."* They go onto explain that she is *"thinking that NO-ONE knows her"*.

The children responded directly to the Headteacher: *"Allow Rosie to be free and let her do whatever she wishes for a while."* (Fig 8). Ian identified the rich variety of responses that individual children made, acknowledging that Rosie *"has no voice."* He described how they made assumptions of potential bullying and attributed this to low self-esteem. One young person referred to the possibility that the character might have been previously hurt and a number of young people mentioned the potential of trauma in her life. Identity was a key issue, related strongly to Rosie ripping the quote out of the dictionary, which says, *"my face does not belong to me."*

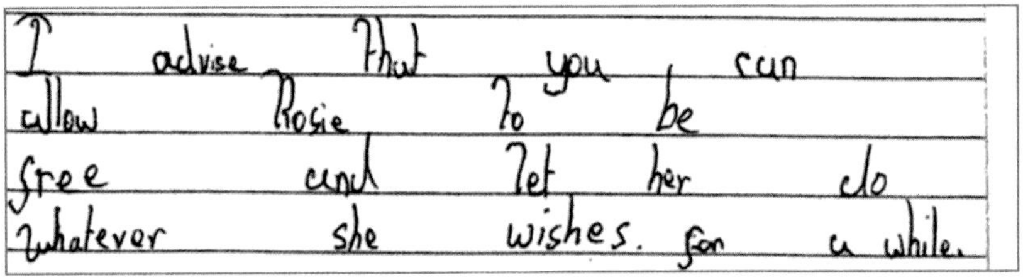

Fig 8: *"Allow Rosie to be free"* - Rookery child.

The children raise issues around depression and anxiety: the level of empathy and concern is palpable (as one child explains, *"nobody should feel like this, it's very sad and students need to be more kind"*). In comparison with the pupils from Outwoods, Miranda was struck by the sophistication of the responses from the (slightly older) children at Rookery School; she referred to the seriousness of the situation the children were grappling with. The children were aware that Romeo and Juliet had committed suicide and they were being asked to identify the issues for Rosie: *"I just felt that the children from Rookery felt more equipped to really think about that stuff."* They were grappling with the enormity of the emotions that Rosie was feeling and they didn't shy away from this: *"I think stress could drive such hate and anger but also jealousy"* (Fig 9).

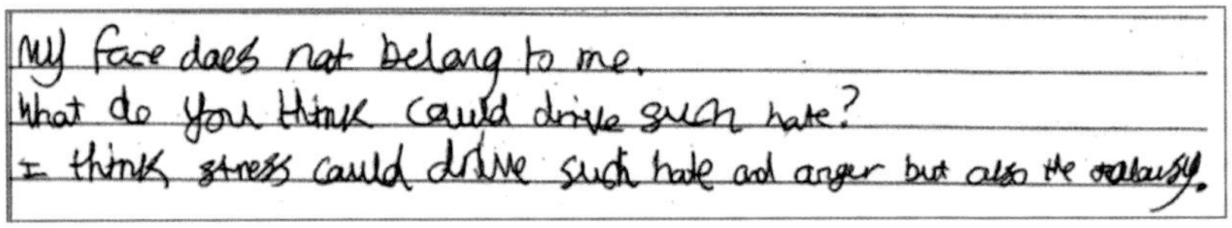

Fig 9: *"I think stress could drive such hate and anger"* - Rookery child.

The nature of the interventions suggested

Similarly to the way they identified the nature of Rosies' problems, the children from Outwoods School moved more readily to action and intervention than the children from Rookery. Observationally, in keeping with the 'Zones of Regulation' framework, they tended towards more practical solutions focused around how Rosie could support herself. Whilst Miranda acknowledged that there were real merits to having a wellbeing framework where children could 'ground' themselves, she was conscious of the limitations with regard to the interventions they suggested: *"they go to the framework, rather than exploring the context"* and this results in *"a tick list"* of how Rosie can be supported. The suggestions from Outwoods pupils included a whole range of responses, as well as the overwhelming response urging Rosie to work with the 'Zones of Regulation'. They made particular suggestions around actions she could take herself, including: to speak with friends; go for a walk; play with a fidget or stress toy; keep a diary of her thoughts; ask people to play with her; make a hideout.

Miranda draws attention, however, to how confident the children in Outwoods are with regard to approaching adults, as a result of working with an understood framework. *"I think when they say you can go and speak to a trusted adult, that is included in their understanding of 'Zones of Regulation'."* Other suggestions included writing down thoughts for a teacher to read and talking to an adult or family member. The children understood that Rosie needs to be listened to: *"Help Rosie feel respected, listened to"* (Fig 10).

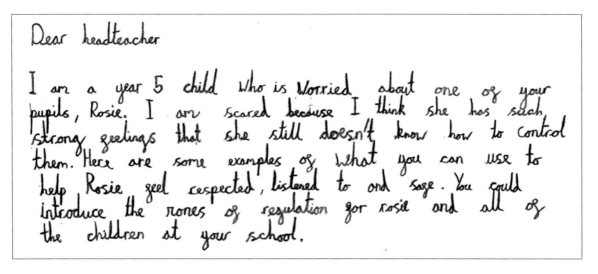

Fig 10: *"Help Rosie feel respected ..."* - Outwoods child.

In Ian's view, the children from Rookery School seemed to have a greater grasp on the gravity of Rosie's situation. He described it as *"a much bigger picture, what is the journey to be able to support that person?"* He describes how they identified "a greater situation at play here" and this was reflected in the people the children put forward to help Rosie. Many of them wanted Rosie to receive therapy or to see a Doctor or at least to talk to someone. Seven of the pupils suggested talking with the teacher or someone in school: *"Talk to someone she feels comfortable with, someone she fully trusts like close friends or caring teachers or you [Headteacher]"* (Fig 11).

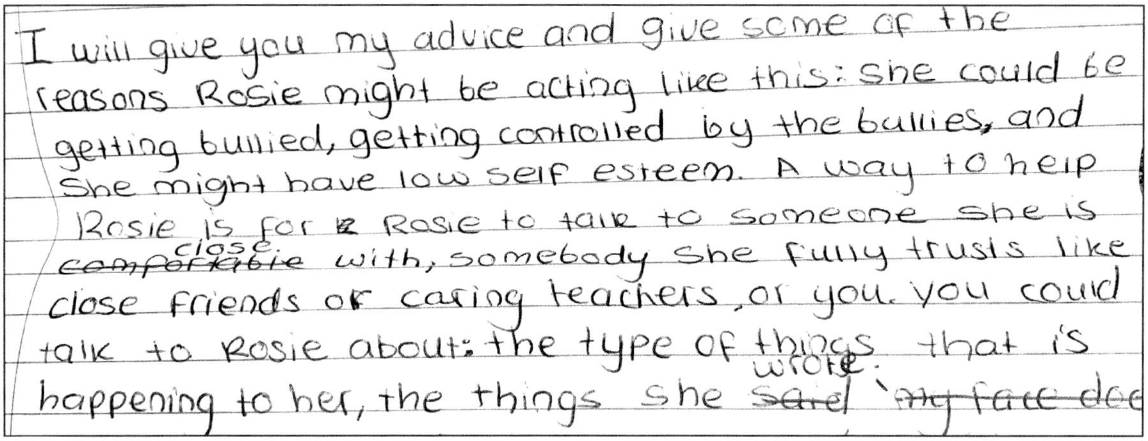

Fig 11: *"Talk to someone ..."* - Rookery child.

Miranda described how, because the children at Rookery had been encouraged to imaginatively engage with Rosie, they had more grasp on the level of engagement she required and the urgency of the situation. *"What is most interesting about children from Rookery, many of them talked about the need for a professional intervention, they recognised that maybe this is beyond them, beyond parents"*. The question of involving parents was of interest to Miranda because the premise of 'Romeo and Juliet' is of parents who seriously let down their children and are proven to be untrustworthy. Therefore, it is unsurprising that so few children suggested parental involvement to Rosie. However, in the opening quotation of this study, a brave child suggests to the Headteacher that he should try and broker relations between Rosie and her parents.

This led onto a key area of discussion with regard to Big Brum's work. As Miranda queried *"in the end, if we really want to help children, helping parents for me, from where I stand, is part of the issue."*

The Role of Big Brum

Through the exploration of the children's letters from Outwoods and Rookery, Miranda and Ian were drawn into the imaginative world of Rosie's situation, and how the children were choosing to advocate for her. Of course, through this, the children revealed, at times directly and at other times imaginatively, their own concerns about the world of school, home and community. Miranda highlighted the strength of Big Brum's work in achieving this outcome and also a concern that in wanting to broaden the scope of their work they should not dilute the richness of their Theatre in Education practice. This has brought about the ability for children to open up to their teachers in such a significant way. As she describes it, *"I think that most of the time the endeavour of Big Brum is to produce outstanding, high quality theatre in education interventions ... I think you have to be really careful you don't dilute it."*

Miranda queried whether - in relation to Big Brums work - it is better to make small and meaningful interventions rather than try and be all things to all people. She suggested that the company could have opened up a small but meaningful space for children and parents, just by suggesting that the children take the letters home, or possibly they could have invited in a small panel, including a couple of parents, to review the letters that were sent to the headteacher and give feedback to the children.

Miranda's previous work exploring youth arts practice with parents from working class and diverse backgrounds has challenged some of her own assumptions about how parents engage with artistic practice, particularly involving their children (Ballin, 2015). She also drew attention to the national Creative Partnerships programme in England[21] that involved thousands of schools but was honest in its assessment that there had been very little direct engagement with parents throughout the programme ... and which viewed this as a missed opportunity.

Ian held a potentially different viewpoint. He pointed to the fact that many of the children, particularly from Rookery, were actively seeking engagement outside of the school gates: *"I could interpret it the other way round as well, that the young people are asking for something else as well that is beyond the school gates, that isn't interacting within the school gate."* Ian posed the question as to whether schools should be better at signposting and supporting young people to access support and help outside of 'the school gate' that can benefit them but also strengthen schools. He felt that being independent and standalone gave Big Brum better scope to broker partnerships than being too tied to schools.

---

[21] Between 2022 and 2011, 'Creative Partnerships' served as the UK government's flagship creative learning programme.

Miranda's concern with this model was ensuring that Big Brum had the skills and capacity to truly sustain long term and embedded work in a community setting. In her view, this is a different discipline than Theatre in Education. Whilst Big Brum has run a Youth Theatre and supported initiatives like The Gap in Birmingham[21], sustaining this activity long term is a huge challenge and may involve an even more radical rethink than Big Brum imagines. Her concern here rested with the role of trusted adults in young people's lives, the need to be consistent and long term. While schools provide this, in her view a traditional Theatre in Education Company doesn't always have that capacity. In developing 'Communities of Recovery', she comments, *"the only way I can see them doing that successfully is if they have a real arm of their work that is dedicated to that, and that is a big ask".*

Conversely Ian's concern was that in his role in Lead Creative Schools in Wales[22] he had never really seen integrated work taken to the next level. He feels that the pressure on schools to deliver other objectives mitigates against this. Ian felt they were two different avenues to consider and asked *"do you bring the outside of the school gate in or do you bring the inside of the school gate out?"* This feels like a useful provocation for Big Brum in the next stage of their development.

Further discussion points

• Should Big Brum have a role in brokering relationships between schools, parents and children – if so, what does that look like?

• Should Big Brum consider in the creation of their TIE Programmes whether they could open these out to enable parents/ community members to be more part of the process? If so, is this feasible within the current school structure?

• If Big Brum are considering community interventions in the next phase of their work, 'Communities of Recovery,' how do they build on the strength of their current imaginative theatre practice rather than fall into a more 'skills based model'?

• Do Big Brum need to be a more standalone community-based organisation which provides a 'home', particularly for more disadvantaged young people, and which enables them to build independent partnerships with health and wellbeing, community-based organisations, parents and schools? If so, would this benefit the young people they work with? Do they have the skills and capacity for this? Where is Theatre in Education in this model?

[21] The Gap is a youth arts organisation and cultural space based in Balsall Heath, Birmingham.

[22] Lead Creative Schools is a programme for schools in Wales where *"pupils, teachers and creative professionals work together to implement creative projects."*

- Do Big Brum need to re-imagine and radically rethink their model of work and practice if they really want to support the recovery of schools and communities? What role do Big Brum's partners and advisory groups play in this?

- How do schools, health organisations, arts and community based organisations work more collaboratively and collectively to ensure that young people have a network of trusted adults they can call on to support them?

Potential recommendations

Big Brum to review tasks and follow-up work, so as to investigate the potential of parental involvement and to explore the possibilities of such involvement with trusted and long term schools and partners.

Big Brum continue to advocate with teachers to enable children to respond freely and imaginatively to their follow-up tasks and programmes of work, encouraging teachers to enable these tasks to be as child centred as possible.

Big Brum to review their 'Communities for Recovery' programme plans and consider the methodology and activities attached to this, to drill down into their methodology and ways of working and ensure it is informing their process.

Big Brum to take full advantage of the links and partnerships that have flourished around 'Creating "Schools of Recovery"' and to see how these can be strengthened and developed in the next stage of their work and programming.

Methodology

As stated in the introduction, we re-visited our initial process and began to explore a different approach to this evaluation. In order to find a way forward we worked collaboratively to explore the data and information available to us.

This included reviewing the following:

- Fictional letters written by learners from both Rookery and Outwoods Primary Schools, in response to activities set by Big Brum;

- Evaluation recordings taken place during and post engagement with teachers and school leaders;

- Written documentation from the evaluators;

- Revisiting the pre-engagement interviews with two class teachers from Fordbridge Community Primary School (one of whom who is a member of the Senior Leadership Team).

Review of Letters: Miranda and Ian read all 60 letters produced by the children and individually made detailed notes regarding them. They categorised them (Fig 12, below) into how the children had responded to Rosies' dilemma and their suggested interventions.

Interview and Transcript: Miranda and Ian met online and recorded a detailed conversation where they reviewed the letters, and spoke in depth about the way the children had responded. They compared and contrasted their notes and observations and began to draw out key themes and areas for exploration.

Miranda transcribed the interview and with Ian began to categorise the areas in order to draw out more fully the findings and to highlight the areas of discussion, so as to highlight potential recommendations for Big Brum's future work and to prepare the study.

Fig 12: Children's responses and suggested interventions

Rookery School - 31 letters

Descriptions of how Rosie is feeling		Suggestions to support Rosie	
No Voice	1	Parent	1
Lonely	3	People	1
Cannot control her thoughts	1	School/Teacher	7
Identity ('My face does not belong to me')	16	Therapist	11
Control/Forced	12	Other Friends/Students	3
Bullied	5	Let time pass	1
Low Self-Esteem	2	Stay away from strangers	1
Anxiety	4	Talk to someone	2
Previously Hurt	1	Stay away from people forcing her to do something she does not want to do	1

Outwood School - 28 letters

Descriptions of how Rosie is feeling		Suggestions to support Rosie	
Doesn't know how to control her feelings	22	Zones of Regulation	19
Needs attention, and needs to be seen	1	Speak to a friend	1
Anxious	1	Play with her	1
Doesn't know how to express her feelings	1	Get people to understand how she is feeling	1
Insecure	1	Needs to be listened to	1
Stressed	1	Wants others to feel what she feels	1
		Go for a walk	1
		Write thoughts down for a teacher to read	2
		Stress toys	2
		Diary for her thoughts	4
		Make a hideout	1
		Talk to an adult/family member	3

References

Ballin, M. (2015) *If Only We Asked: A qualitative study exploring the role of parents in a youth theatre and youth arts context:* Clore Leadership Programme & Arts and Humanities Research Council

Big Brum Website. *Artistic Policy* (January 2011) https://static1.squarespace.com/static/60d061bcd571dc3fb7554ef9/t/60da28adc343fd57d8339fd4/1624910001086/Big+Brum+Artistic+Policy.pdf [Online] Accessed 29/4/2024

Kuypers, Leah.(2023) *The Story Behind the Zones* https://zonesofregulation.com/about/ [Online] Accessed 29/4/2024

Solihull MBC website. *Children and Young People in Solihull 2022* Available https://www.solihull.gov.uk/sites/default/files/2022-11/202207_CYP%20in%20Solihull%20Finalv1.2.pdf [Online] Accessed 29/ 2024

Zones of Regulation Website. https://zonesofregulation.com/ [Online] Accessed 29/4/2024

About the contributors

Dr Konstantinos Amoiropoulos is currently working as an Associate Professor in Drama in the Department of Early Childhood Education at Oslo Metropolitan University. He has worked as a primary school teacher and an Early Years teacher in Greece for 24 years. He was the founder and artistic director of the Drama and TIE company 'Diadromes in Drama and Educational Praxis', in Athens, Greece, for ten years, where he delivered drama workshops and seminars for adults, children and young people and directed TIE programmes for Early Years students.

Miranda Ballin, is the Artistic Director of Sparc, Valleys Kids, Youth Arts Project, specialising in drama and theatre. Miranda is also a qualified social worker with a particular interest in how we work more effectively with parents and guardians in a youth arts setting. This was the subject of her paper for AHRC Clore Leadership Programme, 'If Only We Asked' (2019).

Dr Adam Bethlenfalvy is Associate Professor at Károli Gáspár University and CEO at InSite Drama, Budapest.

Dr Gill Brigg is a theatre-maker and cross-phase educationalist, who serves as Additional Needs Officer for National Drama. Gill lectures in Sensory Theatre at Rose Bruford College with BA, MA and MFA students. Within SEND settings, Gill provides CPD and mentoring for schools both nationally and internationally.

Gilroy Brown is an Education Consultant, Pastor and Mentor, who worked for 10 years as a Primary Headteacher and 11 years as a local authority school advisor in Birmingham.

Dr Chris Bolton is Senior Lecturer at Birmingham City University, where he leads the Drama PGCE, International PGCE and Masters courses.

Emma Davis is a Lecturer in Education at University College Birmingham, a former Nursery Manager and Early Years teacher. Emma also writes regularly for Nursery World, Teach Early Years and Early Years Educator.

Dr Rebecca Patterson is Senior Lecturer in Education and Lead for the Secondary PGCE Drama Programme at Manchester Metropolitan University. She is also a former Drama Teacher.

Alison Ramsay is a Lecturer on the BA and PGCE Primary education programmes at Manchester Metropolitan University, specialising in Drama education. She is also a former Drama teacher.

Balbir Sohal is an Education Consultant and former teacher who has worked closely with Coventry City Council (including as Prevent Officer), the Anne Frank Trust and Peacemakers. Her Masters degree specialised in Race and Ethnic Relations.

Rebecca Taylor is Head of Education at University College Birmingham and a former Primary teacher. Her MA investigated the effective mentoring of Newly Qualified Teachers.

Ian McAndrew is CEO and Joint Artistic Director at Think Creatively CIC, Ponyclun. Ian has worked for the Arts Council of Wales as a Regional Lead for the Lead Creative Schools programme. His theatre and drama practice is mostly in a community development setting: outside of the classroom, he is a Sparc Associate with Valleys Kids.